Learning and Growing

*a guide
to child development*

Laurie and Joseph Braga

A SPECTRUM BOOK

Prentice-Hall, Inc., Englewood Cliffs, New Jersey

Library of Congress Cataloging in Publication Data

BRAGA, LAURIE.
    Learning and growing: a guide to child development.

    (Spectrum Books)
    Bibliography: p.
    1. Children—Management. 2. Learning, Psychology
of. 3. Parent and child. I. Braga, Joseph, joint
author. II. Title.
HQ772.B67   649'.1   74-26845
ISBN 0-13-527614-4
ISBN 0-13-527606-3 pbk.

HUMAN DEVELOPMENT BOOKS is a series designed to bridge the gap between research and theory in the behavioral sciences and practical application by readers. Each book in the series deals with an issue important to the growth and development of human beings, as individuals and in interaction with one another. At a time when the pressures and complexities of the world are making increased demands on people's ability to cope, there is a need for tools that can help individuals take a more active role in solving their own problems and in living life more fully. Such information is not easily found or read by those without previous experience or familiarity with the vocabulary of a particular behavioral field. The books in this series were designed and executed to meet that purpose.

HUMAN DEVELOPMENT BOOKS

Growing with Children, by Joseph and Laurie Braga
Growing Older, by Margaret Hellie Huyck
Learning and Growing: A Guide to Child Development,
    by Laurie and Joseph Braga
Death: The Final Stage of Growth, by Elisabeth Kübler-Ross
Culture and Human Development, by Ashley Montagu

10 9 8 7 6 5 4 3 2 1   75-7178

PRENTICE-HALL INTERNATIONAL, INC. (*London*)
PRENTICE-HALL OF AUSTRALIA PTY., LTD. (*Sydney*)
PRENTICE-HALL OF CANADA, LTD. (*Toronto*)
PRENTICE-HALL OF INDIA PRIVATE LIMITED (*New Delhi*)
PRENTICE-HALL OF JAPAN, INC. (*Tokyo*)

To the Reader

*Children are the world's most valuable resource
and its best hope for the future.*

JOHN F. KENNEDY

This is a book about children—how they grow and how they learn. It will tell you what kinds of behaviors you're likely to see at different stages of children's growth, and it will suggest some activities to stimulate their learning and growing in ways that should be fun for you as well as for your children. We've written this book with the expectation that you, our reader, are a parent, teacher, or friend of young children and that you share in our commitment to the happiness and growth of children, our most valuable and precious resource.

Young children are the continual hope and renewal of humankind, and they serve to remind us of our own humanity in its most basic, uncomplexed form. In our last book,* we stressed that the most important and powerful source of learning for young children is the model provided to them by adults. But growing with children should be a mutual process, and just as we give them a picture of what they can be, so they should be a mirror for us of what we may have forgotten about ourselves.

With recent attention to the importance of the early years for human beings' total growth, many parents, future parents, and teachers of young children have become both overwhelmed by the amount of information there is to know and frightened by the awesome responsibility of child caregiving. It is true that there is a great deal of information available, and child-rearing *is* the greatest responsibility a human being can assume. But the needs of infants and young children are fairly basic and logical. They need to know that you care deeply for them; that you can be counted on when they need you; that they can trust you not to hurt or betray them, either deliberately or through negligence; and that you respect them as well as love them. In addition, children need to be supported in their attempts at increased independence and responsibility for their own actions as they grow; they need to be provided with a variety of experiences through which they can try out their own resources with the expectation of success, or, at least, without the *fear* of failure.

The most valuable thing you can do for the children in your care is to help them achieve a stable and consistent sense of their own worth as persons. The kinds of interactions they have with you and others can make the difference in whether your children come to feel about themselves that they are good, worthy people who can be successful at most things to which they set their energies or whether they are filled with fear and self-doubt. The key to children's learning and growing into happy productive human beings is developing feelings of confidence, of competence and self-worth, of belief-in-self.

Thus, we ask you to read this book, with its behavioral descriptions and suggestions of stimulus activities, with the constant reminder that it is children's self-

* Joseph Braga and Laurie Braga, *Growing With Children*. Englewood Cliffs, N.J.: Prentice-Hall, Inc., 1974.

concepts that must always be given primary consideration, not their meeting of behavioral norms or their ability to accomplish specific tasks. There is a danger in overly self-conscious childrearing and in developing the mind *without also providing nurturance to the heart.* Time spent participating in organized learning activities with children is no substitute for honest, spontaneous, loving care. "Educational toys" are never as stimulating as interactions with interesting and interested adults in real-life activities. Language is always learned better through real communication with children—talking with them about their thoughts, interests, and feelings —than through teaching them isolated words that have nothing to do with their own real lives. Thinking skills are developed more meaningfully and enduringly through capitalizing on children's spontaneous interests and through guidance in solving their real-life problems than through contrived "learning activities."

We give you descriptions of characteristic behaviors of children in different stages of development so that you may understand their behavior better—so that you may know what behaviors are to be expected and how to plan for and deal with them in order to promote learning and growing. We suggest activities because we understand that just being with children can be physically and emotionally draining, and a few suggestions can go a long way to spark a tired mind. But we ask you to remember that the style with which you conduct these activities will make the difference in whether you are a facilitator to children's learning or an obstacle in their paths. Learning should always be fun, not a drudge for you or the children.

It is our deepest hope that the information provided in this book will be helpful in providing some guidelines to you for your children's happy and healthy learning and growing as well as in reassuring you that it is safe and important for you to learn to rely on your own *gut,* human judgment and your children's signals to guide your behavior as a caregiver to children.

Sharpen the mind like a tool; give nurturance to the heart as if it were a tiny infant—it needs the food of love; and inform the gut—make it the child of the marriage of the mind with the heart.

Laurie and Joe Braga

general editors of
HUMAN DEVELOPMENT BOOKS:
A SERIES IN APPLIED BEHAVIORAL SCIENCE

Drs. Laurie and Joseph Braga, both developmental psychologists, are on the faculty of the Department of Psychiatry at the University of Miami School of Medicine. The Bragas are co-authors of *Child Development and Early Childhood Education: a Guide for Parents and Teachers,* published by the City of Chicago, and *Growing with Children,* published by Prentice-Hall.

Contents

We dedicate this book to
each other,
our son Tommy,
and
all kindred spirits
who are friends of children

To Michael Hunter, Director of Spectrum Books, thank you for your commitment, belief, intercession, and faith in our books and in this series.

To John Mills, production co-ordinator for this book and for *Growing with Children,* thank you for your commitment, hard work, competence, and aesthetic judgment in designing and executing the production of these books.

1

Learning
and Growing:
An Explanation

. . . the most important job in the world is
the making of another human being,
one to whom we have given roots and wings.
—ASHLEY MONTAGU

At times in human history it has been thought that children did not begin any serious learning until they entered school. The years before school were viewed as a time when children "just played," and the only kind of teaching that was undertaken was that of "training" young children to enter civilized society. These views reflect not only a misunderstanding of learning and playing but also a lack of appreciation of the importance of early childhood as the foundation of all learning.

Learning has popularly been equated with schooling and thought to consist primarily of the accumulation of information. For this reason, parents and preschool teachers occasionally have misunderstood the focus of early childhood education to be the learning of skills such as reading, writing, and arithmetic. This is a very narrowly defined view of learning. Actually, young children are continuously learning, from exposure to different kinds of information and experiences, opportunities to practice newly developing skills, and so on, not simply when adults are deliberately and purposefully "teaching" them.

Children learn from all their experiences, and in a number of different ways. First, and most important, they learn from doing, through direct experience and practice. They learn how things look, sound, smell, taste, and feel, for example, through seeing, listening, smelling, tasting, and feeling. You may provide the opportunity for these experiences and talk with children about them, but still they must experience things for themselves in order to learn about them.*

Children learn many of their behaviors through modeling—i.e., through watching and copying others. They try out behaviors they have seen, play at being people they know, imitate the actions of others, and so on. For example, your children will be more likely to learn to read, draw, play sports, and so on if they see you do these things than if you simply tell them you want them to do it. A large part of children's defining who they are in relation to others is learned through this process.

There are some things that children learn as a result of direct, deliberate training or through being told. Such matters as table manners and other social amenities (e.g., "Please" and "Thank you") as well as prohibitions (e.g., against touching certain things) are learned through deliberate instruction. But this is the least effective way for children to learn even though it seems to be the most prevalent kind of teaching they receive from adults.

Children's real learning occurs through their own active, responsive involvement with stimulation from their environment. They need stimulation and experience, but they will use it at their own pace and in their own way. For example, a young infant may enjoy watching a small stuffed toy that is hung above her† and bat at it with her fist to try to make it move. Later she will try to grab and feel it and will put it into her mouth to investigate its taste and texture. At a later age, when she begins role playing, she may cradle and cuddle her stuffed animal and treat it as a pet or baby.

The early years are a time for learning about the world, for figuring out how things work, what things are, and what the rules are—with

---

* Clearly, most of us learn about many things that we have not experienced. But that is one of the differences between how we learn as adults and how we learned best as young children; and we all learn more fully when we can experience something ourselves rather than merely be told about it.

† An unusual aspect of this book that you will no doubt notice is our use of pronouns. Our language is structured in such a way that the masculine singular pronoun is always used to stand for both sexes. In many books on child development you will find an apology by the authors and an explanation that they know children come in two sexes, but that it is necessary to use "he" for clarity. We have given this much thought and have come up with an alternative: Wherever possible, we have used "they"; when it was not practical because it would lead to confusion, we have alternated between the use of "he" and the use of "she." If you notice yourself feeling a bit startled or uncomfortable each time you see "she" used to stand for both male and female children, let it be a reminder to you of how important language really is in forming impressions. It is hard to know, since we're so used to it, how the exclusive use of the masculine pronoun affects the self-concept of the growing female child; but it's an interesting question to ponder.

people and with things. It is also the time when children learn about themselves—what their place in the world is, what they can and cannot do, how people feel about them, and as a result of all this, how they feel about themselves.

From birth through the preschool years, children are learning how to learn. Learning may be thought of as the construction of reality,* like putting up a building. Children must start from the ground floor and build upward, and each part of the structure is dependent on the one before it. Each step children go through serves as a foundation or basis for later learning. This is true for each particular skill young children learn as well as for the combination and working together of these skills. Once individual skills have been learned by children, they put them together in various ways to acquire new, more complex ones.

For example, children learn to move around; then they move around to learn. First children learn to use their hands as tools—to pick up, grab hold of, and manipulate things; then they learn to use their hands in the use of tools such as cups, spoons, forks, scissors, and crayons. Having learned to use some of these tools, they can use them to learn other skills. For example, children must learn to *use* scissors before they can begin to use them to cut out things.

The early years of childhood can be compared to the foundation and frame of a house. Whatever is built upon the foundation is influenced by the quality and strength of this structure and the materials used. The form of the completed structure of a house is at least partially decided by the beginning foundation and frame, even if additional parts are added later. In a similar way, the foundation of the person a child will become is formed in his early years. A person's mind is not "formed" in the preschool years; there are many important stages of growth ahead for a child before he will be able to think like an adult. But much of what will influence how, how much, and how well children will learn during the rest of their lives is developed before they enter school.†

* As adults, we assume that reality simply exists, and that children absorb it like a sponge. We don't remember what it was like to be a baby and to exist in a world of confusion with enormous amounts of unorganized input. We each build our own reality as our brains apply organizational structure to our individual experiences and make them conform to the organizational structure that is defined by our cultures as meaningful. But each of us still always sees things through our own eyes, and an important part of learning is learning to see others' point of view in addition to our own.

† There is some controversy among those who study children about the existence of "critical periods"—times when children must learn certain skills or lose the capacity to do so—and about whether the period of early childhood in some ways constitutes a critical period in itself. We do not feel that it is ever too late to learn basic skills if the capacity is there and the teaching is good. However, we do feel that there are "optimal periods" in which it is easier for children to

Children develop more skills and at a faster rate between birth and the time they enter school than in any other period in their lives. For example, from birth to school age, children change from dependent beings incapable of moving on purpose to very mobile persons who can walk, run, hop, jump, skip, twirl, and do various simple athletic stunts. During this period, children master most of the underlying rules of their language; they learn how to put words together to make a variety of different kinds of sentences. From birth to age five, children proceed from not even knowing there's a "me" that's separate from what's "out there" to being able to express their thoughts and feelings through words and actions so that other people can understand them.

All of these accomplishments represent essential learnings that take place in early childhood. And most of them, complex as they are, are undertaken by children in the form of play. Learning is child's play, and playing is child's work. It is through playing that young children learn their most fundamental skills, and children's play should also provide the direction for our teaching. That is, through capitalizing on children's own self-chosen activities and interests, we can extend and expand their learning. For example, many children around four or five enjoy "playing" with words by rhyming or making up silly words, and so on. If you, as a parent or teacher, observed this in your children, you could teach them the word *rhyming,* concoct some fun activities based on rhyming words, and build some additional vocabulary, all through something you noticed your children engaging in on their own.

The Puritan ethic, which regards pleasure as sinful, has had a strong influence on our culture. This, in turn, has had a significant impact on child rearing and educational practice—so much so that a number of subjects were made a part of the school curricula in the past simply because they were distasteful and learning them was thought to build the will. As a result of this underlying, almost unconscious, attitude toward pleasure-oriented activities in our culture, children's play has been viewed as frivolous and nonproductive, having no value in their learning.

---

learn certain skills and that early childhood does constitute such a period for building the foundations on which future learnings will be based. A good example of this is language learning: children growing up in a home where two languages are spoken usually learn to speak both languages with ease and without a "foreign accent" in either language. Those of us who struggled through many years of studying a foreign language in school and who still are not fluent can understand the principle of optimal periods. Although part of our problem may stem from poor teaching techniques, it is really more a matter of our having missed that period in early childhood when it would have been much easier and more natural for us to learn languages.

The fact is that children (and all other human beings as well) learn best when they enjoy what they're doing, and taking pleasure in an activity is in no way inconsistent with hard work. The infant who is actively learning to walk is both working hard and enjoying herself. Very creative persons typically get great pleasure from their work. You, yourself, if you are like most people, probably are most productive and successful at activities that you enjoy. This, then, is what we mean when we say that learning is child's play, and playing is child's work.

As a reaction against the views held in the past that children did no important learning in their early years, some would now do away with children's spontaneous play and replace it with structured teaching of academic skills. This is as much a misunderstanding of the purpose of the early years as was the earlier view against which these people are reacting. There is certainly a place in early childhood education for teaching skills that will help children prepare themselves for reading, writing, and arithmetic. But children's time and energy at this point in their lives is too precious to be used in learning these skills to the neglect of others far more basic and fundamental.

The basic skills that young children should be learning in their early years can be grouped into four interrelated areas: motor, language, cognitive, and socioemotional development. Motor development is the growth of the ability to control and coordinate movement. Language development is learning to understand and use language to communicate with others. Cognitive development is the growth of thinking skills. And socioemotional development is the learning of skills for relating to and coping with others while, at the same time, gaining increased understanding of oneself as a person. Neuropsychological development underlies and guides all areas of development. It involves the growth of pathways to the brain from various parts of the body, from the brain to various parts of the body, and from parts of the brain to other parts of the brain. Neuropsychological development forms the circuitry through which the brain and spinal cord control and direct behavior.

There are rules that govern each of these areas of development. An understanding of these rules can be helpful to you in providing the conditions for your children's learning and growing as much, as well, and as happily as they are able.

MOTOR DEVELOPMENT

There are two kinds of motor development: gross (large) and fine (small). The first is the movement of the arms and legs, or coordinated body movement. The second is the refined movements of smaller parts of the body such as the tongue, lips, wrists and fingers, and toes. Gross motor is accomplished by the larger muscles of the body; their control and coordination generally precedes that of the many smaller muscles that must be brought under control and into coordination with each other for children's fine motor development.

Gross motor is involved in such skills as sitting, walking, running, climbing, jumping, hopping, and skipping. Fine motor is involved in using the hands and especially the thumb and fingers in picking up, letting go, holding on to and manipulating tools such as a spoon, crayons and other art materials, dressing oneself with buttons, zippers, and so on. It also includes growth of the ability to use the lips and tongue efficiently for eating and talking, and the toes for tiptoeing and pointing, and so on.

Children's development of motor skills follows a regular pattern. Control of the muscles through growth of pathways connecting them with the brain occurs, more or less, from the head downward and from the center of the body to the outermost parts. Thus, the first muscles of children's bodies to be brought under control are those directing the eyeballs, then the neck and shoulder area. Controlled arm movements precede control of the hand, and control of the palm of the hand for grasping comes before controlled use of the fingers and thumb.

This rule is helpful to know because you can observe what part of a child's body is under control and easily predict what the next step will be. Knowing this, you can provide stimulation to strengthen the child's capabilities while providing her or him with challenges to move on to the next step. For example, if your baby is beginning to hold her head up herself when you're holding her at your shoulder and when she's lying on her stomach, you can play some games with her to strengthen the control she's gaining of her neck muscles while also helping her develop strength and control in her shoulders. With her lying on the floor facing you, you can call to her and attract her attention with a toy until she raises her head to look at you. Gradually, you can raise the toy higher and move it to the side to get her to follow it with her head and eyes.

In general, control of gross movement precedes control of finer movements. For example, most children learn to walk some time around one year, whereas they don't learn to use their hands and fingers skillfully for several more years. Parallel to this, "mass" movements come before "specific" movements. For example, tiny infants startle with their whole bodies to a loud noise. Later they learn to turn only their head and eyes or only their eyes toward the source of a sound.

The process of motor development initially involves achievement of control over individual portions of the body. Then, super-imposed on that process is a continual reorganization of the different parts of the body in relation to each other as new skills are developed. For example, the arms and legs must be brought into coordination with each other for creeping; for walking, the arms serve a different function in relation to the legs and to the rest of the body.

Development of control over the muscles, continuous reorganization of motor skills, and changes in body proportion due to growth of different parts of children's skeletal structure all combine to require children to continually shift their point of balance, postural control, and consequently, their relationship to the world. For example, an infant's first achievement of balance occurs when he holds his head up when lying on his stomach; then as he begins to sit up with support he must learn a new state of balance through the reorganization of his head, neck, and shoulders in relation to his back in that posture.

Young children's motor development leads and directs their development in all other areas and is therefore important for a variety of reasons. First, as children gain control over their bodies, they gain control over their environment; they become able to move around and to act on the world. Various self-help skills including toileting oneself, feeding oneself, dressing oneself, and washing oneself all require the development of motor skills. The development of the ability to produce sounds for speech is dependent on control and coordination of the muscles of the mouth and tongue.

In addition, motor development is the basis for many of children's thinking skills. Children's first learnings about the world come from their direct sensory-motor interactions with it; that is, through their own reactions to and actions upon it. Subsequent learning will be related to children's internalization of these early motor-based experiences with the world. For example, children's understanding of such concepts as up and down, big and small, here and there, and so on are first learned in relation to their own bodies and are later transferred to understanding of relations among objects apart from them.

Finally, children's motor development indirectly affects the development of their relationships with other people and their feelings about themselves. As children become more competent motorically, they are able to be less dependent on others. They actively pursue, through continuous practice, achievement of independence skills, such as moving around on their own, feeding themselves, and undressing and dressing themselves. How you respond to this period of active motor involvement is important both to the growth of your children's self-concept and to your relationship with them. If you are supportive of their attempts to "conquer the world," your children will feel good about themselves and will see you as an ally. On the other hand, if you meet your children's attempts at independence with resistance, they will begin to feel incompetent and insecure, and the battlelines will be drawn between you and them.

LANGUAGE DEVELOPMENT

Children's understanding of language comes before they are able to use it meaningfully. Therefore, before you can expect children to speak, you must provide them with plenty of experience hearing you speak to them. Your speech should be concrete and meaningful; it should relate to the objects, people, and events in their lives. One way you can achieve this is by talking along with your activities, giving words to whatever you're doing with your child, even when he or she is a tiny baby. If you're a person who has always been able to carry on one-way conversations with animals, asking questions and answering them yourself, then this kind of talking will be easy for you. Anyway, do your best. For example, when taking your child outside, you might say something like, "Let's go outside. Here's your coat. Here's your hat. Where are your mittens? Here they are . . ." The point is that you can't wait until your children start talking to talk to them.

Typically, children first learn to say a few single words, and they sprinkle these in with a lot of jargon—speechlike sounds with the melody and intonation of real speech, but with no real meaning. They use the few words they have to "point to" things, and they use gestures to supplement their speech. Gradually, the jargon is replaced by more conventional words, and children begin to string words together into "telegraphic sentences," leaving out connectives, articles, even verbs: e.g., "Daddy coat," "Ari car." As children get more practice, and as time goes on, they begin to fill in their sentences, until by school age, children can use most of the different kinds of sentences contained in their language system.

The important thing to understand about children's language learning is that it proceeds at *their* own pace. You can enhance your child's language by talking to him a lot, and you can help him build a larger vocabulary of words. But what is more important than the number of words children know is the kinds of words they can use and the ways in which they can put those words together into sentences. And that you cannot speed up. Children go through very definite and predictable stages of language development during which they filter different information from the language they hear spoken around them and make up rules by which they construct their own language.

Therefore, there is no place in your language stimulation for correction of your child's speech, either in terms of sound production or of how she strings words together to form sentences. What you can do when your child makes a "mistake" is to give her back the correct form, but not by telling her she's wrong. For example, if she says, "I ain't got none," you might say, "You don't have any?", but it's best to avoid saying, "No, you should say . . ." First, it doesn't make any difference; she'll learn to say it correctly when she's able to, and your model will be sufficient; and second, being corrected hurts children's feelings and makes them defensive.

Just as, in motor development, children proceed from mass to specific movements, in language development they proceed from using single words to represent whole sentences and many different thoughts (e.g., "Mama" might mean everything from "Come here" to "I'm hungry") to learning words and combinations of words to say exactly what they want to say. You can help extend and expand your children's language when they're just beginning to use single words by reading into their intonation patterns and the kind of expression in their voice just what it is they want and then providing the language for them (e.g., "You're hungry? Let's eat. Here's a cracker"). The more tuned in you are to them, the better you can help your children give words to their actions and especially to their feelings. That's one of the more important functions language serves for us—letting us express things verbally that without language we can only express awkwardly and not very clearly through bodily action and gestures.

There is some disagreement among people who study young children about whether language development helps children think or whether there is no direct relationship between the development of language and children's increased ability to form rules about their world. Certainly there are things which children understand before they have the words for them, and teaching them the words will not teach them the concept. For example, children do not learn the concept of size by being taught such words as big and small. They learn about size by experiences which allow them to see how the bigness and smallness of a thing are related to what it is and to other things. For example, a small elephant is bigger than a big dog. A small dog may be a puppy or it may be a small kind of dog.

In helping children develop language skills, it is important not to teach them words which relate to adult's rules for thinking, but rather to guide them in using language through direct experience to describe their own way of thinking, to communicate to others what they already know though they lack the words to express it. It is important to realize that when a young child cannot answer a question using words, it may be because of the way the question is phrased, not because he doesn't know about the thing asked. A child who, when given a piece of chalk, uses it to write on the chalkboard, knows things about chalk even though he cannot name it or say that it's used to write with. Also, he will not know anything more about chalk if he knows those words.

However, children need words in order to communicate with others more easily. You should, therefore, try to find out from children, in ways other than talking, what the children know and then help them develop the language to communicate this to those around them. Having the idea or concept allows children to understand and deal with the world; having the word allows them to communicate the idea.

The development of language is a very important step in young children's growth. Most people rely very heavily on verbal communication to share their thoughts and feelings with others. In this exceptionally verbally oriented culture, preverbal children are at a great disadvantage. Unless their caregivers are very sensitive to nonverbal cues, children who can't yet speak have a hard time getting across to others what they want and need. This accounts for a great deal of the frustration and resulting temper tantrums we see in children who are just learning to talk but who cannot yet do so very articulately. Thus, as children become increasingly more verbal, they also become better able to affect what happens to them—they become more in control of their own lives.

In addition, as children become better able to put their thoughts and feelings into words that others can understand, they also become able to express those thoughts and feelings in more socially acceptable ways. When angry at someone, they can express that anger in words and work it out rather than striking out bodily. They can ask for a turn rather than grabbing a desired toy out of another child's hands. And, because they can understand a language shared with others, they can learn to see others' point of view, to understand why someone acted in a particular way toward them, and so on.

All of these benefits of being able to communicate, however, don't occur automatically just because children learn words. You must help them use those words in some of the ways described above—to communicate with others, to share their thoughts and feelings, to work out problems, to see things from others' point of view. It is essential that you talk *with* your children and listen *to* them. Too often, adults talk only *at* children, never communicating with them as equal human beings.

If you want your children to use language for communication and not as a disguise for their true thoughts and feelings as too many adults do, then you must be willing to communicate with them. That means sitting down together, so that your eyes can meet, and discussing things that are important to each of you. Don't ask children questions that can be answered by yes or no and expect to start a conversation. And don't assume they can't carry on a conversation with you. They can if you can. You need to be open, receptive, and respectful of them as human beings. You need to be sincerely interested in communicating with them. If you do these things and let them know that you haven't forgotten what it is to be a child, you'll find that even the quietest child will open up to you in time.

Language arises out of children's motor behavior. They learn to give verbal labels to the things they have learned through direct experience. Later, they will learn to use language as a substitute for experience and as a tool for manipulating thoughts in their heads. In helping children develop language, it's best to start with what they already know and help them to express it in words. You do this not through teaching them words, but through encouraging them to express their thoughts and feelings about what they're looking at, listening to, doing, and so on.

Because of our culture's dependence on verbal language, and because tests of intelligence are too often just expanded vocabulary tests, children's intelligence tends to be judged on the basis of the level of their language development. This is really unfair and inaccurate. Children know many things they don't know the words for and they know many words they don't really understand. Although language certainly is an important tool for thinking because of the shortcuts it provides, it is not, particularly in early childhood, synonymous with thinking. We must be very careful about judging children's intelligence by the number of words they know. There is much more to intelligence than words.

COGNITIVE DEVELOPMENT

There seems to be some confusion among those who study and those who care for children as to what is meant by cognitive development in early childhood and what is included in its realm. There are those who seem to confuse it with learning the 3 R's, and there are those who think it consists of learning color names, how to count, the alphabet, and other isolated bits of information. There are those who feel it occurs naturally if children are just allowed to play on their own, and there are those who are attempting to define it somewhat more systematically, but not rigidly. If we borrow from a dictionary definition of cognition, then we may define cognitive development simply as the growth of "the mental process by which knowledge is acquired." * The important thing is, then, not the development of specific, concrete skills so much as the development of generalizable and

---

* *The American Heritage Dictionary of the English Language.*

adaptive skills which can be applied to the acquisition of a variety of different kinds of skills and information.

Generalizable skills are those that can be applied to a variety of problems, challenges, and other situations. For example, there are certain procedures which go into solving a problem, whatever its nature:* 1) recognizing when a new situation is a problem situation; that is, understanding that problems exist and that they can be solved; 2) calling on search techniques in seeking a solution—to find strategies that have worked in the past with related problems; 3) actively taking initiative—starting problem-solving behavior right away, trying out strategies that might work; and 4) responding to the problem with persistence until a solution is found and the problem is solved.

You can help your children develop this essential generalizable cognitive skill by working through all levels and varieties of problems with them in this way and helping them develop strategies which they can bring to bear on problems—strategies that will then be available to them in the future when they apply search techniques. A simple way to express the importance of teaching children generalizable rather than specific skills is the following saying: "Give me a fish, and I eat for a day. Teach me to fish, and I eat for a lifetime."

Adaptive skills are those that enable people to adapt their own behavior to cope with change and with a variety of situations, including ones they may never have encountered before. These skills are particularly important in getting along with different kinds of people. Children who have had extended contact with many people with different styles and personalities seem better able to shift gears easily, changing their behavior in an adaptive way so as to deal effectively with all types of people. Children whose contacts with people have been limited seem less able to adapt their behavior to changing situations and people of different temperaments and styles.

Perhaps the most significant and helpful rule of cognitive development is that proposed by Piaget.† He has suggested that human beings, like all living organisms, develop through a process of active adaptation to the environment. Two complementary processes are part of this: assimilation and accommodation. Through their interactions with the world around them, children are constantly taking in information;§ each new bit of information taken in is *assimilated,* that is, filtered through and made to fit with what the child already knows. In addition, children *accommodate,* that is, adjust what they know to allow for (to fit with) the added information. Through this ongoing

---

* Jerome Bruner (Ed.), *Learning About Learning* (Washington, D.C.: U.S. Government Printing Office, 1966), p. 4.

† See Jean Piaget and Barbel Inhelder, *The Psychology of the Child* (New York: Basic Books, Inc., 1969), pp. 5–6.

§ "Information" is used here very broadly to mean any kind of input.

process of adaptation to the environment, children progress to increasingly higher levels of functioning.

Each time children assimilate new information into their structure of thinking and accommodate their structure to fit that new information, they broaden the territory covered by their cognitive category. For example, suppose you take your preschool child to the zoo and she sees a penguin for the first time. As with most children of her age, one of her primary criteria for defining an animal as a bird, unless she's already learned otherwise, is that it flies. But a penguin is a bird, and it doesn't fly. So from the other things she knows about birds (and perhaps with your help in identifying this creature), your child concludes that this strange-looking winged animal is a member of the bird family; she assimilates it into her idea of birds. But she must also accommodate her concept of birds to allow for this exception to the rule about birds she'd learned before—that birds are creatures that fly. Now she knows that a bird can still be a bird even if it doesn't fly.

The reason why assimilation and accommodation are such important concepts to understand is they provide a simple and logical explanation of how children learn as well as a guide for helping to enhance their learning. The point is that children will only assimilate information that is close to what they already know and understand, so if you want to teach them something new, you have to relate it to their past experience and storehouse of information.*

You can see in the above example what your role as a facilitator to children's learning should be. You can take children to the zoo, and although they will undoubtedly enjoy themselves, without your help they may not really learn anything new from the experience.† But with your help, guided by your understanding of the processes of assimilation and accommodation as the bases for children's learning, each new experience at the zoo can be related to ones you know the children have already had. For example, you can talk with children who have cats at home about all the members of the "family of cats," including the lions, tigers, and other cats at the zoo. This, in turn, might stimulate a later discussion about different "families," leading ultimately into how that relates to human beings. The amount of

---

* By the way, this rule applies to your learning also. Think about the school subjects that gave you the most trouble—you probably had very little in your background to relate the new information to, so you couldn't assimilate it until you translated it into more familiar terms. As you read this book, you'll learn most when the information presented is close to what you already know and least when it's very foreign.

† However, don't ever let your teaching become more important than your children's enjoyment of experiences. You should add to their enjoyment, not get in the way; besides, as we've said before, people learn more when they're enjoying themselves.

talking on the issue versus acting out, drawing pictures and murals, "writing" a book, and so on would depend on the children's individual interests and abilities.

Learning, seen in the context of assimilation and accommodation, proceeds in small steps as children gradually accommodate what they knew before to allow for differences between their old ideas and the new information.

Thus, it's wise to take your children's leads as to what they can readily assimilate. For learning to occur, there must be what Hunt* refers to as a "proper match" between what children already know or can do and stimulation from the environment. Input must contain just the right amount of novelty. Children learn best from things similar to but slightly different from what they already know. Once a child has explored an activity or material in every possible way, then it will no longer be interesting, and he will not learn from it. In contrast, if it's too different, too new, he won't be able to relate it to something he knows, and he will not learn from it.

Related to the amount of novelty a material or activity contains for a child is the degree to which it challenges her or his thinking skills. To be interesting (and thus intellectually stimulating) it should be a little puzzling or challenging. Thus, when choosing things for children to play with or when thinking of good activities, try to provide just the right amount of difficulty, coupled with just the right amount of novelty.

The response you receive from children when your choice of materials and activities is not matched to their interests and abilities may be fear and avoidance, or it may be lack of attention or some other sign of boredom. In order to find out what children are interested in, what is "just right" for them (not too hard but not too easy, not too new but not too familiar), watch them. See what interests them, what they pay attention to for more than a very short time. Then find other activities and materials which are similar, but a little different. If the children become involved with the new materials and activities, you've chosen well; if they're not interested or if they avoid the task, it may be too easy, too hard—try again.

In our discussions of motor and language development, we noted that development proceeds from mass to specific responses. There is a related process in cognitive development. At first, children respond to the world around them in a more or less global way. For example, in early infancy, babies smile at anything resembling a human face; they stare at all visual events with about equal regard; they have a limited number of actions they can perform on objects, and they apply them similarly to everything. Gradually, they begin to make some order

* J. McV. Hunt, *Intelligence and Experience* (New York: The Ronald Press, 1961), pp. 267–88.

out of their world: they differentiate among people, events, and appropriate actions on objects according to their specific meanings. For example, by three and a half months, most babies will look only at what holds particular interest for them, not at just anything that happens to be around. By six to nine months, most babies begin to differentiate between friends and strangers and will smile only at the former. Toward the end of their first year most babies will begin to respond to objects in an individualized manner, e.g., squeezing a rubber squeaky toy; ringing a bell; "drinking" from a cup; banging on a drum, instead of applying the same actions—touching, banging, shaking, tasting, and so on—to all objects encountered.

In addition, an important aspect of cognitive development is that children combine formerly separate ways of knowing about a thing or previously unrelated things and events into more integrated patterns. For example, tiny infants when hungry can be comforted only by being fed; their knowledge of their mother revolves around the feel and taste of her breast, or if they are bottle-fed, of the bottle. Gradually, they begin to differentiate her voice, her smell, her footsteps, her face from others' and to integrate all these separate characteristics into a definition of mother. Then, on exposure to any one of the characteristics, they will come to expect the others. Thus, on simply hearing their mothers' footsteps, babies will often stop crying, knowing that they'll soon have their needs met.

Another example of the processes of differentiation and integration can be seen in children's learning of categories—what things go together. To very small children, everything that walks on four legs and has a tail may be classified as a "doggy" (or whatever other label they apply). Then, slowly, children begin to differentiate among different kinds of animals, learning to identify each of them as separate and distinct creatures. At the same time, they are learning to integrate all these things into the general category of animal.

It should be noted that classification—grouping together like things and separating them from things that are different—is very much culture-bound. Although children do not simply absorb their culture's manner of classifying things (they actively extract rules and consistencies from their own experiences to come up with their categories), they do learn the classification system of their own culture. For example, in our culture, there are a large number of classifications for colors: we define not only the basic hues of red, orange, yellow, green, blue, and purple, but many combinations and shades of these. The Kpelle,* (a tribal group in Western Africa) in contrast, have words only for white, red, and black. Their color "red" would include what we would call red, orange, dark yellow, and even certain shades

---

* M. Cole, J. Gay, J. Glick, and D. Sharp, *The Cultural Context of Learning and Thinking* (New York: Basic Books, Inc., 1971).

of purple. This is a particularly interesting example because colors in the natural environment are not divided into separate units; all colors blend into one another. Color names, like other words, demonstrate the way human beings use words to group things together which, for their way of life, are similar.

Human beings of all races and cultures are basically more alike than they are different in terms of potentiality. But different cultural priorities tend to encourage and allow for development of different potentialities of the human mind and body. Children both model their behavior after the adults around them and are reinforced by adults to behave in ways that are consistent with the cultural norms. The cultural impact on children's cognitive development is important to understand even within our Western culture, because we are actually not one culture but many subcultures. We should try to recognize our own culture-boundness and in our interactions with children present them with a maximum of alternatives even though these may still lie within the constraints of our own cultural boundaries. The ultimate goal of human development should be to become more human and thus less restricted by our cultural differences and more bound together by our shared human attributes.

We have already talked somewhat about the relationship between cognitive development and the other areas of development. Cognitive development is grounded in children's motor development: children learn about the world first through their direct, motor-based interactions, and these experiences in turn "inform" their minds. For example, in learning to move about on their own, children learn about spatial relations—how things are positioned in space in relation to themselves and to each other. Learning to walk around without bumping into things, how to move in order to avoid obstacles, is a matter of cognitive development as much as it is motor development. Learning to maneuver a spoon so that more food gets into the mouth than on the floor is another example of the interrelationship between motor and cognitive development.

The example used in explaining differentiation and integration —that of classifying animals—and the discussion of the cultural aspects of cognitive development, in which we noted how human beings in different cultures give names to things according to the function they serve in their lives, both illustrate some of the interrelationships between language and cognitive development. In the first example, it seems reasonable to assume that having the words to describe the various characteristics that distinguish animals, as well as having the word "animal" itself, would facilitate children's learning of those concepts. This is in contrast to a concept such as "bouncing a ball" that is understood on the basis of the experience itself; here the words are useful more for communication than for clarifying the concept. In the second example, you can see how the words people use can help structure their thinking about things. Anthropologists have always looked at a culture's language to get some ideas of the kind of life its people lead as well as the relationships existing among them. Finally, as we noted before, many people judge the intelligence of others by how articulate their language is, and this is reinforced by the kind of schooling we have and the kinds of testing we do to assess people's "intelligence." Actually, intelligence is not a thing in itself; it is a function, that of information-processing, and information can be processed in many forms other than spoken or written language. We should avoid, in early childhood education, too great a reliance on these sometimes limiting aspects of intelligence.

The relationship between cognitive development and socioemotional development is complex. In a sense, learning to relate to others and to be in control of one's own behavior is as much cognitive as it is socioemotional in character. But these aspects of cognitive development have been largely neglected or left to chance in our educations. Those people who have good skills for relating to others and who feel in control of their own behavior have usually had good models as well as a nurturing, supportive environment in which to grow when they were young. And there is a strong relationship between how you feel about yourself and your competence. Children whose cognitive skills enable them to be successful tend to feel good about themselves, and children who feel good about themselves tend to believe that they can be successful.

But we all know children who are very "smart" in that they are very articulate and can do many things, but who, nevertheless, fail miserably when it comes to relating to others, understanding themselves, and feeling in control of their own behavior. This type of child is usually the result of child rearing that emphasizes development of the mind without equal concern for the development of healthy, loving interpersonal relationships. Ideally, of course, child rearing and early childhood education should stress both as intimately related and equally important. A mind without a heart is both a dangerous and a sad thing.

SOCIOEMOTIONAL DEVELOPMENT

Whereas motor development is the most predictable and firmly established area of human growth, socioemotional development is the least. It is the easiest to disrupt and impede, and it is extraordinarily vulnerable to both cultural and individual social influences, since, by definition, it is within the social context that children develop socially and emotionally. It is also the most important area, because its influence pervades all the other areas of development, and because it is with us all the time. Long after you have forgotten most of what you learned (or failed to learn) in school, and the greatest effect you recognize of the success of your motor development is whether or not you are awkward or graceful or good at physical sports, and your language development is adequate for communicating fairly effectively with others, you will still be strongly influenced in your day-to-day life by the effectiveness of your development of socioemotional skills.

We come into contact daily with many apparently successful and well-adjusted adults who nevertheless often function in their relationships with others and in terms of their feelings about themselves as though they were two and a half years old. Many behaviors that might be considered neurotic by some can be viewed instead as failures to grow in the socioemotional realm. They are maladaptive because they don't make people happy and they are not productive, but they are inappropriate mainly because they are found in people who are chronologically far too old to be showing such behaviors, and not so much because they are in themselves problem behaviors.

One of the major reasons why a relatively large number of people find it difficult to cope with others and themselves in a consistently harmonious and productive way is that the major avenue for learning social and emotional behavior is through modeling. If those around you in your childhood did not present you with an effective model, it is very difficult (even when you know how intellectually) to cope effectively yourself later on. The only behavioral models available to you are those in which you have been a participant or an observer.* This is why many parents find, much to their chagrin, that they treat their own children in many of the ways they swore they would never treat anyone because they hated being treated that way when they were children. It isn't because they're not decent, well-meaning people. It's that when you learn a role, you don't just learn one part of it; you learn a role set, incorporating all aspects of the role interaction. So when you find yourself in a behavioral setting calling for any segment of a role interaction in which you have taken part, you will find yourself automatically beginning to play whatever role is opposite that played by the other person(s) in the interaction.

For example, suppose when you were a child your father always made you feel very stupid and insecure whenever you made any kind of a mistake; imagine that he yelled at you, talked sarcastically to you, and called you names, reducing you to a very weak and submissive atti-

---

* Some of the behaviors people adopt from others and make their own are modeled from ones they've observed in others with whom they've never interacted. But the most powerful models in your behavioral development are people with whom you have interacted on a regular basis and whom you care about and want to please.

tude by the time he was done. You might find in your adulthood (or even before) that when interacting with someone who was weak, rather than empathizing with that person, as you would think you would, you act toward him or her as your father did to you. If this happened, as it does with many people, it would be because the only two parts of such an interaction you learned as a child were either to be the weak one or to be the bully. On the other hand, if your mother usually stepped in to console you and make you feel better, then you'd have learned this role too. Therefore, you'd be more likely to be able to react to someone who reminded you of your childhood self in the empathic way you'd prefer.

We do not mean to alarm you into thinking that you are forever a victim of your childhood experiences. This is not true unless you let it be. By recognizing those behaviors in yourself that do not reflect how *you* really feel and would like to be and by realizing that they are habits that can be changed, you can begin the process of changing them. The first step in problem-solving, as we noted earlier, is recognizing that a problem exists. In this case, those of us who are responsible for the care and nurturance of young children must become conscious of those behaviors in ourselves that are maladaptive and nonproductive and begin to try to behave in ways that are more conscious and more productive. We must make sure that "the buck stops with us." Life is getting too difficult to burden our children with these same behavior patterns that we've all been unconsciously passing through each generation.

What is the answer then? If the only behavior patterns we know are those we've observed or in which we've taken part, and these don't work very well, then what are the options? The first answer is to look within yourself and around you for individual behavioral interactions that *do* work. Everyone has some times when they are very successful at coping with others and with themselves. Make note of these times in yourself and others, examine them, and try to repeat them. Second, and most important, is a rule by which you should judge all your behaviors toward others and theirs toward you: *You may do whatever you will as long as it is not at someone else's expense,* or, stated another way, *Your rights as an individual extend only to the point at which they infringe on someone else's rights.*

The rule stated above is directly related to an age-old human rule—The Golden Rule—which states that you should "Do unto others as you would have them do unto you." Unfortunately, this is meant in a much broader way than it is usually interpreted by many who think they follow it. It does not mean that you should do something nice for someone because you wish they would do it for you. Interpreted in this limited a way, it would be better stated that you should "Do unto others as they would have you do unto them." In too many relationships, including parent-child relationships, we see people "unselfishly" giving the other person all the things they want themselves, never realizing that they're rarely giving anything the other person really wants. The real point of the Golden Rule is that, in the most general sense, you should try to put yourself in the shoes of other persons and treat them as well as you would like people to treat you if you were in that same situation. In a specific sense, this means that you need to try to find out, through observing and through asking, what particular things would make other persons feel comfortable; don't assume that they want the same kind of treatment that you want.

This rule of human interaction incorporates the two aspects of human behavior that are important for individual and collective human development: individuality *and* cooperation. Individuality by itself can, and often does, develop through competition with others, and therefore, ultimately, at others' expense. Cooperation by itself limits the human potential, since it is through the creative acts of individual self-expression that the whole of humankind develops new insights, levels of consciousness, and visions of what human beings can be.

You may be wondering what this discussion has to do with child development in general and socioemotional development in particular. The answer is that it has everything to do with it. Ultimately, our goal in child development should be to help children develop well enough individually that they can contribute collectively to the further development of the human race. The Golden Rule and the variations of it that we've offered should be the basis of all human interactions. We need to understand how it applies to us as adults, because the model we provide to the children in our care (both in terms of how we treat them and in terms of how we treat others) will have a significant impact on their behavioral interactions with others. And if we can begin to change our own behavior in productive directions, we can save our children from having to undo maladaptive habits learned through nonproductive interactions they observe or participate in.*

One aspect of socioemotional development is learning to interact with others. The other, which develops within the context of the first part, involves how you feel about yourself (in relation to others, in terms of your expectations of success or failure, in terms of the amount of control you feel capable of over your own life). In our preface, "To the Reader," we discussed the importance of helping children develop feelings about themselves of competence and self-worth. The rule for

---

* The whole point of *Growing With Children*, our last book, was that an understanding of how children develop and how your own childhood experiences influence your present behavior can help you begin to grow yourself, whatever your age; and if you want to guide children into happy and productive adulthood, you have a responsibility to grow yourself. If this idea appeals to you, we recommend that you look at this book for details.

social interaction is to try to see things from the other person's point of view and to treat others as they would like to be treated. The rule for individual development is "belief-in-self"—if you want to be able to do anything, you must believe in your ability to do it.

All of us, no matter how good a facade we may present to others, are crippled to some extent and in some areas by the poison of self-doubt. This poison is injected into us at an early age, usually by well-meaning people who don't want us to get too puffed up with a sense of our own importance. The problem is that they have confused the issue of concern for the rights of others with belief-in-self. If your belief in yourself were to take the form of your feeling that your rights were more important than others' rights, then belief-in-self would, indeed, be a dangerous thing. In fact, however, it is usually those who do *not* believe in themselves—who are insecure about how others feel toward them—who are more likely to be blind to other peoples' needs in relation to their own. Those who have a greater degree of belief in themselves are freed from constant concern about themselves and therefore have more energy to devote to concern for other people.

Children first develop feelings about themselves in the context of the feelings they receive from those who care for them. If their caregivers love them deeply and unconditionally (that is, without regard for what they do or fail to do, but simply because of who they are) and communicate this consistently, then children will feel good about themselves; they will develop a sense of themselves as persons whom other people care about and think well of.

Much attention has been paid to the importance of the first year of life for children's developing a basic sense of trust about the world as a good, predictable, comfortable, loving place to be; this trust in others, in turn, enables babies to feel good about themselves—if the feelings they get from others are consistently loving and responsive to their needs, then they must be persons worthy of such feelings. (Clearly, children this age don't think in those terms, but such connections are being made on a nonverbal, emotional level.) We agree that infants' first experiences should, ideally, promote such feelings of trust, but it is not impossible for it to happen at a later age; it's just much harder, because the child would have built up that much more of a habit of expecting the world to be unloving and unresponsive. Undoing a habit is more difficult and more time-consuming than establishing one. Also, it should be noted that it is not enough for babies to feel loved when they're tiny; if their caregivers suddenly become very restrictive and ambivalent in their feelings when children begin to move about on their own, they'll still become insecure even if they did have a positive, loving early experience.

The key, then, to helping children develop positive feelings about themselves is to 1) give them consistent, unconditional love (which doesn't mean that you can't get angry at something they do; it just means that nothing they do can threaten your love for them and that they know that to be true), 2) allow and help them to assume increasing amounts of responsibility for themselves as they become interested in doing so (they won't always be able to be successful right away, because responsibility takes practice), 3) provide them with challenging experiences through which they can develop their skills and, as a consequence, feelings of competence and confidence that they can meet challenges in the future. (They should not feel under pressure to achieve or to compete with anyone else; fear of failure is an obstacle to success and to feelings of self-worth.)

One thing that will help your relationship with your children to be a good one is to let them know what you expect of them. Children really want to please and win the approval of their caregivers, but they often don't know what it takes. You may have specific things that you expect, and if you do, you should let your children know what they are. We propose that, in general, all we should expect of our children is that they be human beings. That means two things: 1) that they be themselves and 2) that they be concerned with the rights and feelings of others. It is important that you make a point of communicating to your children, in words and by the way you treat them, that you want them to act in ways that feel right to them as long as it doesn't hurt anyone else; that you will be pleased with them when they are pleased with themselves, and that they should not, therefore, do things just in order to try to please you; that you will let them know when they can do something specific to please you, and you will tell them if they do something that displeases you, but that you really want them to learn to do the things that feel right to them.

The one basic rule for children's behavior, then, should be that they may do what they will as long as they respect the rights and feelings of others. Since children spend their early years trying to discover and make up rules about how things work in the world, this should be a welcome, ready-made one that can be generalized to almost every behavioral situation. It should be the basis of your behavior management, and its eventual goal is people who think about the consequences of their actions, in terms of others as well as themselves, before they act—a breed of human beings we can surely use more of.

In addition to the general goal of helping your children develop good feelings about themselves as persons, you should also try to help them get in touch with and understand all their emotions. Our emotions are at the core of our being, and they influence our behavior all the time. If you feel good, happy, elated, enthusiastic, you will feel able to do whatever you set your energies to. In contrast, if you feel depressed, lonely, angry, or sad, you probably won't have much energy for anything other than those emotions. It is not that the latter are "bad" emotions, and they should not simply be dismissed. If you can help children to identify just how they feel and to focus on who or what they feel that toward and why, then they can learn to harness those emotions and turn them into positive energy. At the same time, if you can help them recognize when they're feeling good, why, toward whom and what, then they'll be more likely in the future to be able to reproduce those positive emotions when they're needed.

Emotions are not something outside ourselves that take control of us; we are in control of them, and they are ours to harness and use productively if we choose. Human beings, unlike other creatures, have choice. If they choose not to choose—if they choose to be controlled rather than to be in control—then they should at least recognize that they have made a choice by not choosing. You can be most helpful to your children by examining your own experiences and getting more in touch with your own emotions. In the process of your own explorations, you can share with your children and ask them to share with you how they feel.

We have emphasized repeatedly the importance of children developing a healthy self-concept, and we have asserted that this is fundamental to all other areas of development. For any of you who doubt the enormous impact emotional climate has on developing children, we refer you to Dr. Ashley Montagu's book in this series, *Culture and Human Development*. In it, he includes readings that dramatically illustrate the extent to which the emotional environment children are brought up in can interfere with their growth in all areas; the articles report numbers of cases of physically and intellectually retarded children whose disorders were the result, not of organically based problems, but of nonsupportive emotional environments.

Certainly not all children respond to a cold and unresponsive emotional climate by becoming stunted in their physical and intellectual growth. For most children, the results are probably much more subtle. And we know that children are born with different temperaments that affect their capacity to cope with stress. Some babies seem to be able to take things in stride, not becoming upset easily, and quickly establishing their own very stable life rhythm. Other babies are set off easily by the slightest irregularity or tension and have a hard time adjusting to life and the people around them. Most babies display some combination or more moderate variation of these extremes. But all babies filter their experiences in terms of their own capacity to endure and adjust to change, tension, inconsistency, and so on.

What the dramatic cases cited in Dr. Montagu's volume tell us about the effects of the social environment on children's growth should not be dismissed, however, with the excuse that babies have different capacities for coping and these children were weaker than most. The important message of these extreme examples is that less obvious and more subtle instances of failure to grow probably occur with more regularity than many of us would like to admit. Most children will grow physically, and they may grow intellectually enough not to draw attention to themselves; but it is clear that, overall, human beings' social and emotional growth has a long way to go. Those persons who are healthy enough to function effectively, and even sometimes outstandingly, nevertheless still suffer from feelings of self-doubt that impede their full effectiveness as human beings. The world is desperately in need of healthy, whole human beings who can interact harmoniously and cooperatively with others and who are at peace with themselves. The hope for these kinds of human beings is with the children, and their hope is with you.

NEUROPSYCHOLOGICAL DEVELOPMENT

You cannot observe the development of connections within the brain and between the brain and other parts of the body except indirectly through the behavior that it makes possible. Nevertheless, we think it is helpful to your understanding of child development to have some knowledge of the underlying neurological basis for development in all areas. Your provision of optimally stimulating conditions for your children's learning and growing will not affect their neuropsychological development in any way that you can see; but studies of animals have shown that stimulating environments in early life do result in an increased capacity for profiting from new experiences at maturity.[*]

As stimulation occurs, pathways are formed in the brain to carry the information that comes in from the environment and to carry response information back. Conclusions about the relationship between neurological development and learning seem to indicate that the amount of stimulation the brain receives sets a stage for the amount of information it continues to be able to handle and to anticipate. Pathways for carrying information develop from being used to carry information. This doesn't mean that you should bombard your children with as much stimulation as possible. Studies of human infants[†] indicate that too much stimulation is disturbing; too much input at one time cannot be processed, and infants will react by tuning out. The trick is to be very observant of your children's behavior so that you provide them with just the right amount and kind of stimulation at the right time.

[*] J. McV. Hunt, *Intelligence and Experience* (New York: The Ronald Press, 1961), Chapter 4.
[†] Burton White, *Human Infants* (Englewood Cliffs, N.J.: Prentice-Hall, Inc., 1971).

For example, in earliest infancy, it is the repetition of the same consistent, predictable experiences (such as being fed when hungry by the same person) that enables the first connections to be made in the infant's brain—connections between the infant's actions and the environment's response ("When I am hungry and I cry, someone comes") and connections identifying the source of the satisfaction (babies learn very early to distinguish their mother's voice, for example, over others'). In turn, early experiences that provide information for initial hook-ups also give the baby's brain a repertoire of information with which to then compare new information. And, as explained in the section on cognitive development, the brain is able to assimilate new information that can, in some way, be related to previous experience and stored information. Babies' alertness or lack of alertness to new information is your cue of what they are ready and able to take in.

Children's development follows a regular sequence which is decided in advance because of the way their brains are "programmed" to follow a sort of built-in maturational code. The brain is the most rapidly and completely developed part of the young infant's equipment, and it serves as the master controller of all the rest of the child's development. Although new connections and pathways continue to be formed past the period of early childhood, a baby's brain has nearly all its quota of cells at birth.*

Although newborns have most of the brain cells they're going to have, they are not all in working order. When they are born, children's behavior is not purposeful. They can't control it because the higher, peculiarly human parts of their brain aren't yet functional. Newborns' behavior consists of a large repertoire of reflex, automatic responses that are governed by the lower parts of their brain. Gradually, more and more of a child's body comes under his conscious, deliberate control as the higher parts of his brain develop working pathways which "tell" him about information coming in and "tell" the parts of his body what to do.

Nerve cells are the "messengers" of the brain; they carry coded information from within and outside parts of the body to the brain and from the brain to the other parts of the body to tell it what's happening and what to do. Before they can be in full operation, neurons

---

* There is enormous growth in the size and weight of a baby's brain in the first three years and especially in the first six months. (The brain nearly doubles in weight in the first six months "and by the end of the third year, the brain of the average three-year-old has achieved more than four-fifths of its maximum adult size." Ashley Montagu, "Sociogenic Brain Damage," in A. Montagu (ed.) *Culture and Human Development.* Englewood Cliffs, N.J.: Prentice-Hall, 1974.) This growth is not so much the number of brain cells but rather, as explained in the following pages, in the development of pathways within the brain to carry information. The fantastic growth that occurs in this time period is further confirmation of the importance of early childhood to a human being's total development.

must become "connected" * to each other, forming pathways through which messages are carried to and from and within the brain. Also, different groups of cells must learn to carry different kinds of messages; and each of these different groups or pathways must become covered with another kind of cell which will keep it separated from other pathways so that their messages don't get mixed up. As these changes happen, babies begin to learn to sort out and construct the meaning of the things in the world outside themselves and to respond to that world.

The brain works in two directions. First, different kinds of information from the outside world—sounds, sights, feelings (touch, pain, temperature from outside), smells, and tastes—are carried to the brain to be registered and interpreted. You don't "hear" a sound because it is there; your ears carry the sound from the outside, then the auditory nerve takes over, and finally, if the "sound" reaches the necessary parts of the brain, your brain "hears" the sound. In a similar way, the brain gets messages from inside your body telling you if you are hungry, if you have pain inside your body, and so on. The other direction in which the brain works is in sending messages to different parts of the body, to different muscles, telling them how to move.

In addition, connections must be made within the brain, integrating all the different kinds of information that come in with each other and with motor responses. One of the parts of the human brain that distinguishes it from the brains of other animals is called "the association area." (It is much larger in the human brain, relative to the sensory area, than in the brains of other animals.) This part of the brain is responsible for hooking up the otherwise separate parts of the brain for receiving different kinds of information (e.g., auditory, visual, touch, smell, and taste) and for acting on the world, making possible such peculiarly human abilities as verbal language and thinking. As the association pathways and their connections to motor pathways begin to work, babies begin to associate the different ways of exploring and recognizing objects.

There is a relationship between the development of different parts of children's brains and the development of new skills and behaviors. For example, the cerebellum, the part of the brain which is responsible for coordination of movement, undergoes its most rapid period of growth between the ages of six to fourteen or fifteen months; this is the time period during which children learn to sit, crawl, creep, stand, and walk. The brain's growth, activated by experience, directs children's development.

This information is useful for you to know because there are

* There actually is no *physical* connection between neurons; rather it is a chemical and electric "connection" that forms a sort of "bridge" from one neuron to the next.

certain times when children's brains are ready to develop each new skill or ability, and that is the time when they should learn it. The readiness of a child's brain is related to her or his human and personal heredity as well as to experience. Trying to teach children a skill that their brains are not ready to develop is a misuse of their energy and yours. For example, the connections between the brain and the sphincter muscles which are necessary for voluntary and deliberate control of holding in and letting go are not fully developed before eighteen months to two years. You can waste a lot of valuable energy and create problems for yourself and your children by spending time trying to toilet train them before the muscles enabling them to accomplish it are under their conscious control.

It is important to keep in mind that we cannot observe the development of children's brains; it is only useful to understand the relationship between their neurological development and their development in other areas in order to recognize that there is a biological foundation to the sequential regularities of development. But it is children's behavior that reflects the stage of their development and signals their "optimal periods" for learning specific things.

SOME GENERAL PRINCIPLES OF CHILD DEVELOPMENT

There are regularities to human development that weave a common thread through the entire human species. As a human being, every child will follow certain orderly, predictable rules of development. The specifics of development, such as what kinds of tools children will learn to use when they are ready to learn the use of tools, what language they will learn to speak, and to what particular use they will put their thinking skills, are culture-bound; but the generalities of development cut across cultural boundaries. Each culture selectively stresses certain aspects of the range of possibilities for human development. But the possibilities are, nevertheless, fundamentally the same for all children of the human race regardless of the particular human culture they are born into. And the rules of development apply similarly across cultures.

1) Development occurs in an orderly sequence. The expression "You must walk before you can run" illustrates the sequence of development. There are experiences through which children must go before they go through others. All children go through a similar sequence of steps (the order is always the same, the specific behaviors may be somewhat different). Thus, if you know the sequence and the steps, and you know what step your children are at, you can predict

what their next step will be. Then you can think of appropriate stimulation which will enhance their development at the step they're at and which will help them get to the next one. You can also prepare yourself for the next stage. For example, when your child is going through the steps preparing him to walk, you can help him and, at the same time, clear the child-level places in the house of breakable items in preparation for his new stage.

2) Most children reach certain developmental milestones, such as standing, walking, and speaking single words at about the same time. There is a general age range within which most children normally develop these different skills. It is this kind of regularity that allows us to talk of the behavior of the "average" two-year-old or clothing manufacturers to put age sizes on children's clothes. But just as you would not expect any child to be a perfect size two, i.e., to wear size two in all of her clothes—shoes, hat, shirt, pants—when she's exactly twenty-four months old, so you would not expect her behavior to resemble exactly that of the "average" two-year-old discussed in this or any other publication about child development.

3) When we make the statement that most children develop skills within the same age range, we assume that they are given the opportunity to develop that skill. Children left lying in cribs all the time, as in institutions where there aren't enough people to love them, hold them, fondle them, talk to them, play with them, provide interesting experiences for them, and give them a chance to grow and learn, will not develop skills at the same time as other children. Children's abilities do not, as once thought, simply unfold. Children need stimulation in order to develop skills just as they need food in order to grow. And, just as their food must be varied to give them the right amount of different kinds of nutrients, so must their stimulation be varied, including the right amount and kind of love, different things to look at, listen to, feel, taste, and smell, and opportunities to act on the world.

4) Children need different kinds of stimulation and treatment at different times. For example, during the period between about eighteen months and three years children are most "ripe" for learning language skills. During this time, they need a chance to listen to and practice talking with people in order to develop their language skills as well as possible. If for some reason they were not exposed to language at this time, it would be harder for them to learn it later. This, of course, doesn't mean that children don't need language stimulation before eighteen months; they need it from birth in order to be ready to talk some time around one year. But their needs for practicing and using their newly developed language skills are particularly important between the ages of eighteen months and three years.

The best way to know when your children need a particular kind of stimulation and what kind and how much they need is by heightening your responsiveness to their cues. Children tell us very clearly what they need from the time they're tiny; all we have to do is learn how to "listen" to them. They tell us more from their actions than from what they say. This is probably why adults often miss their "message."

For example, if you try to feed solid food to a tiny infant and she coughs and sputters and spits up all the food you give her, her behavior is telling you that she's not yet ready to handle solids. Knowing that babies generally are *not* ready for this step until about the age of three months will give you confidence that your baby's response really does "tell" you correctly that this is so; but ultimately it is your baby's behavior that should guide your care of her.

In general, if children are happy and attentive, that is, if they watch, listen intently, get involved with something, you're doing the right thing for them at the time. With preschool-age children, if it takes a long time to teach something, and you have a hard time keeping the children's interest, you're on the wrong track. If they're developmentally ready to learn something, children will show interest in and be excited about it.

5) Different amounts of energy go into different areas of development at different times. For example, in the first year of life, infants expend a great deal of energy learning to move about. At the same time, they're learning to make sense of the world around them, which includes trying to understand conversation. Developmental norms suggest that many children begin early attempts at walking at about one year and also begin speaking a few words. Again, this is the imaginary "average" child. In reality, children who are actively learning to walk may forget about talking for a while and devote all their energies to walking. On the other hand, children who are actively trying to talk —to name the things around them—may fall behind for a while in other areas and spend all their energies learning to talk. Many things occur simultaneously for children; but when they are learning and practicing a new skill, they will put more energy into it and less into other things, sometimes appearing to fall behind.

6) Finally, children's development does not proceed in a straight path toward each developmental goal. Rather, the path of development is more like a spiral, with stops and starts, progressions and regressions. Children make forward strides in which their growth seems to be progressing well. These stages are usually followed by what seem like steps backward. In fact, children are simply pushing their newly gained abilities beyond their limits or, having mastered one skill, they're starting at ground zero on a new one. These periods are usually followed once more by stages of good equilibrium in which children seem again to be moving forward, well in control.

Whatever skills children develop require practice before they are accomplished with ease and efficiency. Every time children complete the refinement of one particular skill or set of skills, this sets the stage for the emergence of a new challenge to be mastered. Each newly emerging ability must be tried out, practiced, and consolidated; it must be fit into children's repertoire of automatic skills and behaviors. So, just when a growing child seems to be well under control, to be becoming self-contained and competent (i.e., when one new skill is mastered), a new behavior emerges, and once again he becomes off-balance as he goes about developing the new skill and fitting it into his repertoire.

SOME THOUGHTS ON DISCIPLINE

Children learn more from the way you act, the way you treat them and others, than from what you tell them or try to teach them. You should, therefore, be aware of what things your behavior is teaching your children, especially if it's different from what you want to teach them in words. Children do not follow the directions to "Do as I say, not as I do." Thus, it doesn't make sense to hit your children to punish them for hitting other children. By hitting them, you teach them to hit others; your behavior shows them that temper and violence are acceptable forms of expression.

Also, be aware of what behaviors you are reinforcing in your children by the way you react to their behavior. Many behavior problems are created by well-meaning adults who intended to keep their child from showing just that kind of behavior. For example, suppose you can't stand whining. Every time your child whines, you get very angry at him and/or you end up giving him what he wants to stop him from whining. Either way, and especially if you do both, you are making sure your child will whine every time he wants something: (1) you pay attention to him when he does it; and (2) it works—it gets him what he wants.

On the more positive side of the coin, and as a general rule, it's wisest to ignore behaviors you don't like (unless they are harmful to you, your child, or anyone else), and to respond positively to behaviors you do like. Children (and adults) crave attention,* positive or negative. Try to pay more attention to positive behaviors and less to negative ones. Your children will learn to stop the behaviors you don't like

---

* Attention from others is as important (and normal) a psychological need for human beings as hunger is a physical need. It's important that you do not simply dismiss this need with "Oh, she's just trying to get attention." Rather, you should help your children learn to satisfy their need for attention in acceptable and productive ways.

and continue the ones you do like. Remember, however, that if you're trying to undo a behavior which has been around for a while, it also will take a while to get rid of it.

Another important rule is to *be consistent*. Be consistent with your love, so that your child knows that you can be counted on for support and help when you're needed. You can never, never spoil a child with love. Your children should be able to take your love for granted; they should never have to worry about it. This will make discipline easier for you too, because you can teach your children that they have done something which you didn't like without also causing them to fear that you don't like them because of it. Don't threaten to stop loving your child, and don't withdraw your love as a punishment. You can withdraw positive attention, but your love should be a constant.

Be consistent with your discipline. If there are things which your children are not allowed to do, they should never be allowed to do them. Do not let them get away with something one day because you're feeling good and then get mad at them another day for the same thing because you're in a bad mood. If it's not important enough to be consistent about, then it's not important enough to be angry about. Inconsistency is confusing to children; they need to know what behaviors are okay and which ones are not so they know where they stand and so they can learn to predict the consequences of their behavior.

Of course, even with the best intentions, everyone loses his cool sometimes. Don't be afraid to apologize for losing your temper or responding unjustly to a child. We're all human, and it's a good lesson for a child to learn about admitting one's mistakes. Also, don't let your concern with consistency make you inflexible. Sometimes children whine for a reason. If you ignore it every time, never checking to find out the cause, you could hurt a child's feelings unnecessarily. Before ignoring or punishing a negative behavior, give children their "day in court"; see if they had a valid reason for acting as they did.

If children are going to be punished, then do it at the time they're doing something to be punished for, not later. If you see them beginning to do something wrong, stop them right away; don't wait for them to finish the deed. Don't threaten anger or punishment, and don't build up to a punishment in little steps (e.g., starting with "Don't do that," said hesitantly as if you don't really mean it, and building up to a spanking). A firm "No!" said with real conviction is much more effective than "If you don't stop that, I'm going to . . ." Also, if you tell children you're going to do something, carry through with it. Don't promise things you're not going to do. You'll only teach them not to believe you.

If you punish children for something, tell them why. You want them to learn from their mistakes and not to repeat them any more often than necessary for them to remember that they're not supposed to do certain things. And give them a good reason, not just because you said so. If not used as a catchall, it is certainly valid for you not to want them to do something because it really bothers you. But, if you know that it's really your problem, let children know that too. Whenever possible, show and tell children what they can do *instead* of the problem behavior (e.g., ask for a turn instead of pushing).

Don't have a large list of "no's." Decide what's really important, such as not playing with matches, not running into the street, not touching a hot stove, and be absolutely consistent about those things. Structure the environment so that you avoid as many potential problems as possible. For example, remove things which could be problems, such as breakables when your child is at the stage of grabbing everything. Don't expect self-control from children when their natural developmental urges tell them to explore and investigate the environment, and don't make them think they're bad for following their own inner drives toward mastery. Just try to keep things not meant for exploration out of their reach.

Children inevitably develop habits that can be annoying to those caring for them. Many annoying behaviors, such as whining and playing with food, only stay around if you pay attention to them; consistently ignore them, and they will go away after a while. Others, of course, like thumb sucking or constantly carrying around an old blanket, toy, or other "prized" object, may persist in spite of you because they are intrinsically satisfying to the child. On those things, decide whether your dislike of a behavior is really as important to you as the behavior is important to the child. When it no longer serves any function for the child, she will give it up.

Nail biting, thumb sucking, bed wetting, rocking back and forth, and various tics are common ways children have of expressing temporary anxieties. If they continue over a long period of time, you should examine whether you're being too demanding (e.g., expecting children to be too controlled, mature, and responsible for their age), overly critical or evaluative of the child. Ease the pressure, and many of these kinds of habits will disappear. If you find that your child is lying a great deal, especially to cover up for misbehavior, examine your relationship: are you accepting enough of him that he can feel safe in telling you the truth?

Discipline should be seen as a way of protecting children and teaching them responsibility for their own actions as they get older; it should not be viewed as punishment for misbehavior. It's like preventive medicine: if you do a good job with behavior management all the time, misbehavior will be minor, seldom, and easy to deal with. Punishment should be reserved for very important things, and it should be the kind that requires the child to learn something from it.

For example, if a child hits another child, she should be given a time out from playing while she thinks about her behavior; when she can change it, she should be allowed to rejoin the group. Harsh and abusive punishment (e.g., yelling at a child or hitting him) only stops bad behavior temporarily, and what it teaches best is avoidance of punishment, and, through modeling, harsh and abusive punishment teaches children that kind of behavior toward others; it does not teach the child to refrain from repeating the problem behavior.

Use problem situations and misbehavior as opportunities for teaching. For example, talk calmly to children about why their action or behavior was unacceptable. If they understand and use language fairly well (usually by three years), ask them how they would feel if someone did something like that to them. Using the modified form of the Golden Rule discussed earlier, relate their behavior, if you can, to a similar situation that they have experienced: e.g., "Do you remember when Noah took away your toy? How did you feel? . . . Well, it made Kim unhappy too when you messed up her picture." As much as possible, listen to your child's version of the story, and direct your questioning to get him to talk about it rather than to telling him what you think about it. Don't turn your teaching into a moral lecture.

In a preschool setting, you can use common problem situations as a focus for occasional organized dramatic play. Have a couple of children play the roles of two children squabbling, for example, and have a few more watch. You can stop the role playing, have the children switch roles, trade with a couple of children in the audience, and so on. Then, you can talk about what happened, why, and what should be done about it. You can learn a great deal from listening to the children's responses. It's generally a good idea *not* to use children who were actually involved in a problem situation to act it out at first; it could get out of hand. Let them be in the audience. Also, if it's slow starting, you can help by playing one of the roles.

Let children settle their own disputes as much as possible without your interference. They learn important social skills through working things out among themselves.

Most important, react to problem behavior appropriately, according to the age of the child. In general, hitting children is not a good idea because it only teaches them that hitting is an acceptable form of behavior. But never hit children under two years. They won't learn anything from it, and it will make them afraid and confused. The part of the brain that would enable them to evaluate the punishment in relation to their behavior, and thus to understand *why* they were hit is not fully developed in children this young. Instead, pick them up and remove them from the problem situation without a fuss, and distract them with a toy or other activity. If problem behavior persists, ignore them until the behavior improves. Don't threaten to or actually withdraw your love, but do withdraw your attention.*

Use eye control and touch control instead of yelling or hitting, especially in that period around two years when children begin to have tantrums. Place a firm, but gentle hand on the child's shoulder or arm, or hold both her hands in yours while you look into her eyes and keep up a soft, rhythmic talking (it doesn't matter what you say; it's the soothing quality of the sound that's important). This will stop or calm down a tantrum much more effectively than yelling. Eye control for children as young as one year can be very effective; the child will learn to "read" the message in your look, and you won't have to yell.

Talk to children over three and explain simply what the problem is. Don't make them feel guilty. Never make them feel that they were bad, but only that you didn't like the behavior. Don't embarrass children in front of friends. Give them a chance to save face by telling them to go off, think about the behavior and come back when they think they can change it. (This is especially appropriate if the child has been hitting or taking things from others.)

Don't expect behavior from a two-year-old that you'd expect from a five-year-old, and you'll save headaches. By five, most children, given good behavior management up to that time, can be expected to have assumed a good deal of responsibility for their own behavior; they have developed some inner controls. But the two-year-old still needs a great deal of outer control, preferably in the form of avoidance of problem situations as much as possible; actual restraint should be kept to a minimum.

Two can be a difficult time, but if handled well, those two-year-old behaviors won't carry over into later ages. Remember that two-year-olds are trying out their new independence. They're still part baby, but trying to be child. So it appears that one minute they're reasonable; the next they're angry. Their anger usually comes from frustration— not being able to do something, or having something turn out differently from what they expected (at this age children know certain things about the world; they have developed rules for the way that things work. If a routine changes or something unexpected happens, it can be cause for a tantrum). You can help not by getting upset, but rather by ignoring the temper. Sometimes you will need to reassure them too, because children frighten themselves with the strength of their tempers, and often they can't control them.

---

* When we say you should withdraw attention, we do not mean you need to leave the child's presence. Just stop paying attention to the child while the problem behavior persists.

It is impossible to give you all the answers to handling behavior problems, especially since each child is different. In general, if you remember that you're reinforcing any behavior you pay attention to, even by yelling at children, and if you examine your responses to children, you can begin to handle their behavior better by being more aware of your own.

A FEW NOTES ABOUT
WHAT'S TO FOLLOW

The rest of this book is a discussion of behaviors that are characteristic of children within different age ranges and descriptions of activities that might be useful in stimulating children to develop their skills more fully. Clearly, many of the behaviors described and, especially, specific skills are characteristic of children developing within the cultural context of a Western, industrialized society. The examples used in relation to language development are given in Standard English.

Readers whose culture or subculture has a different focus should translate, where necessary, into terms more consistent with your own cultural context. We recognize that this is asking you to do what those of "the majority culture" cannot do—function in multicultural contexts—and we hope that with your help in the future multicultural education will be expected for all human beings, not just for those of minority cultures. The place to begin is in preschool education when children are still delighted with what is new and different and have not yet been taught to fear and distrust people and customs different from their own.

Differences in the development of children of different cultures and between individual children are more in specific timing and the particular use to which basic skills are put than in anything else. And although there are many individual differences among children, there are enough characteristic similarities among most children of one age group and differences from another for us to make some generalizations about children within each group.

It is useful to place children's developmental patterns within the context of age ranges, both because it provides a logical organization to the information and because it will help you locate behaviors that you see in your children or to find out about when you might expect other behaviors to occur. But we hope you will use this information in a very flexible way. The ages should be used only as guides to children's level of development, not as yardsticks against which to measure a particular child. The age levels noted are averages. They represent only signposts of developmental trends. No individual child is expected to achieve these steps of growth at exactly the ages given here. A particular child might be ahead in some areas and behind in others. This is normal. So, for example, the picture of the two-year-old or three-year-old that we give will describe many children in some ways but probably no child in every way.

There are wide variations among children in the times that they develop different skills. Each child is an individual; his particular growth pattern, though generally similar to the growth patterns of other children, will be unique to him. Each child must be considered individually in terms of her own special developmental pattern within the general trend of development, so that opportunities may be provided to help her move smoothly along the sequence at her own pace and in her own way.

One final note about the contents of the remainder of the book. This is not a catalog of all the behaviors you might expect to find in children within each age range. There are many behaviors that you will not find here, because there simply isn't room to include them all even if we could, and you would certainly find it overwhelming if not boring if we did. We have tried to select behaviors which both characterize or typify children within a particular age range and seem to be of concern to those who care for children. Because of the range of behaviors that are discussed, however, you should be able to fill in the gaps yourself, and the bibliography at the end of the book will lead you to further sources of information about behavioral norms if you are interested.

A baby is no clock and there is no timetable that can tell exactly when to expect a baby to reach a new landmark in his life.

—JEROME BRUNER (1915–   )

Suffer little children to come unto me, and forbid them not, for of such is the Kingdom of God.

—ST. LUKE 18:16

2

Birth to One Year: The Beginning

Just as the twig is bent, the tree is inclined.
—ALEXANDER POPE
(1688–1744)

The first year of human life is both the beginning of something new and a continuation of something already begun. It is the beginning of life in the outside world where one must ultimately learn to care for oneself—to become less reliant upon others and more responsible to oneself and for oneself. But it is also a continuation—of the development, dependent and symbiotic with another, that was begun within the womb. For if it is ever to become a self-sustaining individual, the human infant must first complete its gestation. The nine months it spends in the womb is not enough time to do that, and it takes an equal amount of time outside the womb before gestation is fully completed. "The human infant must be born when it is, because if it were not, its head would be unable to pass through the birth canal. It is very immature at birth and still has much growing to do before it can control its own movements, eat solid food, and so on." * While a colt or calf, for example, can get up and walk right after it is born, the human infant will not even be able to roll over for months. Like baby kangaroos, who must live in their mothers' pouches after they are born, human infants must be carefully protected and nurtured by adults.

The need of human babies for care and nurturance does not mean, however, that they should be sheltered from the world like a

* Ashley Montagu, Introduction to "The Origin and Significance of Neonatal and Infant Immaturity in Man," in Ashley Montagu, *Culture and Human Development* (Englewood Cliffs, N.J.: Prentice-Hall, Inc., 1974). We recommend this article to those who would like to know more about the "exterogestation period" which Dr. Montagu has described.

baby kangaroo until they are ready to go out and meet it on their own terms. In order to develop, babies need stimulation and opportunities to exercise new skills as they begin to emerge. They need adults who care for them and about them; who give them many different kinds of sensory experiences (e.g., things to look at, listen to, feel); who play with them, and make them feel loved. They need to be moved around and to have things brought to them before they can move around on their own. They need to have regular changes in the things around them to stay interested and keep learning. When they begin to move around, they need to be encouraged to do so and should be given lots of room and different kinds of areas in which to move. They need adults to talk with them, to provide them with a reason and a model for developing language for communicating with other people. They need encouragement in trying out new skills, in exercising their growing independence and freedom to do things for themselves as they become able to.

In general, babies need the people caring for them to be tuned in to them and responsive to their needs. It is sometimes difficult for adults to do this, because they are so dependent on words and babies don't use words to communicate what they need. But their behavioral signals are really very clear once you've begun to learn to read them. When they're tiny, babies cry to communicate because they don't have more effective methods yet. But if you're immediately responsive to their cries and if you try to be alert to all their signals, then the two of you will soon establish an effective communication system. Babies need a lot of holding, cuddling, rocking, and, in general, tender, gentle skin-to-skin contact. This is their first avenue for communication, and, if developed, it should continue to be a very satisfying and effective one.

The first year is a very busy and productive one, full of changes and marked by remarkable amounts of growth. Between birth and one year, children learn about the connections between what they do and how things and people react. They learn to recognize familiar things and people. They grow, get some teeth, sleep less, seem to become "more human," smile at and enjoy playing with people. They learn to reach for, grasp, and hold on to things. They learn to sit up, and then begin to move around, pulling up on things, crawling, creeping, standing, perhaps even walking. They begin to be able to eat solid food cut into small pieces and to be fed from a spoon and a cup; they even try to feed themselves. Before the first birthday some children may say a few words, and they begin to listen to and understand people talking around them. In general, the period from birth to one year is a time for babies to learn the basic skills of how to move, how to make sounds, how to perceive things (give meaning to things they look at, feel, hear, smell, and taste), how to respond to things, and how to relate to other people.

THE NEWBORN

Newborn infants spend much of the first month of life adjusting to their new world. The world inside their mother's womb was a protective one in which they were not required to act on their own, eat, or breathe for themselves. Nourishment, safety, comfort, and security were assured (assuming a normal pregnancy and a healthy mother). The birth process upsets this pleasant state of equilibrium, and life outside the womb requires a whole set of major adjustments for the newborn human infant.

Fortunately, infants enter the world with a set of reactions which are on "automatic pilot" and help them adjust to the world outside their mother's womb. These reactions, called *reflexes,* allow infants to function during that period when they cannot yet do things for themselves. Furthermore, many of these reflexes are designed to coordinate with maternal behavior so that mother and baby can develop a mutually responsive relationship outside the womb that reproduces the need satisfactions that occurred automatically within the womb.

For example, human babies cry reflexively to signal needs such as hunger or pain. The automatic, reciprocal response of mothers is to go to their babies, to relieve the cause of the crying.* Unfortunately, cultural influences on human beings are so strong that they can interfere with "what comes naturally." Mothers have been "taught" (by "experts" in the past who were trying to make child rearing more "scientific") not to respond to their babies' crying "because it might spoil them," and many resist this natural response, thinking they're doing the right thing, even though it feels wrong.†

Babies' reflex actions also allow them to react to things in their world as they're learning to control their bodies themselves. They en-

---

* For further discussion of the relationship between infant crying and maternal responsiveness, see the discussion and articles on that topic in Joseph and Laurie Braga, *Growing With Children* (Englewood Cliffs, N.J.: Prentice-Hall, Inc., 1974), pp. 46–55.

† This is a good example of what we meant in the preface when we said we hoped you'd be reassured by the information in this book that it's safe and important to learn to trust your own gut intuition. This "first feeling" tells you that you should go to a crying baby. Experts in the early 1900's told mothers that they should not do so, nor should they cradle, cuddle, rock, or hold their babies, for fear of spoiling them and interfering with their development of self-control and self-reliance. We are still suffering the effects of this "scientific" advice, both through the process of modeling and because it takes quite a while for new information to become part of public practice. As we learn more about how children develop and what they need to become happy, healthy human beings, it becomes more clear that much of child caregiving is good common sense and following your (hopefully informed) intuition about what *feels right.* If your child is happy, you can be assured you're on the right track.

able babies to do such things as grasp a finger or object put in their hand; turn their head to the side when placed on their tummies in order to free their nose for breathing; follow a moving object with their eyes; and suck and swallow in order to eat. Then, with the development of babies' muscles and their connections to the part of the brain that "tells" the muscles how to work, the reflexes which provided them with automatic movement gradually disappear. Meanwhile, the reflex movements allow babies to exercise their muscles and help teach them how to make them work themselves. For example, the grasping reflex causes infants to hold on tightly to a finger or pencil put inside their hand. But they can neither hold on nor can they let go on purpose. By the time they're about four to five months old, most infants' grasping reflex will be gone. During that period of time, they will be developing the ability to reach out and grasp something on purpose and hold onto it.

Knowing that babies come into the world with a large repertoire of automatic reflex actions should reassure you that your newborn is equipped to cope in the world as long as his needs are met by a person who is attuned and responsive to him. Thus, it is possible for you to relax a bit in your concern with doing the correct thing and in your possible alarm at the baby's seeming helplessness. Because babies enter the world with some wired-in responses to help them survive until they have voluntary control of their movements, you can insure their survival through responding to what their reflex behaviors enable them to "tell" you they need. You can, if you are very tuned in to your baby's signaling system, trust her behavioral cues to guide your care for her. For example, if your baby cries, you can be assured that there's a valid reason; thus, you should try to discover what she needs, letting her behavior guide your responses to her. When feeding your baby, you should let him take the lead in how much milk he needs, and you should let him establish his own schedule for when he eats.*

_____

* There is, of course, an exception to every rule, and there are some babies who, for some biologically based reasons, are temperamentally prone to crying for reasons that would not concern most babies, and who never seem to establish a regular life-rhythm on their own. Trying to meet their needs simply by responding to their cues can be frustrating and harrowing for any parent, and special considerations must be made for these special children. For a more in-depth discussion of this issue, see Stella Chess, Alexander Thomas, and Herbert Birch, *Your Child Is a Person* (New York: Parallax Publishing Company, Inc., 1965), which focuses not only on this issue, but more generally on the whole issue of how a child's temperament (which is evident from birth and, in some ways, even before) affects the caregiver-child relationship in very significant ways: it's not just what you do that counts; it's also how your child responds to you and how your temperaments work together. This is a good book for you to look at as an accompaniment to a book such as ours which focuses more on the commonalities and similarities among children than on the differences. Another excellent resource which looks at differences in the patterns of development in individual children in

One important element in establishing an effective communication system between infant and mother is timing. Ideally, immediately after a baby is born, he or she should be put to the mother's breast. This immediate contact is reassuring psychologically to mother and baby and it sets into motion important physical recovery systems for both. It is felt by some that if this critical period for mother-baby interaction is missed (as it is automatically in modern hospital settings where babies are routinely taken away from their mothers and put in a nursery, a generally sterile physical and emotional environment with nothing but other crying babies for company) there is a resultant loss in the case with which mother and baby learn to adapt to one another.

Fortunately, there are many new movements in the "civilized world" aimed at making childbirth a more natural, relaxing, comfortable and even enjoyable process for all concerned. Midwifery is becoming popular again, and some women are having their babies at home. Even within the hospital setting, regulations are becoming more flexible to allow for rooming-in arrangements, having fathers present during the birth, and feeding babies on their schedule rather than on an arbitrary one set by the hospital. These movements are very important, and if you feel strongly about them, you should be sure that you insist on being allowed these things when you are having a child. If more women and men ask for changes in these directions, hospitals and doctors will become more responsive to making them.

You may assume from the above discussion that we would suggest that mothers should nurse their babies rather than bottle-feed. In fact, we do strongly recommend it for some very good reasons: It is physically preferable, because it provides the baby with many important immunities against disease and it helps the mother in the process of returning her body to a prepregnant condition—the baby's nursing sets off contractions in the mother's uterus. It is nutritionally much better for babies than bottle-feeding, and mother's milk is much more easily digested than formula. Breast-feeding insures that mother and baby will have skin-to-skin contact, so important to the baby's psychological and physical development. And the psychological benefits of breast-feeding are substantial, because it provides a very close bond and the basis for the symbiotic relationship so important in the mother-child relationship.*

However, there are women who simply are not comfortable with the idea of nursing, and there are some (but a much, much smaller

the context of mother-child relationships is T. Berry Brazelton, *Infants and Mothers* (New York: Dell Publishing Co., Inc., 1969).

* For a detailed discussion of the benefits of breast-feeding for baby and mother and for an explanation of the importance of putting the baby to the breast right after delivery, see Ashley Montagu, *Touching* (New York: Harper & Row, 1971), Chapter 3.

proportion than think so) who cannot nurse for physical reasons. There are no psychological benefits to a baby being nursed by a very tense mother who cannot let go and engage in the very pleasant interchange that nursing can provide. It would be better not to nurse than to try to do so under stress. The whole question of nursing is one that should be given very serious thought by prospective mothers, including considering waiting to have a baby until they can unlearn some of the negative feelings they have about it. But it's a very personal matter that must be decided in a way that is most comfortable for both parts of the nursing couple.

We'd like to say a few more things about the role of mothers *and* fathers in relation to childbirth and the beginning period of a baby's life. There has been much said about the period of depression that many women go through after having a baby. There may be a letdown, simply because something that has been so anxiously awaited has finally occurred; and there is often a feeling of fear and self-doubt about one's ability to successfully assume such an enormous responsibility, especially when there is no preparation in our modern society for having and caring for children (other than what you undertake on your own initiative). There are no support systems for new mothers; they often have to come home and not only recover from giving birth and take care of the baby, but also take care of their house. But the whole process can be a very different one if the father is a full participant in it—if he is genuinely involved during the pregnancy, present at the birth, and supportive and sharing of responsibilities after the baby is born.

Before having a baby, therefore, both partners should consider very seriously whether child rearing is going to be a mutual process or one that becomes only the mother's responsibility. Babies need to be born into a loving, harmonious environment in order to grow to be people who can have such relationships themselves. You should think hard, before having children, whether you can provide that for them.

Once you and your new baby are at home, you will notice that aside from their reflex movements, which are accomplished with relative efficiency and organization, newborn babies' movements are random, disorganized, and uncontrolled. When awake, babies kick, squirm, jerk, and writhe. Their kicking may be so strong that they turn themselves over, so make sure you don't leave your baby lying unwatched in a place from which he could fall. When your baby is sleeping, you should adjust her position occasionally so she's not always lying in the same way; her muscles aren't strong enough for her to turn herself over, and lying in the same position puts a strain on them. Sometimes babies become upset by all their random movements. It has been found that swaddling babies snugly sometimes quiets and comforts them, but swaddling that is not secure is more upsetting than none at all. For the cold months, some babies like sleeping in tiny "sleeping bags." This prevents them from kicking off the covers or getting tangled in them.

Babies' neck muscles are very weak at first, so be sure that when you pick them up, put them down, and hold them you provide good support for the head and neck. For example, when holding the baby at your shoulder, hold her head gently but firmly with one hand, your forearm supporting her neck and back; with your other hand, support her buttocks. When you sit with your baby, maintain your support, lowering him almost to your knees and then shifting him so that his head rests in the crook of your elbow or securely against your forearm.

For the first month of their life, babies spend the largest proportion of their time either sleeping or eating. They drift in and out of sleep, often waking at first only when they're hungry. They are recovering from the shock of being born, and they are learning to adjust to having to cope in this totally new, more demanding, and more stimulating environment. Although this is the time when some parents have constant visitors coming to see the baby, it is probably better, if you can do so tactfully, to ask people to wait until baby and parents have had a chance to adjust to one another and to their new life together (unless the visitors are friends who can help relieve some of the responsibilities rather than further draining your energy).

In spite of the task of recovery and acclimation babies have at this time, however, they're busily learning from the start. Just lying in the crib or cradle,* feeling the motion of the air upon their bodies, looking around, and feeling their own movements are sources of interesting stimulation for newborns.

Eating can be a real adventure, between the feelings, tastes, and smells that accompany it. In addition to satisfying babies' physical needs, eating is at the center of newborns' waking lives. Being fed, therefore, should be a satisfying experience in all ways for babies in order to develop in them feelings of trust and security about life. Use the times when feeding babies to cuddle them, talk to them, sing to them, comfort them, play with them, enjoy them, and, in general, let them know you love them. When you're feeding your baby, if you're nursing, you'll automatically switch him from one side to the other. If you're bottle-feeding, don't forget to do this; its important for your baby's visual development and the development of the muscles in her neck for turning her head, and it gives her a more extensive view of the world around her (although at first babies close their eyes while

---

* A cradle is a much more comfortable and comforting environment for a newborn than that large space with bars we call a crib. Babies probably won't suffer from being in a crib, but cradles are nicer if you have one.

they're sucking; they can't concentrate on both looking and sucking at the same time).

Babies have built-in motivation and energy to learn—they want and seek stimulation, and they learn from everything around them. As your baby spends more time awake, you'll want to make that time interesting for him. Because they are helpless in controlling their own bodies, babies are totally dependent on others to care for them and to provide them with the stimulation they need to develop and learn so they can later do things for themselves. Babies need to have things done for them, to have things brought to them, or to be brought, themselves, to new things so that they may learn.

Although babies cannot fulfill their own needs for care, love, and attention, and must be given stimulation of all types in order to develop, they are by no means passive creatures. When given attention and stimulation from people and things in their environment, babies begin learning and developing the foundations for thinking from birth.

Recently, researchers have shown that "infants are smarter than we think." They learn from everything around them; they respond to things they see, hear, feel, smell, and taste from the beginning of their lives. Research has shown that even the tiniest infants can distinguish different sights, sounds, and so on, and react to them according to which ones they like and which ones they don't like. For example, they are quieted and soothed by pleasant voices and upset by angry ones; they prefer voices to other sounds; they show preference for complex rather than simple visual stimuli and particularly respond to faces. They respond happily to gentle touching and holding, and they are upset by rough handling. It is important, therefore, to be aware of the stimulation you provide for babies from birth on, and to try to make it as pleasant and interesting as possible.

Babies spend their first month or so exercising their automatic reflexes. In this stage of their lives, they get used to their new surroundings, and through using their ready-made equipment, begin to change and add to their abilities and apply some organization to their experiences. For example, they become better at finding the nipple in order to suck and thus to eat, and their sucking becomes stronger and more efficient. Newborn infants do not "think," and they do not "know" either themselves or things outside them. With your loving attention to their needs, they will soon develop these capacities.

The priorities of newborn babies are to be fed, changed, kept warm, and to have physical and emotional needs taken care of. They have less need for play objects than for people, since they don't have the working equipment necessary for playing with things. They can see, however, though they don't focus well on things which are too close to them. They like complex visual sights which have sharp contrast. A black and white picture, bright piece of cloth, or bright mobile might be hung on the side of your baby's crib, about two feet in front of her. Set it us so that it faces toward her head. Babies can't move their heads much at first, and they usually lie in the same position, with one hand extended and their head turned toward that hand.

Don't worry about waking or disturbing your baby by having lights on or noise from people talking, the television, radio, and so on. First, it would be creating an unreal situation to keep the home quiet and dark; babies should get used to the everyday sights and sounds of their surroundings. Second, they will like the stimulation and learn from it when they're awake; when they're asleep, a little noise and light will soothe them. Too much silence would wake them up.

Since babies learn very early to turn toward a sound and enjoy soft melodic kinds of sounds, you might want to make or buy a set of wind chimes which would hang by a window and make sounds when the wind blew or the door was opened. Chimes can be made with pieces of wood, metal, glass, or plastic hung on string, yarn, or elastic. Make sure they're far enough away that your baby can't get tangled in them. Some babies might also enjoy having music played in their sleeping room; you can try out different types from the radio or a record. Better yet, talk and sing to them yourself.

The most important things for newborn infants are love, attention, and consistent, responsive care. They must feel that the world is a good place to be in and that they can count on someone to take care of their needs when they have them. They can't "think" about these things, but they can feel; they can sense the feelings of the people who care for them. Built into human infants is a capacity and drive to adjust to and learn about the world around them. But their reactions to that world, and, most importantly, to the people in their lives, will affect the ways in which they will continue to seek out stimulation, and thus to learn.

ONE TO THREE AND A HALF MONTHS *

At the beginning of the period from one to three and a half months, babies are just coming out of the newborn stage in which most of their energies are spent in getting used to the world. Most babies still can't move around, roll over, lift their head, or move their arms or legs on purpose at one month. They sleep a great deal, though not as much

* The divisions are made first into three-month intervals, then into intervals of six months and a year because of differences in the amount of change that occurs during a particular time period. The divisions also correspond to times of changes in the child's thinking and/or skills development.

as before, and their sleep is deeper than it was. They are more alert when awake, but they still tend to drift in and out of sleep. They are stronger than before; their breathing, heartbeat, and temperature are more regulated, and their muscles seem to tighten as you pick them up.

By the end of this period (i.e., at three and a half months), although babies still can't move around, they are awake and alert almost half the daylight hours; most have gained good control of their eyes and head and some over their arms and hands. And they have entered human society—when you smile at them, they will smile back.

Infants make these changes and more if the world they live in allows, supports, and encourages their growth. As we have said before, children's development is neither something that just happens regardless of what their environment provides them, nor is it something entirely dependent on what is done to and for them. Development is interactive; children will develop those skills which are made possible by their human and personal inheritance and which are required of them in order to live in the environment within which they grow. They do not simply absorb experience; they actively pursue it and act upon it, gradually changing the way they think and behave as a result of what happens to them.

This period in infants' lives is marked by growth in their ability to make some sense out of the world around them—to apply some organization to all the information coming in through their eyes, ears, and other sensory channels.

When a healthy baby is born, all his sensory receivers—eyes, ears, nose, mouth, and skin—are in good working order. But babies need experience before any of the information coming into these receiving stations makes any sense. With repeated experience with the same people, things, and events, babies begin to recognize the familiar. This is the first sign of memory and learning. Infants show their recognition of familiar people and things by their responses to them. For example, by the second month of life, babies will quiet when they see their mother or are picked up. They will make sucking movements when they see the breast or bottle.

At first, when they're about a month old, babies seem to be drawn to stimulation—any stimulation—without much choice. For example, they tend to "stare" both with eyes and ears, as if taking in and memorizing every detail of sights and sounds. But their "staring" seems more one of fixation than of interest, as though the sight or sound were demanding their attention rather than the infant's choosing to attend to it. By the time they're about three and a half months old, infants no longer are such captives of stimuli; they're beginning to have a "take it or leave it" attitude toward some kinds of stimulation. Now they will look at those things which they're interested in, not just at anything that happens to be around. Before, they just looked; now they look in order to see.

In the beginning of their life, babies pay attention to anything around because they know nothing; they have nothing with which to compare incoming information. After the first month or two, infants have begun to stabilize some of their impressions of the world; they are able to recognize some things that they have previously seen (or felt, heard, and so on) when they appear. But although they recognize some things, they don't remember them when they're not there; they still don't know that things exist apart from their attention to or action on them. Of greatest interest to babies in this stage are, at first, the things that they have experienced before, and then, as they gain more experience, things which are similar to but slightly different from things they have already experienced and found out about.

This probably explains babies' great interest, from two to three months, in their hands. They will watch them and play with them for as long as a half hour at a time. Babies have had plenty of time to get used to their hands because of the way they usually lie when they're awake. This changes in the period from birth to three and a half months. At first a baby's head is always to one side, facing one of her hands. Gradually, her body straightens out; she lies flatter on her back with her head straight up and with her hands freed to come together in the middle and clasp each other. To young babies, watching this "spectacle" of their hands playing together is fun and will help them learn to look at and reach for things in a few more months.

Infants a few months old already have built up some organizational schemes (ways of grouping information or experiences) within which they can "take" or "leave" new information. If the new information is too close a match to information that they already know, they won't be very interested in it. Thus, if you hang a mobile over a baby's crib, after a while he will cease to be interested in it. If you then replace that mobile with one that is just the same, but a different color, you probably won't get much additional interest. On the other hand, if you replace it with one that is similar but with different figures, is made out of different materials, or reacts somewhat differently to the baby's hitting or batting it with his feet or fists, you might find more sustained attention.

You can make your own mobiles, hanging common household items and inexpensive things from the dime store such as pieces of colored paper and yarn, a spoon, a man's tie, large plastic rings, pieces of tin foil, buttons, clothespins, etc., a few at a time, on a piece of thick elastic pulled across the top of the crib, tight enough so that your baby can't wind it around himself. Change its location and the things on it to fit his changing posture and interests. For example, if he seems to be doing a lot of kicking with his feet around two months, you could hang a rubber ball with a bell inside around his feet so that when he kicked, he'd hit it and make it ring. If your baby's head is still turned to one side, you'll want to hang things on that side so she can see them. As she gains increased movement of her head, you can hang more things in the middle and to the other side.

Through the experience infants have with things and other people in the first few months they begin to learn that they are separate beings. They learn that touching a toy feels completely different from touching their own hand. In feeling the difference, they learn that that moving thing they see is *their* hand, a part of them. By being held during feeding and changing and cuddling, babies learn that there are two kinds of feelings, one type that comes from outside themselves and the other (for example, when they touch their own hand or chew on their own toes) that does not.

Once babies feel that they are individuals, they must discover what kind of persons they are and what they can do. For example, their first cries were the reflex response to a need such as hunger or cold or a need to be held. Now they learn that crying brings someone to help. If they find that adults will solve their problems and fulfill their needs, they will learn that crying brings this comforter. They learn that they can have some control over what happens to them (a cry brings another to them); and through this they begin the crucial basic step in learning to communicate.

The baby's feelings of security and the feelings of happiness from communicating with other persons during this time are extremely important to later being able to build close relationships as an adult. Young infants are very aware of the feelings and emotions of other people. They feel all these emotions as part of reactions to themselves. They do not have the knowledge that would help them see that anger or disappointment in their world are not always because of them. For this reason, infants begin to feel toward themselves what they feel in others around them. Adults must be loving and happy in order to make their babies feel loved and happy and secure.

At this stage babies' primary interest still is other people rather than toys. At one month, they may look briefly at a face which comes into their view. By six weeks, they may brighten and smile at the face. Gradually, during this period, they will become more and more sociable. By three and a half months, most babies will smile back when you smile at them and react more happily to a familiar than to a strange face.

Babies are learning to communicate with other people. At first all they could do was cry. As they develop more skills, infants find more ways of getting their needs and feelings across to another. Real words won't appear in many children until the end of the first year or later, but the process of learning to speak begins through listening to other people and practicing making sounds.

Babies enjoy making sounds now, and may copy you when you make a sound. At one month, they make small, throaty sounds; by three and a half months, they coo, gurgle, laugh aloud, and make some noises that resemble speech sounds.

Making the same sounds over and over again is just one example of a kind of learning game which children in this stage begin playing with themselves and which you can sometimes play with them. When they discover something they can do that they like (such as making a sound or sucking their thumb) they will try to do it again. Once they rediscover how to do the thing, which at first was done by chance, they'll do it over and over like a game. This is a way they have of practicing new skills and expanding them to include more things. When your baby makes a sound, repeat it after her; then she may say it again too. She's not really copying you; it's more like copying herself, but it's even more fun because you're both doing it.

Another way that infants in this stage show that they're learning more about the world is through putting together some different ways of knowing about things and thus reacting to the presence of one with an apparent expectation of the other. For example, babies begin to connect what they hear with what they see. When they hear a sound or a voice, they will look in the direction from which it came. If it is the familiar sound of his mother's footsteps and/or voice, and she picks him up as she does when she's going to feed him, the baby may begin making sucking movements in anticipation of being fed. He will do this too if he sees the breast or bottle. Even if he's not hungry, if he's used to good experiences with his parents or caregivers, he will stop crying when they approach him, before they pick him up.

In spite of this kind of developing "intelligence," however, babies still react to the world as if they were its creator, as if they caused things to exist or disappear—if they are looking at it, it exists; if they don't see it, it doesn't exist. If someone or something disappears from their view, babies at this stage will keep looking at the place where it was before it disappeared, as if waiting for it to come back. If it doesn't return, they'll probably forget about it. If it's a person who's important to them, they may cry. They would not, however, think of looking elsewhere for it. If your baby is playing with a toy and you cover it up, she'll act as if it were never there. Out of sight is out of mind during this stage.

In addition to changes that occur in this stage of infants' view of the world, some changes occur in their developing motor responses. The greatest gains made are in developing control of the eye muscles. At one month, babies pay attention to things which move within their view. If you take a bright colored toy and "dance it" about two feet in front of an infant, you can play a game in which he follows the toy with his eyes from the side his head was on to the middle. By three and a half months, your baby will follow an object or person with her eyes from one side to the other; now she has good control of her head. Although infants are still attracted by movement, by now they pay attention on their own to something that is not moving. You no longer need to wave a toy in front of their face to get them to look at it. In addition, they can now focus well on objects that are as close as five inches from their eyes.

Babies "grasp" with their eyes before they can use their hands for grasping—they study visual events so carefully now that they seem to be grabbing for them with their eyes. They also are beginning to direct their reaching by looking, so that in the next stage they'll be able to look at, reach for, and grasp something in one smooth motion. From two to three and a half months, meanwhile, babies are developing skills leading up to that. They can swipe fairly accurately at nearby things, looking back and forth from their hand to the thing. Their hand may still be fisted, and they won't try to grab with it. By three and a half months, they may bring both hands together, approaching a nearby object such as a dangling ring, but they still won't grasp it. At a month, if you hand a rattle to most infants, they'll probably not open their fist to take it; if you put it inside their fingers, they'll drop it. By three and a half months, they'll have learned to open their fist (and gradually they'll keep their hands open more often anyway) when their hand is touched with a rattle, and they'll hold on to it for a while.

By knowing some of the steps of the "sequence" that infants go through in developing skills such as reaching and grasping, you can provide them with experiences and materials to promote their development. For example, while babies are developing control over their eye muscles, they will enjoy different things to look at, including homemade mobiles placed at an angle so that they can see them, or the light from a window, or a revolving lamp, and the various sights that can be seen when carried around at someone's shoulder.

When babies begin to swat at things, toys with bells or squeakers inside could be hung near enough so that they'll hit them as they swat. Something might be hung near their feet too, so that when they kick it, it moves or rattles. These types of toys will prepare babies for the next stage, in which they will repeat actions on objects in order to see them happen again. When babies begin to bring both hands together, you might make colorful sock-mittens, like racing gloves, for their hands, so that their thumb and fingers stick out. They'll enjoy looking at their hands anyway, but this might be an interesting variation. Also, you might add a few large plastic bracelets to the homemade "mobile" or display area, now in front and above them, which they can perhaps grab on to by chance when they clasp their hands together. A wooden rattle or a large clothespin could serve for holding on and maybe even chewing; you'll have to help get it into the baby's hand, since he can't grasp on purpose yet, but he can hold on to it for a while by himself.

By three and a half months (and often starting before that) infants enjoy being in a position which allows them to look around at the world. By this time babies have enough control of their neck muscles to hold their head up themselves when carried at your shoulder and to lift it and turn it to the side when lying on their tummy. They like to lie on their stomach and peer about, especially at the level of a big bed (make sure they're in the middle and can't roll off). And they like to be carried around so that they can see. Babies' shoulders and upper back are coming under control too, so they are beginning to enjoy sitting supported, either on someone's lap, against some pillows, or strapped into a car seat or similar device. Their muscles aren't yet strong enough to sit for very long though. A seat with a table in front is beginning to be good at this age, because you can put some toys on it for babies to play with. At first, they'll be more interested in your hands or their own than in the toys. Later, they might begin to enjoy household items like a cup and spoon.

Also, by the end of this stage, they might begin to enjoy things with different feelings. Toys can be made of such things as vinyl, foam, latex, plastic, rubber, and sandpaper. For example, you might make a "feelie board," mounting small pieces of different kinds of materials on a piece of plywood to hang on the side of the baby's crib. Even the feel and sound of a piece of crumpled paper can be interesting. Some of the more interesting ways of exploring new toys and materials will have to wait until the next stage when infants have more control over their hands. But even now they can begin to make their appearance, and your hands can help where your baby's are not yet in control.

Toys should be given to children one or two at a time; they should not be bombarded with stimulation. They will learn more if allowed to explore thoroughly one thing at a time; when they have too many interesting things around them, they won't get involved with any of them but will simply look at them. Watch to see when your baby is tired of a toy, and then give her another.

As they begin to find out about the world "out there," as they find some organization and begin to recognize things they've experienced before, infants begin to find out that they are separate from the world. They make this discovery through such experiences as feeling the difference between biting a toy or their mother's nipple and chewing on their own fingers, and watching and feeling their own hands clasp each other in front of their face. With this developing awareness of the world around them, babies become more interested and excited about investigating it. When given an object, babies will explore it in all the ways they have available to them—through seeing, feeling, hearing, smelling, and tasting, and using any motor responses they are capable of at the time.

As soon as babies begin to know that they are separate from the rest of the world around them, they also begin to develop feelings about themselves and who they are. The foundations of children's self-concept are based on how other people and things react to them. They need to find pleasure in their interaction with people and objects. Infants will learn that they are separate from the surrounding world of feelings and actions by contact with a warm, loving person who is responsive to their needs. That person does not have to be their biological mother, and it may, in these early months, be more than one person, as long as infants' needs are met *consistently*. Babies do need the security of having one or two people primarily responsible for their care. They will learn to trust and eventually to love only if, in the early part of their life, they receive care and attention when they need it and have a close, dependable relationship with at least one person.

Infants need stimulation of all kinds; that is how they develop and learn. The most important stimulation of all is that which they receive from people. Infants react to the feelings and attitudes which they sense around them. If they sense happiness, they will feel happy. If they sense unhappiness, they will feel it too. It is critical that babies' needs be met, that they be fed when they're hungry, changed when they're soiled, and so on. Equally important is that infants' emotional needs be met; they should feel loved, wanted, enjoyed, and, generally, that you are glad they're around. They need to be talked to, sung to, cradled, rocked, cooed at, held gently and securely, played with, and treated, in general, with tender loving care.

THREE AND A HALF TO SIX MONTHS

The greatest achievement in this time period is visually-directed reaching. Babies gain control of the muscles which enable them to support their head and move their arms, and they begin to reach out for and grasp things. At three and a half months, you may remember, babies can bring both hands together toward an object, but they can't yet grasp it. By four months, they begin to use one hand again. They bring their open hand near the object and slowly bring it closer to the thing attracting them until they finally grasp it crudely. Finally, by about five months, infants begin to be able to look at something, reach for it, and grasp it accurately in a quick, smooth motion. Almost all six-month-old infants can reach with accuracy for objects offered to them. This accomplishment is called *visually-directed reaching* because infants' eyes direct their hands in the reaching. This makes sense because in the last stage, babies gained good control of their eye muscles. Now they can be used to guide newly developing muscles.

At three and a half months, infants enjoy sitting on someone's lap or being propped up for ten to fifteen minutes. They hold their head fairly steady: but after a while their back begins to droop because its muscles aren't yet strong enough to support the weight of their body. By six months, babies sit well in a highchair, well enough so that they don't have to put all their energy into sitting. Their energy is freed to try out the newly developed skills of their hands. Although they can reach and grasp now, they grasp crudely, using their thumb and fingers to hold "hand-sized" objects against their palm; they can't yet use their thumb and forefinger in grasping, and they scoop things to themselves.

In the last period, infants were chiefly lookers; in this stage, they are becoming touchers and manipulators. As they develop the ability to reach and grasp, when they see something they'll reach for it, feel it, transfer it from one hand to the other, put it in their mouth to see how it feels to their tongue and gums, play with it some more with their hands, and so on. Infants at six months can entertain themselves in their crib, playpen, or highchair for as long as a half hour or more; it depends on the children and your treatment of them.

Babies in this stage are very interested in their own hands and their new powers. This is the stage when babies really enjoy toys to grab, feel, or chew on. The toys mentioned before will be even more interesting now. Be sure you take small things off the mobile and cradle gym since babies at this stage are beginning to put everything into their mouth. Substitute, instead, larger things to be grasped, held, and felt, such as big wooden or plastic beads and blocks, plastic bracelets, a piece of cloth with bells sewed securely onto it, small homemade balls of different materials that they can grasp and feel, a big wooden spoon, etc.

In addition to having objects attached to their crib for grasping and manipulating, babies will enjoy having a variety of kinds of objects in other places where they spend time. A good toy for their eating tray or table is a rubber suction toy with "handles" for grabbing, that will stay in place while they're practicing their new skills. (This will save your back too; it'll be soon enough that your baby will insist on playing drop and retrieve, with you as the retriever.) The best "toys" to satisfy children's "touch hunger" in this stage are common household items such as metal or plastic measuring spoons and cups, plastic bowls, wooden salad bowls, spoons (not forks or knives, since babies can hurt themselves with these), pots and pans—anything that can be touched and grabbed. Hand-sized items such as plastic or rubber blocks that make a noise are also good for practicing grasp-and-hold techniques.

One of the ways to stimulate the development of grasping behavior is by providing babies with interesting things to look at and try to reach and grab. In this instance, you are providing the stimuli and relying on your child to make use of them. Another avenue for stimulation of these skills, which has the added pleasure of shared time together, is to play games with your baby. For example, you can take an object such as a stuffed animal with "handles" (e.g., an octopus or a starfish) and dance it to your baby, making sure she's watching the toy. Dance the toy from her eyes to her hand while she watches; then place the toy in her hand. When she can grasp on sight, hold the toy a short distance from her hand so that she has to reach for and grasp it herself.

As we mentioned at the beginning of this section, the prime attraction of this time period is the development of visually-directed reaching. But there are other very important motor milestones in the making as well. Babies are gaining increasing control of the muscles in their trunk, enabling them to learn to sit well with support and briefly, by six months, on their own. In some ways an even more significant consequence of this increased control of the trunk is that babies are learning to roll over purposefully, their first instance of self-propulsion. In fact, we've observed babies, anxious to get about on their own, who used this method to slowly but surely make their way across a room long before they had the muscle strength or co-ordination necessary for crawling* or creeping.

Babies will gain increasing control of their trunk through the practice they get sitting with help and learning to roll over. You should provide numerous opportunities for your baby to sit—propped up by pillows, in your lap, in a car seat with a strap, in a highchair or baby-tender. But babies in this stage shouldn't be left sitting too long at one time since their back muscles, especially those in the lower back, are still weak, and sitting for a long period will put too much of a strain on them. When you notice your baby's back sagging, put him in another position—perhaps on his tummy, since the efforts he makes in that position to raise himself onto his arms or hands is, in itself, a back strengthener.

You can help your baby learn to roll by playing a game with her: place her on her side and stand behind her. Then call her name

---

* Many babies, when placed on their bellies, will begin trying to crawl by the end of this time period (five to six months). They draw up their knees or make swimming movements, but are unable to move from the spot on which they're placed. It is rare (though certainly not impossible) for babies to learn to achieve any forward motion before seven months.

softly or make a noise with a sound toy. She should roll to her back toward the source of the sound. When she can do this easily, expand the game to get her to roll from one side to the other. First roll her playfully back and forth from one side to the other, giving her a chance to experience the feeling. Then place her on one side and stand behind her. Call to her, and when she turns to her back, move away from her, and entice her to turn to the side facing you so that she can keep you in sight. Finally, put the baby on her belly. Hold a favorite toy just beyond her grasp. As she reaches for it, move it up and to the side so that in order to keep it in sight and grab it, she has to roll over. Repeat the game with the baby on her back, and do it in both directions.*

Except for the rare baby who has devised some means by which to propel himself along, most babies are still stuck to the spot on which they are placed. However nice this may sometimes be for weary caregivers, we must ask you also to look at it from the point of view of the poor baby. Life in a playpen, crib, or even on a rug on the floor—when you're unable to go anywhere other than where you're put—can be fairly frustrating, especially when you're struggling to try to do something about your dilemma. So, please, be alert to your baby's needs to get about before she can do so for herself. Sometimes she may be very pleased to be just where she is, because there's something or someone interesting there with her. But other times she may really need to be taken for a walk outdoors or just around the house or put in another location. Be alert to your babies' signals and try, when you can, to meet their needs.

A further development which occurs in this time period is that babies learn to eat solid food. (This doesn't mean that you should stop nursing; studies indicate that babies should be nursed for at least nine months. But, they can begin in this period to add a few solids to their diet.) Babies show their readiness for handling puréed or well-mashed foods by drooling and biting. This is usually around the third month, at the time that swallowing begins to be voluntary, the digestive system begins to be able to handle more complex foods than milk, and babies begin to need some supplements to the nutrients contained in a diet of milk alone (e.g., vitamin C).† Between three and six months,

---

* This stimulus activity, like the behavioral descriptions, covers a time period of several months; it's not something you'd expect to do all at once.

† By the way, the best source of information about the nutritional needs of infants and young children that we have found is Marian Breckenridge and Margaret Murphy, *Growth and Development of the Young Child,* 8th ed. (Philadelphia: W. B. Saunders Company, 1969), Chapter 5. The information is presented in a simple and readable form but in all the detail you may have looked for and failed to find before. The authors explain nutrition in the context of children's changing needs for and ability to handle different kinds of foods—they give you the whys as well as the whats.

although babies are beginning to be able to swallow voluntarily, their sucking is stronger than their swallowing, sometimes resulting in choking. At the beginning of this period, infants' tongues may still work reflexively in such a way that food put on the front of the tongue will be pushed out of their mouth. As the reflex tongue movement fades, babies become better able to eat from a spoon without choking or coughing.

Babies must *learn* to eat solid food, and the approach taken in this early period of introduction to solids will influence their later feeding habits. Eating should be a pleasure, not a task. It is important, therefore, to go slowly, following your baby's lead, and to make sure not to force him to eat any food he doesn't seem to like or any more food than he wants. At first, for example, one-half teaspoon of a new food is enough. If you have to put the food at the back of your baby's tongue in order to keep her from spitting it out, perhaps you should wait a little longer before introducing solids. As she gains control of her tongue she will be able voluntarily to get the food from the front to the back of her mouth. Remember not to give your baby any foods containing lumps or foods that require chewing since he is not yet capable of handling them. His food should be puréed or mashed well.

Within this time period, babies also become able to drink a little water or juice from a cup, but only a few sips at a time and with drooling and spilling. They need to develop more control of their lips so that they fit well enough over the rim of the cup to keep the liquid in their mouth both when they're drinking and when you remove the cup from their mouth. Be sure to make the cup a treat and not an obligation. Practice with it now may make weaning from the breast or bottle easier later. By then the cup will be an old friend, and switching from sucking to sipping may be presented as a positive achievement of independence and mastery rather than as deprivation.

The period between three and a half and six months is important as a prelinguistic stage of infants' speech and language development. The maturation of the oral mechanism for eating also affects infants' sound-making. They will gradually introduce consonant-like sounds to their previous repertoire of vowel-like sounds. Although some of these sounds may resemble speech sounds, at this stage they really aren't; they're sound play. All babies at this stage, from any part of the world, make the same kinds of sounds. Babies are motivated to babble more by their own internal feedback system than by outside stimulation—it feels good to their mouth, and it sounds good to their ears. Only later in the year, after hearing their own language for a period of time, do children begin selectively to make sounds which are really like those that the adult speakers around them make.

Part of learning to make sounds is learning how to hear them.

As they are practicing their sound-making, babies are also beginning to attend to the sounds around them. They are attracted to voices and listen to their rhythm patterns and tone changes, which by the age of six months they will begin to imitate. By this time they may also respond to one word—they may turn when they hear their name. In addition they can distinguish a friendly tone of voice from a scolding one. When babies make a sound, you can make a game out of saying the sound after them. Talk to them all the time, even though they don't understand the words yet; they will learn to make the sounds and learn the meanings of words through hearing people talk to them and around them.

At this stage, infants' behavior is becoming increasingly more purposeful as they find out that they can make things happen. They learn, for example, that the ball they hit makes a sound because they hit it; so they'll hit it again in order to make the sound again. Infants in this stage, however, see their actions as the direct cause of what happens, as if by magic. You can observe this if you hang some toy from the ceiling and attach a cord or elastic to it that will dangle within a baby's reach. He'll soon learn to pull the cord to make the toy move. Then, if you take away the cord and leave the toy, now out of his reach, your baby will probably move his arm as if pulling the string and look up at the toy as if waiting for it to move. He doesn't yet understand the relationship between the cord and the movement of the toy.

A sign that babies are beginning to understand more about the way the world works is that they will begin to enjoy playing a game in which you make part of a toy disappear and then reappear. They are learning to anticipate the whole object, seeing only a part. You may remember, from before, that if an object disappeared, they just forgot about it or continued to look in the direction where they last saw it. By six months, if they drop their toy or if you drop something in front of them, most babies will begin to look toward where it fell rather than back at the place from which it was dropped. They also will try to follow with their eyes a fast-moving object or attempt to find one they looked away from. They are learning to judge space and distance. This is what enables them to reach out in front of them for something in the right direction. You can help them to learn these things by playing short games with them (for as long as they enjoy them).

For example, hide part of a toy under a cover and ask, "Where's Teddy (or whatever it is)?"; then uncover it and say, "There he is." When the child discovers what has happened, she may laugh or indicate pleasure in some other way. As your baby gets better at the game, cover up more and more of the toy; make a toy "disappear" in front of her by moving it under a table or behind your back. Then make it reappear. Put something the baby wants a short distance away in front of him so he'll have to reach for it. Then, do it again with the object to the child's side. Talk to him all the time you're playing.

Babies are beginning to have some memory now, for people, events, and action schemes—they recognize familiar things and people, react to people differently according to what activities they routinely perform for them, and so on. In the time period between three and a half to six months, infants begin to become more aware of strange people and places as they become more attuned to the familiar. Whereas at three to four months they are friendly to everyone, by six months some babies may smile at a friend and look warily at a stranger. At four months babies may cry when someone leaves their presence; by six months, they will cry if the person leaving is their primary caregiver.

In general, the period beginning at about three and a half months marks a great change in the lives of infants. Prior to this time, they were totally dependent, relatively immobile creatures. They have been learning since birth and becoming increasingly more competent; the changes are gradual and cumulative, not sudden. But about this time, babies seem to be becoming separate persons rather than just extensions of their caregivers. Through experience, babies are becoming more aware of themselves in relation to other persons and things; they're developing new modes of action and communication; and they're beginning to make more sense of the world around them.

Around the third month, babies' crying begins to occur much less frequently if you have been responsive to them in the first few months. As they develop new means of communicating their needs and desires, crying can be replaced by more mature and effective modes such as cooing, babbling, facial expressions, or body language (e.g., resisting bodily something they don't want). Crying may still serve as a long-distance communicator, but as babies learn to "shout" for attention (usually by their eighth month), crying will decrease sharply even for that purpose (as long as their calls are responded to promptly). Babies who still cry a great deal after the first few months are ones who (1) have been left to cry it out rather than being responded to and (2) have eventually been responded to only because they have been crying for so long (rather than their caregiver trying to meet their needs as they occur, responsibly and flexibly).

During the period from three and a half to six months, because of their new capacity for action and communication, because they are awake and alert for increasingly longer periods, and because it is right now their main avenue for learning, play is becoming very important to babies—play with people, play with themselves, and play with things. People are fun—to be with, to play talking and touching and laughing games with, and just to watch. By four to five months, babies have learned to play, tease, and frolic and will do so continuously even when their caregivers might wish they'd be more serious (such as when they're eating). By the end of this period people begin to be valued not only for themselves but also for what they can do for babies (e.g., give them a toy, prop them up, move them around).

Babies also begin to enjoy some time alone, to play with and "talk to" favorite toys, and to experiment with their growing physical equipment and motor abilities.* But, although infants from three and a half to six months are becoming more self-contained and may enjoy periods of play by themselves, they still very much enjoy the company of people. They will smile at the sight of another person's face. This is both a sign that they recognize it and a form of social interaction. By five or six months, infants will stop crying when they're talked to; they will begin to imitate sounds and movements; and they will reach out to be picked up by familiar people. They may also begin to clown —to do things which bring them smiles and praise from the important people in their lives. By six months, babies are becoming more attuned to people. They're beginning to "read" other people's behavior better and to adjust their own behavior accordingly.

In addition to the types of toys they were given before, some toys babies from three and a half to six months might enjoy playing with include floating toys for the bath, bells and noise-making toys, blocks, balls, small boxes and lids, cups, spoons, clothespins, and sheets of clean, crisp paper. Toys still should provide many different colors, shapes, sounds, smells, and feelings for the child to explore. There should be some toys that have movable parts: strings of beads, rattles, and toy animals. Through trial and error, infants will discover ways to handle toys; however, children also should be shown ways to play with their toys during frequent, short playtimes with an adult. Babies should have things to look at, such as a big, colorful picture on the wall where they can see it, mobiles that frequently change, and a metal mirror on the wall in which they can look at themselves as well as the people around them.

* By the way, if at this time or at any time in the future, part of your children's exploration and manipulation of objects and of parts of their own bodies includes investigating their genitals, please try to see this in the proper context and not get upset about it and make it a problem. When babies bring their hands together to clasp each other, or when they grab their toes, we recognize these activities as valuable opportunities for them to practice motor skills and learn about the feelings of their own body; this is part of defining who they are as separate from the world of objects and feelings around them. Touching their genitals is no different for young babies than clasping their fingers together or chewing on their toes, except that it may feel even better. We want children to like the way they feel, because that's part of them. Don't make problems for them over something that is only a problem because of cultural attitudes. This is another area in which your model will make a difference in whether you give children a chance to grow or burden them with culture-bound problems.

It is important in this stage that the toys and materials you give children are responsive to them. For example, they will develop their new skills with their hands by having things to pick up and handle; they'll develop reaching skills better if things are put just barely within their reach, so that they have to reach out for them. It will help to develop their thinking skills if they have some toys that move or make a noise if they hit them or grab them or pull a cord attached to them. In addition to your changing homemade mobile, now, you might want to have a pole attached to your baby's crib or playpen with different objects attached to pieces of elastic that she can pull down to play with and let go and have swing out of her way.

Babies will become bored if things aren't changed around for them. They still cannot move around on their own, so they must be helped to find new things to look at and explore. They should be moved around to different places instead of always being left in one place. Children should not be kept in a crib or playpen for long periods of time, but should have a chance to explore a variety of environments.

SIX TO TWELVE MONTHS

There are many important motor achievements ahead for infants in the last half of their first year. Having spent their first six months taking in information and trying to make some sense of it, babies are now ready to begin really acting on the world. They begin this period with some, but not complete, use of their hands. They can roll over, they can reach, and they can sit with support; but they're still dependent on others to move them around. In these next six months they will develop the muscular control and skills to put them on the threshold of a new approach to the world—upright and mobile.

Due to the rapid development of areas, pathways, and connections in the brain during this period between six months and one year, infants develop the gross motor control and coordination necessary for sitting by themselves, crawling, pulling up on furniture to stand, standing holding on, creeping, and walking with help. They develop fine motor coordination and control well enough to be able to handle and, at the same time, to watch objects in order to explore them, to pick up tiny objects with a pincer grasp (using thumb and forefinger), and to begin to learn to release objects they've been holding, with some control.

But although a baby may not exhibit the completed and integrated form of a motor achievement until the latter part of the first year of his life, the subskills leading up to that achievement have been developing since he first lifted his head. For example, most infants get around well by creeping (moving on hands and knees or on all fours, abdomen raised parallel to the floor) by the time they're eleven months old. But the steps leading to creeping begin at birth when infants put on their stomachs will move their legs in a rhythmic, reflexive activity that may even cause their body to move forward.

Infants' growth may seem more dramatic and faster to you during the second half of the year because of all of the movements they learn to make. In fact, their growth in this period is somewhat slower than at first if you think back to what they started with. They were like strangers in a strange land. They didn't know the sights; they had no map to guide them and no means to get themselves around. They didn't even speak the language. Now they've learned enough about the surroundings to begin, with you as a guide, to go out exploring.

The first important step in learning how to move about on their own is development of the ability to crawl (moving with arms and legs, belly on the floor) and then creep (moving on hands and knees or on all fours, belly parallel to the floor). At six to seven months, most babies when put on their belly will pivot in a circle, but they won't make any forward progress. You can make a game out of your baby's new pivoting ability by holding a toy on a string in front of her just beyond her reach, and then moving it slowly in a circle so that she'll have to pivot on her belly in order to follow the toy.

You can encourage babies to make some forward progress by squatting in front of them and calling to them. Hold a favorite toy out as a lure, making it talk and dance. As the baby moves forward, move the toy back a little further. After a couple of tries, give the baby the toy. Don't tease or frustrate him; it should be fun for both of you, not a trial. Between seven and nine months, most babies learn to pull themselves forward with their arms, dragging their legs behind, though they may, at this time, end up pushing themselves backwards at first. With practice, crawling becomes more efficient. Babies proceed from pulling with both arms at the same time to extending and flexing each arm alternately.

From eight to nine months, most babies *try* to creep, getting up on hands and knees and rocking back and forth, perhaps pushing themselves backwards; by nine months most begin to creep, at first in a disorganized and inefficient fashion. Gradually, in the next couple of months, babies learn to creep with increased coordination and efficiency, arms and legs moving in a smooth alternating pattern. By eleven to twelve months, babies may creep on hands and feet.*

Make sure your baby has plenty of room to try out her newly developing skills. Set her down on the floor on a rug or mat or, in

---

* Not all babies crawl or creep; some move by rolling, by hitching themselves along on their backs, or by scooting in a sitting position. Most babies find some way of getting about before the time they learn to walk.

good weather, on the ground—on anything that will cushion but not slip and that she can move on with ease. If you're concerned about your baby's safety, then corral off a sizable area for him to move around in. But, don't corral him in as small an area as a playpen; it's not room enough to exercise new skills. When babies have mastered the basic movement of creeping, they will enjoy making a game of it. For example, they will delight in creeping fast around the room while, you, also on hands and knees, chase them.

By the end of the year, creeping is most babies' chief means of locomotion, and they do it with ease and precision. Their efforts are now going into the beginning stages of walking. You should understand that when babies first start to try to walk, they have to go through the same kinds of trial and error and awkwardness that marked their efforts at crawling and creeping. Don't try to push them from creeping into walking. Let them enjoy the efficiency they have achieved in creeping and move into walking at their own pace.

Walking is a very important motor achievement for young children which requires the coordination and integration of various movement patterns, postural control, and balance. It is both the culmination of all of children's previous large motor development and the foundation for their future large motor development. Standing and walking in an upright posture is characteristically human, and the acquisition of a two-footed stance puts infants literally in a new position toward the world. Once mastered, the upright posture frees children's hands to be used as tools.

A mature form of independent walking will not be achieved by most infants until the middle of their second year, but the steps leading to that accomplishment can be traced to the reflex stepping movements which many infants make from birth through the first weeks of life—when held under the arms, they will make stepping movements which may even move them forward a bit. From six to nine months, when held under the arms, babies gradually learn to bear an increasing amount of their own weight and stand straighter with less flexion from the hips. They stamp the ground and make stepping movements with increased coordination as they practice.

By nine or ten months, many infants not only stand well when held under the arms, but they also will make stepping movements when both their hands are held. By this time, infants are becoming very attentive to the act of standing and walking; their eyes brighten and they watch their feet as they step. Their stepping is not yet coordinated, and they don't usually have the balance to stand and walk alone yet.*

From nine to eleven months, most infants learn to pull them-

* There is a wide range of individual difference in the time of achievement of the various steps in learning to walk.

selves up to standing by holding on to furniture. At first they will need help both in getting up to stand and in sitting back down; then, even after they've learned to pull up by themselves, they may still need help getting back down again. Once standing securely, holding on to furniture, babies may begin to practice letting go, first with one hand, then with both. By eleven months, they may also try out their balance for walking by lifting one foot while standing holding on. By twelve months they may begin to walk with someone holding just one hand, by cruising around holding on to furniture, or by pushing a chair in front of them. Although some children will begin to learn to walk on their own by one year, many still won't stand or walk alone for another month to six weeks. Also, although standing alone is often listed as occurring before walking alone, in many infants the two occur at the same time.

As children get older and their emerging skills require more complex coordination of previously acquired bodily control, movement, and balance, more variance can be seen in the timing of the achievement of these higher-order skills. A few infants may already have passed the steps mentioned above and begun independent walking as early as nine months. Others will be just beginning to make stepping motions when held under the arms at nine months and may not walk alone until as late as eighteen months. Each child has her or his own pace, but the sequence is the same.

You can help babies most in the period before they can get themselves to a standing position. Once they're on their feet, as long as they have the space to move in and encouragement (but not pressure), babies will work endlessly at learning to stand and walk alone until they have achieved a basic level of competence. When they are learning to walk, babies are likely to neglect everything else, not wanting to interrupt their work even for eating or sleeping. Be patient, and remember how important a step in her development this is for a baby.

At the beginning of this period, babies will enjoy being held in a standing position and bounced on the ground, perhaps with a song or a nursery rhyme to accompany their activities. As their legs get stronger, you can release more of your hold, letting babies get used to standing supporting their own weight. See if you can get your baby to take a few steps while you support him. This practice will enable him to experience the upright position before he has the strength or balance to maintain it himself. (Babies have been learning to walk through the ages with little or no help from anyone, so you don't have to do these things; but they can be fun for both of you.)

Babies usually can stand holding on before they can pull themselves to standing, so they need your help in getting to a standing position. Take hold of both your baby's hands and pull her slowly and gently to her feet; by nine months, babies should be able to pull back and help get themselves up. When your baby can stand holding your hands, walk with him, leading him by both hands. Face him and walk backwards slowly, encouraging him to walk toward you. You should bend from the waist enough that he doesn't have to raise his hands up to your level. Once he has mastered the above arrangement, try letting your baby walk between you and another person, each of you holding one of his hands.

Before your baby begins to be able to pull herself up by grabbing hold of furniture, check to make sure the furniture around is sturdy enough that it won't topple when she grabs it. Until babies learn how to let themselves down again, they will call for you to rescue them every time they want to escape from the upright position. Have patience; they'll soon learn how to do it themselves, especially if you give them a little coaching.

The Balinese have walking rails for babies to practice on. If you can work with wood, you might want to make one. It's simply a wooden pole suspended at the height of the baby's chest between two supports; the length would depend on how much room you have. When you see your baby practicing standing and walking, holding on with only one hand, you can give her some help walking with you, holding only one of her hands. Bend to the side enough that she doesn't have to reach too far to grasp your hand. As she practices, you can gradually release more of your support as the baby becomes stronger on her feet until she's really holding your finger or your clothes only for moral support.

Don't push babies to stand or walk alone; they are their own best judge of when they are ready. Some babies are more cautious than others and want to wait until they feel secure before they attempt to solo. Please don't get caught up in the "keeping up with the Joneses' baby" game. Each child has his or her own pace and cannot be rushed, and in the long run it makes no difference who walks first.

By twelve months, most babies are quite mobile. They can turn from their back to their belly, get on all fours, and take off. Or they can rise from their back to a sitting position, then go from sitting to creeping. Or they can pull themselves to standing and get about by cruising around holding onto furniture. Some children may even be walking alone.

Although they are still babies and dependent on you to satisfy most of their needs, babies gain a beginning kind of independence through being self-moving. How you respond to your baby at this time will set the tone and ground rules for your relationship through early childhood and will strongly influence both the style and effectiveness of his learning. Within limits necessary to protect them from harm and breakable objects from them, you should let babies have as much freedom of movement as possible. You should realize that since babies can move around now, they can get into things. Therefore, you will avoid problems by "baby-proofing" your environment—removing items that are likely to be damaged by babies in their exploits, and clearing space for them to move in safely. Then, let them roam, keeping a watchful but not overly nervous eye out for them, and be available to them when they need your help.

Children master sitting alone in the period from six to twelve months. The first step in unsupported sitting occurs at about six months for most babies. They can sit well with support by this time, and their backs are strong enough that they can sit momentarily by themselves, but then they will lean forward in a sort of jackknife position, supporting themselves on their hands. From seven to nine months, as control of their back extends downward, most babies begin to sit by themselves, more upright, with a straighter back and without the support of their hands on the floor in front of them to hold them up or of their arms held to the side, like wings, for balance.

When babies' backs are strong enough that they sit for long periods with good control when supported only by pillows, they're ready to try sitting by themselves. Put your baby on the floor, and hold him in a sitting position. If he seems steady and secure, let go for a moment. When he falls forward, you will have to pick him up, since his back is not yet strong enough for him to re-erect himself. When they're first learning to sit alone, babies can get neither into nor out of the sitting position by themselves. They need you to seat them, and, once seated, they are stuck where you put them. You should be sensitive to your baby's plight at this stage and help her out. In addition to the frustration of not being able to move from the spot she's on, it's a strain on her muscles to sit alone for too long until her back is strong enough.

By nine months, most babies can sit with ease for long periods of time, with their hands freed for reaching, grasping and manipulating objects. They can lean forward and sit up straight again, and they can turn their body around in their seated position. Finally, they can get themselves into and out of a sitting position. Now you can leave babies sitting contentedly with some toys to play with for indefinite periods of time. You will, of course, want to keep an eye on them to make sure they're all right, but they no longer need your help in order to sit and to seat and unseat themselves.

In the period between six and twelve months, babies gain increased control of their wrists, fingers, and thumbs, enabling them to refine their skill in reaching and grasping as well as to begin to be able to purposefully release objects they are holding. In this period, babies go beyond their former accomplishment of reaching for and grasping nearby objects. Now they develop sufficient skill in these pursuits to use them for other learning purposes. From six to eight months, babies learn to grasp hand-sized objects such as a small block, first with their whole hand—using their fingers to hold the object against their palm—and then gradually learning to hold it with their forefinger and thumb without the use of their palm. Through practice, babies learn to grasp and hold on to objects with skill. They then use this skill for the purpose of examining the objects to which they have access. Babies use their hands to find about the world around them.

Thus, they need two things from you: First, they need access to a steady supply of materials to pick up, touch, shake, bang, tear, crumple, drop, fold, and so on. The best materials are common, everyday things from which babies can discover more about the world around them. Second, they need your understanding that at this time of their lives they are all hands; they are into everything within their reach. Thus, you need to remove from their vicinity anything that you don't want them to grab and manipulate. Don't get angry at your baby if she does get hold of something that you don't want her to have. Just take it away and give her something equally attractive as a substitute. Babies are not purposefully destructive; they're just very curious, and they're expressing a very natural developmental need to handle, manipulate, and exploit any object they can get their hands on.

From seven to ten months, most babies learn to grasp very small objects such as a raisin, at first dragging it against the heel of their palm with their fingers, and gradually learning to use their thumb and forefinger to pick it up. A good way for babies to get practice picking up little things is through finger feeding. Let them use their fingers to pick up any morsels that drop on their tray when they're eating. They may not be successful at first, either at picking up the pieces or in holding on to them long enough to get them to their mouth. But the practice will enable them to learn to use their thumb and forefinger to pick up very small things. Be careful about leaving objects around that you would not want babies to put in their mouth, since they have a tendency to deposit most things there. For them, the mouth is another, very sensitive, avenue for exploration and investigation of the properties of objects.

From nine to eleven months, babies characteristically gain enough skill in the use of their hands that they can learn to do such things as playing with a toy on a string, pulling it to themselves and swinging it by the string; pulling the plug out of the bathtub, a cork out of a bottle, and the lid off a can; turning the pages of a magazine (a bunch at one time); pulling eyeglasses off a person's face; and squeezing and squeaking a rubber toy.

When babies first began to use their hands to manipulate objects, they usually responded similarly to each thing they encountered, applying the same set of investigative strategies—touching, banging, shaking, tasting—to everything, no matter what it was. With experience, babies begin to learn to respond to each object individually, applying different investigative or manipulative strategies to each object as appropriate, e.g., ringing a bell, drinking from a cup. To help babies learn more about the special properties of objects, you can provide them with a variety of different kinds of things that require different kinds of responses. Let them experiment on their own, and show them special ways they can play with different objects in playtimes with you.

From ten to twelve months, babies' grasp of small objects becomes more refined, approaching that of an adult. They typically can secure a small object between the tips of their thumb and forefinger, and they can hold on to it for visual inspection or to take it to their mouth. Babies should be fairly accomplished at finger feeding by now. They may enjoy the addition of "finger foods" to their meals, e.g., small pieces of fruit, toast, cheese, a few raisins, crackers. Don't give them anything too hard to chew or digest, but coarse, chopped foods are fine.

From ten to twelve months, babies are beginning to acquire the ability to let go of things on purpose. This is shown at first by dropping and then by throwing. Their release is expulsive and the movement of their fingers exaggerated. This is another stage which can be seen by caregivers as deliberate naughtiness if they don't understand that it is a developmentally appropriate and important part of babies' growth. As in every area of their development, babies seek to practice their newly developing skill. In this case, they practice by dropping, and later by throwing, objects to the floor over and over again; this is the drop-and-retrieve game we warned you was coming in an earlier section. It is undeniable that continuously retrieving dropped toys can become tiresome. But if you realize that dropping and throwing provide babies with important motor and cognitive learning, and that this stage too will pass, you may be more willing to indulge your baby in this game when you have the energy.

From seven to twelve months, there is a progressive increase in babies' consistent use of one hand more than the other. Whereas in early infancy, children used both hands interchangeably, now they are beginning to use one for holding while the other maneuvers or manipulates. There seems to be beginning a differentiation into an active and a passive hand. Although some babies begin as early as six months to show a preference for one hand over the other, definite hand dominance should not be expected before age seven. It is very natural up to that point for children to switch hands, especially in new and unfamiliar activities. A child who seems to do so naturally should certainly be encouraged to use his right hand since it will make it easier for him to cope in a predominantly right-handed society. But if your child definitely prefers his left hand, you should not force him to change.

Doing so can have effects on a child's development far more serious than having to bump elbows at the dining room table and use specially made scissors.

Between six months and one year, infants' control over their hands and fingers improves to such an extent that, by one year, they may begin to learn to use a simple tool such as a cup, a spoon, a crayon. None of these tools will be used well by children until they are a little older, but they can begin now to practice. At a year, babies use their thumb and forefinger to pick up deftly even the smallest things, and they use their forefinger to poke at and explore things. Infants' fingers are still their best tools for busy exploration and experimentation on the world.

Between six and nine months, most babies' teeth begin to erupt,* enabling them to handle some chopped foods such as toast, baked potatoes, and eggs. They show their readiness for coarser foods through their behavior at this stage of putting everything in their mouth and chewing on it. Babies improve in their ability to swallow quickly and easily during this time period; they even become able to handle small lumps without any coughing or choking.

It's important to give babies foods that require chewing at the time that their behavior indicates they're ready for them. Their food should be chopped so it isn't too hard to handle, but it should be coarse enough to give them practice in chewing. Again, don't force your baby to eat anything he doesn't like. He may like it better later. Don't force him to eat more than he wants either. Two or three level tablespoons may not seem like much to you, but it may be plenty for him. By nine months, many children are ready to begin eating a regular three meals a day, but their food will need to be chopped until they learn to masticate and have their first molars (usually by about two years).

Infants' oral musculature improves in the last half of their first year so that they can control their lips for drinking from a cup, keep food in their mouth when they are eating, open their mouth to let in a spoonful of food, and close it at the right time. By seven to nine months, most infants learn to hold a cup by the handle but still cannot drink unless someone else holds it. A cup with double handles on the sides and a plastic insert on the top allows infants to begin drinking out of a cup on their own without making too much of a mess. Even if they turn the cup upside down, the liquid will only dribble out. It's important for babies to be able to try things on their own.

Many babies begin to want to hold their own spoon for eating

---

*You should consult your baby's doctor if teething is causing her a lot of pain. In most cases, babies who are teething like to have something they can "gum" and chew on such as a teething ring, a rubber toy, zwieback crackers or toast, and arrowroot cookies.

toward the end of the year. At this stage, since most babies' skill with their hands is not yet adequate for using a spoon really to feed themselves, you may be able to avoid problems by giving them their own to play with while you feed them with another.

Between six and twelve months, babies undergo changes in their ability to understand and use language for communication. Between six and nine months, infants' vocalization (sound-making) tend to increase; they begin to imitate the speech patterns and ryhthm of their language so that their vocalizations sound like real speech, although most children don't usually begin to use real words until about one year, and then only one or two. Babies begin, by about nine months, to pay attention to people talking, both "listening" and watching their mouths as they talk. They are beginning to realize that words are used to communicate with someone and may jabber or shout to call attention to themselves. They combine their jargon speech (wordlike sounds strung together with all the intonation patterns of real speech, with an occasional "real" word mixed in) with facial expression and gestures. For example, they may wave "bye-bye" or shake their head in a gesture of "No." They can respond to gestures and facial expressions, and may get the meaning of a few verbal commands such as "No, no" by the way they sound if not by the actual words.

From nine to twelve months, most children begin to produce several syllables that sound like words, probably including "mama" and "bye-bye." Although these "words" may have meaning to the child, it will probably be both broader and more vague than the meaning assigned the words by adult speakers. Babies seem to listen to conversations around them, and they understand many more words than they can say. They may respond to "bye-bye" with a wave and the words, and they may respond to their name. They are beginning to understand and respond to simple commands such as "Give me the cup" or "Put that down." Some children may be able to point to a few objects as you say the name to them; some may say the words themselves when they hear them. Some infants may practice "talking," jabbering constantly to their toys, to anybody who cares to listen, and to themselves in the mirror.

Babies need to be talked to, but especially at this age the words should relate directly to a specific object or situation. Among the many things you can do to help your child develop his beginning language usage is to take advantage of situations when you are with him to talk to him about things around him, what you are doing, and so on. For example, say "bye-bye" when the child or someone is leaving; ask him if he wants some milk and give him some, saying, "Here's your milk." Talk about eating when he's eating, about taking a bath when you bathe him. Use short, clear sentences. Say, "Do you want to be picked up? Up, up, up we go," when you pick him up and "Down, down,

down you go," when you put him down, so that he'll connect the word and the action.

You can "read" to babies from books with many pictures. Point to and name the objects and actions in the pictures, using short sentences, such as "See the dog." Go slowly and have patience. Set a couple of toys on a table. Say to your baby "Where is the cup?" or "Find Teddy." Be happy and encourage success when the child points correctly; pick up the toy and make it dance to her, or pretend to use it appropriately, saying, "Yes, here is Teddy" or "Yes, here's the cup."

When your baby echoes words, play a game with her, giving her simple words to say after you. Give her simple commands such as "Give me the cup" or "Show me the ball." Sing to her or sing along with her to simple children's records.

In the first half of their first year, babies accumulate experience with the world of people and things around them that enables them to build some ideas about what they know and what they don't know. They are developing a memory storehouse against which they can compare new, incoming information. Due to this, in the second half of the first year babies are beginning to have a more stable, consistent view of the world.

From about eight to twelve months babies are beginning to see the connections and differences between actions and their results. They also are beginning to apply what they know from their own experience to new situations, trying out, for example, strategies that they've found to work with something similar. They are also learning that things have a permanent existence—that even though they can't see them, they still exist. Infants learn to look for a toy that is moved out of their sight, or to uncover an object that they have watched being covered by a blanket. They will get a toy from under a cup when they have seen it hidden and will hit or squeeze a toy to make it squeak. Babies in this stage enjoy putting things into other things and taking them out, playing their own game of disappear and reappear.

Babies at this age may like to copy something someone else does, such as ringing a bell, or opening and closing their eyes and mouth, showing that they are learning to associate their actions with another's and that they are beginning to have an internal image of how to do something they have seen. They are beginning to know something about number; most children begin to see that some things always come in twos (eyes, ears, shoes, socks) and can tell the difference between one and two syllables (for example, ba and baba) when they imitate.

You can play games with babies trying out their new-found knowledge about things. Hide things in front of them and let them find them. Give them toys that they can do things with to make something happen, such as pull toys or ones that make noises. Play copycat games; do something and then encourage your child to do it. Talk in short, simple sentences to the children whenever you do these things to teach them the words for the things they are learning. For example, hide a toy and ask, "Where's the car? Find it. There's the car. The car was under the cup. Good!" Be excited when you play with children. They will learn that learning is fun if they see that you enjoy it. Ring a bell, then give it to them and say, "Ring the bell." When dressing, say, "Here's a sock. Here's a foot. There's another foot! Where's the other sock?" Find it, and say, "Here's the other sock. Here are two feet. Here are two socks. Here are two shoes."

Infants in this stage particularly like to play "peek-a-boo." This is another sign that they are learning that things exist apart from them and that things (and people) that disappear are still there but have to be looked for—in this case behind their hands. Some infants of one year also like being chased around when they creep. They make games out of using their new knowledge and skills. And games are even more fun when played with someone else. In general, babies from nine to twelve months are curious explorers. They want to try things out to see how they work or what made them happen.

By twelve months babies are beginning to be aware of themselves as persons in relation to other people. They are beginning to realize that they are separate beings, and that people and things exist apart from them. Infants may enjoy looking at themselves and things around them in a mirror. They usually know their name and will respond to it. They like to play games with another person; they love an audience and will do again something that got a laugh before. They are beginning to play games in which they imitate actions they have seen others do. They have definite likes and dislikes for particular people. They respond affectionately to people and also to stuffed toys and other things they consider as alive as people. They recognize people's emotions and moods, and express their own.

Babies in this stage may begin to enjoy playing pretend games (e.g., pretending to drink from a cup), and they delight in games like "Pat-a-cake" and "This Little Piggie Went to Market." Toys that babies from six to twelve months might enjoy include stuffed dolls and animals, plastic or rubber toy animals, picture books, pull toys that make a noise, toys that squeak when squeezed, drums, tambourines and similar musical instruments, things from the kitchen such as big wooden spoons and pots, cans and boxes that fit into each other, solid small and large blocks of different colors to build and play with, boxes and baskets to carry things and small things to put in and take out, toys on strings to pull down over their bed or to swing around, bean bags and loosely inflated balls for throwing, and plastic cups with small objects to hide under them.

Perhaps the most significant occurrence in the second half of babies' first year of life is that they fall in love. In the first six months, although they need the love and nurturance of others in order to survive, babies don't know how to love another person because they don't know that other persons exist apart from them. As they learn more about the world and they develop memories, and as they have experiences that help them discover the difference between "what is me" and "what is not me," babies also begin to form a definite image of the person(s), usually their mother, who has been the source of all their satisfactions. And when this happens, babies fall in love.

Two things happen to babies who are just beginning to develop strong attachments to chosen loved ones. One is separation anxiety, and the other is stranger anxiety. The first is an unwillingness on the part of babies in this stage (usually between six and nine months) to part with their love object. Their behavior is not unlike that which any of us show in the first stages of an intense love relationship; they can't bear to be away from the source of their love. As happens in other love relationships, this stage passes as babies become secure that nothing will threaten the relationship and that they can trust their loved one to be there when they need her. At the same time, most babies experience a period during which they are very apprehensive about people they don't know. This can be very embarrassing if it happens at the time when a grandparent comes to visit for the first time, but having mother near will help relieve the anxiety and a friendship can be begun if it's done at the baby's pace.

Obviously this is not a good time to leave babies with a new babysitter, and there may be a period when it's hard to leave them at all. But if you understand that by giving your baby all the love and attention she asks for (in behavior, not words, of course), she'll develop a feeling of security about loving and being loved that will enable her to begin independent explorations of the world around her, and that this stage of extreme possessiveness will pass, then the sacrifice of not going out without her for a short while won't be so hard.

Babies learn to love through being loved, and the love relationship they develop at this early age will form the foundation for their future love relationships. This is a crucial stage in a baby's development, the effects of which will be felt throughout his life. Express your love and receive your baby's love with warmth and joy, and you will give her and all those she touches the most valuable treasure a human being can give or receive.

A loving heart is the truest wisdom.
—CHARLES DICKENS (1812–1870)

3

One to Two Years:
Feeling Their Oats

*Infancy isn't what it is cracked up to be. Children,
not knowing that they are having an easy time, have a
good many hard times. Growing and learning and obeying
the rules of their elders, or fighting against them,
are not easy things to do.*

—DON MARQUIS (1878–1937)

*Childhood and genius have the same master-organ in
common—inquisitiveness.—Let childhood have its way,
and as it began where genius begins, it may find what
genius finds.*

—EDWARD GEORGE BULWER (1803–1873)

*If I were asked what single qualification was necessary
for one who has the care of children, I should say
Patience—Patience with their tempers, with their
understanding, with their progress.*

—FRANCIS DE FENELON (1651–1715)

From one to two years, children continue the development as self-moving, independent persons that they began toward the end of their first year. In addition to adding more motor skills to their list of accomplishments and refining those they began to develop in the first year, children between one and two make significant strides in the development of their ability to understand and use language. As a consequence of their increase in motor and language skills, concomitant with growth in their ability to make sense of and apply organization to things in their world, children in this period begin to be aware of themselves as persons in their own right and to assert their will upon the world, often in defiant and negativistic ways.

This stage is a challenging one for those caring for children, calling upon great reservoirs of patience, resourcefulness, and energy.

Suddenly you look around and realize that your baby is becoming a person; and no matter how much you might sometimes wish you could decide what kind of person (maybe a little quieter or less adventuresome, at least for a few minutes a day?) he is going to be, its becoming clear that that's his job. Gone are the days when you could leave your baby unsupervised, and gone are the days of a neat and orderly house. But in their place is an exuberant, curious, excited small person, just beginning her life's journey toward defining who she is and what she can be. And you have the privilege of helping to light her way.

MOTOR DEVELOPMENT

In the last chapter, you will recall, we took babies through the steps leading up to independent walking. Although some babies begin walking alone before the end of the first year, most do so at the beginning of their second year. From twelve to fifteen months, most babies learn to stand alone, at least momentarily, without using furniture for support. Some begin the steps toward unsupported walking at the same time that they try standing alone, and others practice standing until they become steady before they try walking on their own. A baby's first steps may not be fully intentional. He might just get distracted and let go of his support, then totter a few steps before collapsing. In such a case, the infant may not try again on purpose for another few days or longer, but once he does get up his courage, he'll work at it continuously.

Babies' first steps are typically wobbly with feet wide apart and arms out to the side, poised in readiness to protect them when they fall. They usually take a few steps at a time and fall by collapsing. You can play a game with your baby, positioning her between you and someone else she trusts. Let her walk back and forth between you with support. If she seems secure, gradually move far enough apart that she has to let go in order to walk from one to the other. This should be a fun game with much ado if the baby makes it from one of you to the other on her own. When babies first begin walking, although they'll spend endless amounts of time practicing, when they need to get somewhere in a hurry they usually get down on hands and knees. Some babies alternate between walking and creeping at first, depending on the distance they have to travel.

What babies need most from you at this time is patience and the opportunity and space to practice walking until they achieve some efficiency and sense of confidence. They also need your encouragement and delight at their success when they accomplish their goals, but lack of pressure or concern that they move any faster than they choose. The time that babies are learning to walk is not a good time to put them into shoes; wait until they are secure on their feet. Then get them a pair of shoes with a straight inner border, flat soles, and a firm heel structure against which they can brace their feet in walking. Bare feet are still preferable for walking on grass, sand, or a carpet, but the shoes add support and protection for walking on hard surfaces such as concrete or wooden floors.

With practice over time, babies begin to cover more ground, increase the speed of their walking and the length of their steps, and decrease the width of their steps. They reduce excess movements such as lifting their feet up high each time they step; their steps become more regular, and they begin to walk with a heel to toe progression. They lower the level of their arms and begin to use them (and their hands) to carry things while they walk. This kind of progression occurs, on the average, between fifteen and eighteen months. By the end of that period, infants are generally confident on their feet and trot about everywhere (trotting is the stage between walking and running; the child moves fast with his feet wide apart, swaying from one foot to the other). They seldom fall but their balance may still be unsteady.

Babies need large spaces and different kinds of areas to move about in. When they were first learning to walk, the length of a room was a great distance. Now that's no longer enough to challenge them. Try to take children outdoors to a park or playground in good weather, and let them romp. An area with sand and grass and dirt to walk in and small hills and large rocks to climb on is ideal. Even in cold weather, as long as they're properly clothed, a regular walk outside will provide needed exercise for babies at this age. When you and your baby are walking together, please remember that he has short legs and still is not the master of his upright mobility. He cannot keep up with an adult's regular strides. Have patience, and walk at his pace; don't ever drag the baby along or force him to hurry his steps to keep up with you.

As children become more adept at walking, they will begin to test and extend their skill by various "stunts" such as walking sideways or backwards while pulling a toy on wheels by a string; pushing a wheeled toy along and toddling after it; balancing a toy on their head; carrying around a box or basket full of toys: transporting a small toy in each hand; or lugging a large, heavy object in both hands. It may seem sometimes that your baby is always trying to do the impossible—carrying around things almost as big as she is, climbing on everything, loading her arms up with things to transport around the house, and so on. It's a very natural reaction to move to help her when she's trying to do these difficult things. But try to resist the temptation, and let her do it on her own unless she asks for your help. Babies very deliberately push their abilities to the limit at this age and often frustrate themselves in the process. But this is part of their becoming competent and independent, and they should be encouraged to meet their own challenges.

From eighteen to twenty-four months, children become more sure of their balance and ability to get about on their own. They master all types of locomotion including overcoming obstacles such as hills, ladders, slopes, narrow passages, small planks, and moving surfaces. However, they still watch their feet as they walk so that they'll be able to deal with obstacles in their path. They begin to learn to run, stiffly at first, and then fairly well without falling, but not very fast. Proficiency in running is not finalized until school age. By two years, most children can speed up without losing balance, but they can't stop and start quickly. Because they are still perfecting their balance, children at this age may run into walls or objects when they're in a hurry.

You can set up simple obstacle courses for children to walk and creep through, including such things as steps, inclined planks, and hills (if outdoors) to climb, a tunnel to crawl through, a chair to crawl under or climb onto and slide off of, a ladder laid on its side to step between and over the rungs, a narrow passageway, e.g., between two rows of chairs, to walk through. Once children have started running, it's hard to get them to stop; they seem to run more than they walk. But for those who still need encouragement, try standing at the bottom of a small hill and urging them to hurry; or run with them, holding their hand.

Children from eighteen to twenty-four months often like to go on long walks, as much as a mile or two, stopping to explore, walking slowly, and observing everything on their way. When you have time, take your child on such a walk. Follow his pace, walking slowly and stopping as he wishes, to rest or explore. Long-distance walking is healthy for your child and for you, and it can be a source of many exciting learning experiences as you stop along the way to notice things, collect rocks and leaves or other interesting items, or talk to people. Whether you live in the city or in the country, walking can be a real adventure if you keep your eyes and ears open.

Between one and two years, children learn a variety of large motor skills in addition to mastering the upright posture. They learn to climb—onto ledges and steps, up and down stairs, and into chairs and other furniture; to jump—off low objects, off the floor with both feet, from the bottom step of a stairwell, and over an obstacle; to play simple catch and toss with a ball and kick one; to balance on one foot with help or by holding onto a chair; to squat while playing and alternate quickly between sitting and standing; to walk up and down stairs, holding on to someone's hand or to a banister; to stand on a stool or chair to get something out of reach; and to seat themselves on a stool, low bench, or child-sized chair. Obviously, most of these skills are not attempted until after a child has mastered the upright posture, since they require that she first be able to stand in that position with good balance. So those skills are usually not seen in children before eighteen months. But climbing is begun by children when they're still creeping, and the first stages of it are seen from twelve to fifteen months.

Children need practice in developing these motor skills. You can help by making sure that appropriate spaces and equipment are available—in your home, at playgrounds, and perhaps shared by others you know with small children. In addition, you can play games with your child, trying out newly developing skills. For example, you can climb up stairs with him and teach him how to climb down by creeping backwards or by the bump method (bumping from one step to the next on his bottom); you can lead him up stairs by the hand and then go to the bottom and urge him to come down to join you. You can help your child learn to jump by lifting him onto a large building block and holding both his hands while he steps down at first and then learns to jump with both feet.

You can play catch and toss, at first sitting down with both your legs open to catch the ball if your hands miss it, and placing the ball in your child's arms at first. You can show her how to kick a ball and then hold her hand while she tries it. You can play a modified form of musical chairs, using two chairs and singing to help her practice seating herself with ease. You can both try jumping up in the air to touch the sky, or you can hold up a favorite toy for your child to jump up and touch. There are many simple things you can do with your child to help her practice her new skills; watch her to see what kinds of things she's ready for, use your imagination to think of fun ways to develop those skills, and have a good time.

All the changes that are occurring in babies' motor abilities in their second year make them much less willing to stay put in a crib for naps and at night. To an adventurous child between one and two years, the crib is just another challenge, and you are likely to find your small child practicing climbing over its edge. In addition, many children this age, because they are concerned with asserting themselves as persons in their own right who have choices in their life, may object to being confined in a crib. If your child starts experiencing sleeping difficulties at this time or if he's continuously trying to escape the confines of his crib, that's your cue that it's time for a real bed. He may look very tiny to you sleeping in such a big bed, but you'll all be happier for it.

Between eighteen months and two years, children are beginning to learn how to use simple playground equipment and riding toys. Many children are ready, by this time, to learn to ride a kiddy-car or some type of simple riding toy which they can move by pushing with their feet along the floor. You can buy small, inexpensive and sturdy plastic riding toys. Show your child how to get it to move and give her some space to try it out in any way she thinks of. By two years, with practice, children can ride a pedal-less wheel toy skillfully, steering it well, maneuvering it around obstacles, and backing and turning with speed and accuracy. Some children may begin learning to ride a tricycle by two years, but they usually push with their feet instead of using the pedals. At this age, children can begin to learn to slide on a low slide.

Children should have a chance to practice using different kinds of indoor and outdoor play equipment such as slides with steps up to them for climbing up and sliding down; enclosed swings, low obstacles to jump over and off, tunnels to crawl through, small rocking boats, tyke bikes and other riding toys and boards to walk and jump on.

But more important than either special equipment or organized games with you is that children have the opportunity to run and jump and climb and dig and do anything they feel like in an outdoor space that is large and interesting, with hills or mounds of dirt, flat areas, grassy spots, places with sand, and so on. If there's no such place near you, you could get together with other parents and see if you can get a small area set aside for children to play in. It doesn't take a lot of money, because you don't really need much equipment. The land itself, if divided up into different kinds of areas, can be more interesting and stimulating than expensive playground equipment, and equipment can be made from discarded items such as old truck tires and telephone-wire spools.

Many of children's developing motor skills will get plenty of exercise, also, just in the ordinary process of living in most houses or apartments. Children can practice climbing up and down stairs and onto beds, sofas, and chairs. If they feel like jumping, they'll jump wherever they are. You might want to provide a sturdy stepstool for them to use for getting out-of-reach things; they'll enjoy lugging it around and climbing on it as well as using it to get things up high. In addition, children should have a sturdy chair of their own, small enough that they can seat themselves in it now without having to climb up into it, but large enough that they will still be able to use it for a couple of years. To aid in the early development of good sitting posture, make sure your baby's feet can reach the floor when she's seated. Of course, babies should also be allowed to climb up into adult-sized furniture, since it's good large-motor exercise, but for eating or drawing at a table, babies are best in their own child-sized chair.

From one to two years, children make significant strides in fine motor development also. From twelve to fourteen months, babies show an increase in their ability to let go of objects with control, enabling them to release an object into someone's hand, put things repeatedly into a container and play a game of rolling a ball to another person.* They can remove a round block from a formboard and insert it into the board. They can take the lids off boxes of various shapes and remove a piece of tissue wrapped around a small toy in order to get at the toy. Babies at this age enjoy opening and closing cupboards and drawers and playing with their contents, especially kitchen utensils. They like playing with wooden and cardboard boxes and plastic containers with lids that they can take off and try to put back on (the latter is much harder to do and will take a while).

Control of tools is beginning in this period. Most babies between twelve and fourteen months can hold a crayon in their fist and scribble on paper after seeing someone else do it. They can hold their own cup for drinking, but they can't manage it alone without spilling. They are beginning to feed themselves with a spoon, but they are likely to turn the spoon over, spilling its contents, before it reaches their mouth. Babies' desire to use tools, especially a cup and spoon, probably far exceeds their ability at this point. But try to remember when you become harassed by your baby's insistence on feeding herself that she needs practice in order to become efficient. Even though she may feed the table and floor more than she feeds herself now, be assured that she will improve her performance if you allow her the opportunity to practice. Sometimes you might let your baby practice feeding you. It's an easier task than feeding herself (since she can see what she's doing) and one that she'll enjoy.

From fifteen to eighteen months, babies continue to improve in their ability to place and release objects with control. For example, they can learn to stack pierced blocks on a peg, though not yet in the "correct" order if they're graduated in size. They can, with some trial and error, successfully build a tower of two to three small blocks. And they can replace the lids of a round or a square container. Babies at this age like putting one object after another in and out of a container, but they tend to dump more than to fill. For example, because of their drive to practice their emerging skill of letting go, babies may dump the contents of wastebaskets and drawers. This is not being naughty but rather an expression of their developmental needs. You can help by not getting angry when your baby dumps but instead helping him to clean up when he's done. And you can give him his own basket and some things of his own (e.g., "junk" mail) to dump and fill. It's really a fun game if you play too.

Babies from fifteen to eighteen months enjoy playing with kitchen utensils such as pots and pans and double boilers, taking them

---

* Ball play involves both gross and fine motor control and coordination.

apart and putting them back together again. In addition, they might enjoy a set of small blocks for gathering, dropping, and beginning building; a set of pierced blocks for stacking (round ones are the easiest); a set of lidded boxes of graduated sizes that they can fill and dump and practice putting on and taking off the lids; and a set of cans of graduated sizes. They will also enjoy using a toy hammer. Hammering is not only fun, but it develops important cognitive skills as children learn to aim with greater accuracy and strength in order to pound pegs into a pegboard.

Children at this age are learning better hand and wrist control. They try, usually without success, to turn doorknobs, and they help turn the pages of a book or magazine, a few at a time. They are learning to roll *or* throw a ball with good aim now if they've had the chance to practice, and they can engage easily in to and fro ball play. They throw with one or both hands. Infants at this age are also improving in their ability to use tools. They hold a glass of milk in both hands, though somewhat precariously, and they can feed themselves with a spoon, holding it palm down. If you fill your baby's cup only half way, she can manage it much better. She is still likely to spill when she feeds herself, but that's part of the learning process. It's important that you let her do it herself.

Between eighteen and twenty-four months, children are improving their skill with their fingers in manipulating tools and other objects, but they're still awkward. They work best with things big enough for them to get a good grip on, and at this age they will probably be more interested in common household items or child-sized copies of them than in complex toys. For example, children may enjoy using a sponge, a small broom, and a mop to clean, dust, and sweep as they see others do. In this time period, their developing control of their hands enables children to do such things as put both a circle and a square in the right place in a formboard; build a tower of five to six blocks; put six large round pegs in a pegboard within one minute; correctly nest two or three boxes of obviously different size; unscrew the lid of a small jar or bottle; and put the cover on an oblong box. Children may enjoy a game with different shaped containers, e.g., round, square, and oblong boxes with lids; small plastic jars with screw tops; plastic containers with tops that snap on and off. Take the tops off the containers. Start with two and add more, one at a time, as children get better at the game. Hand them a top, ask them to find the container it goes on and to put it on. Show excitement when they get it right. This, like all learning games, should be fun for both of you. If it isn't, don't do it.*

* By this time, overlaps between different areas of development are becoming increasingly evident. For example, the game just described involves as much cognitive as motor skill—the child must know which top goes with which con-

By two years, most children are beginning to use the same hand more often for one-handed things such as drawing and eating; their passive hand is becoming more passive and taking on a subordinate role in one-handed behavior. At this age, children can usually turn the pages of a book or magazine one at a time, build a tall tower of blocks and a "train" of two or three, and put the circle, square, and triangle in a three-hole formboard after seeing someone else do it and after some trial and error. Other uses to which children may be able to put their hands by now include turning a doorknob to open a door; turning a lamp switch on and off; unscrewing and reassembling a screw toy; inserting a key in a lock; folding a piece of paper after watching someone else do it; driving a nail into soap or soft wood; and snipping with scissors. Most children have enough coordination at this age to work a simple record player, switching it on, putting a record on the turntable, moving the tone arm into position, and adjusting the volume.

A small, easily operated record player and some records of their own (including lively marches and soothing melodies; don't limit them to "children's music") would be a good investment at this time. Children not only practice hand skills in operating the device, but they also get experience in rhythm-related movement. A small wooden hammer and blunt nails with soft wood or a piece of soap for hammering may be enjoyed by some children, but should be supervised.

Children need to learn to use scissors before they can use them with control. Pieces of newspaper to cut with small blunt scissors and then to paste on a piece of paper and to color can form the basis of a good activity for developing fine motor skills. Children may begin now to enjoy art activities such as scribbling on paper with big pencils and fat crayons, "painting" with water, pounding and squeezing with clay or play dough. They like these activities for the process, for practice with the material and with their fine motor skills; most children this age are neither capable of nor interested in making an art "product."

Pegboards with large pegs, simple two- and three-piece jigsaw puzzles, and other equipment of this kind are good for practice in hand skills. You can make your own puzzles by mounting pictures on heavy poster board, cutting them into two or three logical pieces, and covering them with clear contact paper. Children tend to be more responsible with books now. Their finger control is up to turning pages without tearing them. Children will enjoy having their own

---

tainer as well as be able motorically to fit them together; even the fitting together requires knowledge of spatial relations, a cognitive skill. Similarly, eating and dressing skills, though requiring motor ability, have implications for socioemotional development. We will, therefore, mention all these skills in this section and then refer to them again as appropriate in other sections.

books with bright, colorful illustrations depicting common objects or telling a simple story. Because of their new capacity for turning knobs and switches, no such device is safe from children's fingers. It is best to tape over any switches you don't want touched, and to encourage children to help you in turning off lights or switching on *their* record player.

Children should be allowed to play alone with a variety of different kinds of materials as they like; but remember that also at this age they enjoy and need to play with adults who talk to them about what they're doing, ask them questions, and show them new ways to use the materials they're working with. Your role should always be facilitative, not directive, and never interfering.

If children have had sufficient chance for practice up to this point, they are gaining enough control of the spoon to feed themselves with little mess. By two years, most children can eat with a spoon without turning it upside down. Between eighteen and twenty-four months, some children may begin to use a small fork, though not without spilling food off of it; they use it best for spearing chunks of food. Within this time period, children become able to handle a cup well. By two years, they can drink from a cup or small glass without spilling. They hold it with one hand, but with the other poised in readiness to help if needed. By this time, children's oral musculature has matured; they now chew their food almost automatically. If they have gotten their first molars, this is an indication that they are ready to handle unsimplified foods. Thus, as long as you cut their food into manageable pieces and don't spice it too much (this includes not too much salt or sugar), children can now eat whatever the rest of the family eats.

By eighteen months, children should be helping to dress themselves, putting a leg out to go in a pant leg, even trying to put on their shoes. However, they are better at undressing—pulling off mittens, hat, and socks, and unzipping their front zipper if it's not too hard. Between eighteen and twenty-four months, children are becoming progressively better at taking off all their clothes, often to the exasperation of those caring for them. Realize, when you find your child running around outside stripped bare, that for him this is simply another arena to practice his motor skills and not deliberate naughtiness. Undressing is easier than dressing, and the first is a necessary step toward the latter. Let your child help in any ways possible in the dressing and undressing process, and try to explain to him that there are times and places when clothes are a good idea.

By two years, children help actively to dress and undress themselves. They can pull on simple garments such as socks, mittens, a jersey, and their hat if the things are given to them the right way around. If difficult fasteners are undone for them, they will enjoy removing their own clothes. Avoid garments with lots of little buttons, back fasteners, sashes, and so on. With a difficult article like a sock, start it on your child's foot the right way and let her finish it. Let her do as much as she can without becoming frustrated.

Many children by two years are beginning to imitate the superficial actions of grooming, e.g., chewing on the toothbrush or going through the motions of brushing and combing their hair. This is the time to begin good grooming habits. Encourage children's imitative play and help them, once they've had their fill, to learn the correct methods, particularly of tooth brushing. If you make it a habit now, you won't have problems later getting them to do it.

One of the more significant, because of the socioemotional implications it has (due to general societal and specific parental attitudes), motor achievements that occurs in this time period is voluntary control of the bladder and bowel sphincter muscles, readying children for toilet training. This occurs some time between eighteen and twenty-four months in most children, somewhat later in males than in females. By two years, most children have the muscular control, conceptual understanding, and communicative skills necessary in order to be successful at learning to use the toilet. They should, by this time, have sufficient control over their sphincter muscles to hold in and let go purposefully and consciously. And they can learn to recognize when they have to go to the bathroom and tell you so.

When children are motivated to use the toilet, because it will make them feel more competent and grown up, they will almost train themselves. Provide them with a small potty chair, show them how to use it, and let them get used to it on their own time schedule. For some children, this may take a while; for others, it will be only a short time until they're "trained." Don't be competitive with other parents over when your child is toilet trained. He has the rest of his life to use the toilet. It's simply not worth the problems it can create to make an issue of it. If there are older children around who are already toilet trained, sometimes they can help a younger child better than you can. Just make sure they're not too pushy, and take care of cleaning the child afterwards yourself.

LANGUAGE DEVELOPMENT

From one to two years, children's ability to discriminate the sounds and meaning of the language spoken around them improves, as does their ability to imitate and produce speech sounds themselves. Because of their preoccupation with motor learning, children may make very slow progress in language development in the first part of the year. From twelve to eighteen months, babies discover that words refer to things in their environment, and they learn to use words primarily to name tangible, visible things around them. These words typically function as complete sentences, serving different meanings according to the intonation the child uses. For example, "Mama" might mean "Mama, I'm hungry"; "Mama, I want to go out"; "Mama, I love you"; "Mama, hi," and so on. "Papa" or "Dada" is typically used at this age to refer to all men.

Infants from twelve to fifteen months begin to learn words to apply to what they know. At this age they know much more about the world than they have words for. At twelve to fifteen months most infants use three to seven words consistently; by eighteen months, most use one- and two-word "sentences," and their repertoire may include ten to twenty words, about half of which are nouns. Although concrete nouns constitute a large part of children's repertoire of words in this period, many children also include in their vocabulary a number of other kinds of words such as "hi," "bye-bye," "up," "out," "hot," and "eat."

Most of children's talking between twelve and eighteen months is still jargon; it sounds like speech, but the real words they know are used alongside many "words" which have no real meaning. Usually in this age range they learn to ask for at least two things by name. They use words in addition to gestures to get across their needs; they may be able to point to some familiar objects in pictures (even though they may not be able to name them themselves) and they may be able to point to nose, eyes, and hair on a doll and on themselves. They respond to simple commands such as "Open your mouth."

By eighteen months, most children are beginning to claim "mine" and to distinguish between you and me. They are beginning to use words to direct their own behavior by saying such things as "no" or "hot" to themselves when they approach a situation that they have learned they should stay away from. Their words are definite; they may say "eat" when hungry and "no" when they're full. Many children, by eighteen months, understand the word "more" as in "Do you want more juice?"

Children learn fastest those words that they hear in the largest number of different contexts, and the words they learn relate to their lives, thus helping them to define their world. The words given above as examples illustrate the kinds of words children learn in this time period—they are likely to hear "eat," "bye-bye," and so on, used often and within the context of their own experience. You can help children increase the number of words they can use to describe and define their world as well as to communicate their needs by using words along with their activities, and giving them the words for the things they know. For example, when you see them doing something (e.g., climbing, walking, carrying a toy, sweeping), talk to them about it in short, simple sentences: "Megan is climbing. Up, up you go." You can also help by naming the things around them: "Look, there's a bird." "Here's your cup." "See the doll. This is Amanda's doll." Use language with your children, and they'll learn to use it too.

From eighteen months to two years, children's language grows from the use of an average of 10 to 20 words to the use of about 250 words in short sentences. At eighteen months children's language is usually mostly jargon; by two years, it is mostly real words with little jargon. They learn in this time period to use words to ask for needs such as food, drink, or going to the toilet. Children begin, at an average of about twenty-one months, to talk about what they see and are doing, but they do not yet talk about past events or things out of sight. They usually express their needs without gestures by now.

At this time, most children are beginning to use two-word sentence combinations and to imitate two- to three-word sentences such as "Help me" or "Daddy is coming." They may also imitate sounds of cars, animals, horns. Children's speech at this age is *telegraphic,* using only the important words, e.g., "Daddy car," "More milk." Pronouns—mine, me, you, and I—are coming into use, in about that order; but most children will call themselves more by name than "me" or "I"—"Tommy slide down."

By two years, children may combine three and four words in sentences, sing parts of songs, readily name at least four objects, ask for "another" and "more," ask for things by their names, and talk a lot about what they're doing and playing with. Many of their sentences may be almost the same, changing only the subject: "*Shelley* go home," "*Angie* go home," "*Tammie* go home." Children begin to use more pronouns and know expressions of time such as "soon," "wait," "when it's time," and "in a minute" and words to mean something in the future such as "gonna." Knowing these words helps them learn to wait a short time since it gives time a meaning for them.

Children will learn to use language to communicate with other people by hearing language used along with the things they do, by being talked with, and by getting practice talking with others. When you play with children, say the names of toys and simple action words that pertain to what the children do with the toy. Watch what they do and try to fit words to their activities. Try to be alert to their thoughts and feelings and help them express them in words as well as actions. *Listen* when they talk to you and encourage them to use language to communicate with you and others.

It also helps to "read" simple stories to children. Go slowly, and mostly just name things, using short sentences. Ask them to show you pictures of familiar things and actions and to name the objects and activities they know the words for. Point to objects as you name them. Make a word book for children by cutting pictures of familiar objects from magazines, or by drawing them. You may write the name of the object or a simple activity description below the picture. Include in the book such things as foods, daily activities such as face washing or going to bed, toys and play equipment, and so on. Let the children choose what they want in *their* book. Pictures should not be abstract, since children prefer realistic ones.

By two years, children may use words and phrases such as "up high," "there," "where," "go away," "fall down," and "turn around." They sometimes use plural nouns to mean more than one. They can tell the difference between one and many, but they can't count and can't tell which is bigger of two or more things. They begin to use "another," "all gone," "big," "little," "no more," and "much." They are beginning to understand time in the future and to use verbs in the past tense, though often incorrectly.

Play games with children, trying out their new skills and understanding. Talk to them when they're playing, using these kinds of words: "Do you want *another* toy?" "Heres a *big* ball; there's a *little* one." Using objects or pictures, have one of a thing the child knows the name of and a bunch of the same thing. First ask the child to "Show me the apple." Then, "Now, show me the apples." Do the same thing with "big" and "little." Play a "disappearing game," using the words "all gone" or "no more" when you take the thing away. Feed your children language whenever you're together; but remember that verbal language is only *one* way to communicate. Don't make your children just substitute words for their nonverbal communication. Help them develop *both* systems through using words to "check out" their nonverbal understandings and expression.

COGNITIVE DEVELOPMENT

From one to two years, children are continuing to grow in their understanding of the world around them. Their memories are improving for persons, objects, and, by the end of the year, for whole situations and ideas as well as concrete things. By two years, most children can remember something they are told to remember for a short period. The growth in their ability in this time period to remember and *recall* things and events, not simply to recognize things they've experienced before as they did when they were youger, helps children develop their cognitive skills to a higher level than in the first two years. They become able, by the end of this year, to think about things and ideas inside their head instead of having to interact directly with everything in order to "know" it.

From twelve to eighteen months, babies are learning more and more about how the world is organized. They begin to know people by what they do—the person who feeds them, the one who smokes a pipe, and so on. They know what some things are for, e.g., that some things are to eat and some are to wear. If things are usually kept in the same place, many babies can now remember where they belong and look for them there. They like to arrange things and like things to have an order and a place.

As we noted in the discussion of motor development, children in this age period can learn to put together simple puzzles, place a circle in a formboard, and put a few pegs in a pegboard after watching someone else do it. These things require an understanding of spatial concepts in addition to motor skills. Children enjoy filling, emptying, and refilling cups, pans, and boxes with blocks and other things. This marks the beginning of understanding the concepts of "more" and "less." This is paralleled by their understanding and use of the word "more," e.g., "more milk."

Twelve- to eighteen-month-old infants reveal, by their actions and the ways in which they learn new information and skills, that they are beginning to have a desire and need not only to discover a structure and organization in the world around them, but also to make one of their own. At this age, their organization is different from that of older children or adults. It is more fluid and less consistent; it changes, because eighteen-month-old infants still do not have rules for everything, and the rules they make have to be remade all the time as they acquire new information.

You can help infants in their search for structure and organization by deciding some of it for them. There should be a place for everything, and things not being used should stay in their place. When they want something, infants may get it themselves if they're able. You may help them if they need assistance. When they're done with something, have them put it back themselves or help them to do so. It helps if each shelf, drawer, or box that holds things is marked with a picture or drawing of what goes there.

You and your child can play a game with shoe boxes. One box might have a picture of food on it, another box might be covered with pictures of clothing. Then you and the child can find pictures in magazines to go in each box. In a similar manner, there might be a box with a picture of the infant, one with a picture of her mother, and one for father (or for other people with whom the child spends a great deal of time). Once again, magazine pictures may be found and cut out to put in each box. A more structured way to do this activity would be to cut out the pictures ahead of time. Give the child a choice of two boxes to put each picture in, one at a time. This technique would be good to start with for babies at the lower end of this age range. This kind of activity should only be done for the length of time the child is interested in it.

Between eighteen and twenty-four months, most children begin to "think out" actions in their heads. For example, a child may have pictures in his head of what will happen if he moves without actually having to move. By two years children may engage in role playing; for example, playing house, putting a doll to bed, feeding it, and so on. They will follow simple rules such as "No" and "Come." Children's ability to see differences among things gets better. For example, they learn to tell many forms apart (triangle, circle, cross, etc.) no matter what position they are in. By two, while their eyes perceive differences in color, they still don't use color as a cue for discriminating between things. At this age, children do a great deal of looking at things—taking in and digesting the world around them, adding to their store of information.

Many children now can keep track of a toy hidden in a variety of places; they will find a toy which was put into a box and then under a blanket, then taken from the box under the blanket, if they're shown the box. They can find a toy put under one of three boxes in front of them. This is a big change from the infant who would simply forget about a toy that was hidden from her view. Now children know about objects and a world "out there" separate from them.

SOCIOEMOTIONAL DEVELOPMENT

From one to two years, children become more capable of doing things for themselves and on their own, including gaining mastery of the upright posture and of the use of their hands as tools and in the use of tools; learning to undress and help dress themselves; learning to feed themselves; learning to use the toilet; becoming increasingly able to express their needs and desires in words and to satisfy some of them themselves (e.g., getting a desired object off a high shelf by moving a stepstool there and getting up on it); and so on. As a result of these new skills which make children of this age increasingly more independent, their relationship with those caring for them must undergo changes from what it was when they were more dependent.

It has been suggested * that the time period between ten and eighteen months constitutes a turning point in children's development and in their relationship with those adults closest to them that will have a profound impact on whether they grow to be healthy, competent individuals or whether they have problems coping socially and intellectually. The combination of factors occurring in this period

* See Burton White and Jean Carew Watts, *Experience and Environment*, Vol. 1 (Englewood Cliffs, N.J.: Prentice-Hall, Inc., 1973). See also the chapter on this subject in J. and L. Braga, *Growing With Children*.

—the growth in ability to understand language (not yet matched with any significant competency in its use); the development of the ability to get about on their own and get into things; an intense curiosity about things not matched by an understanding of danger (e.g., of playing with razor blades) or an appreciation of other people's property rights; and an emerging sense of themselves as persons having separate identities and who can have an effect on their world—makes this a period that challenges the adults caring for them to the limits of their skills and patience.

White and his colleagues have found that some mothers are very successful in coping with their children during this trying period while others are not. The successful mothers share some of the following characteristics. They enjoy children and are relatively happy about life in general; they are able to live with the mess that children of this age make, and are not overly concerned with their own possessions; they create an environment that is livable and interesting for their children rather than forcing their children to follow arbitrary rules about where they can go and what they can do within an adult-oriented environment; they feed their children's language development by talking a great deal with them at a level they can handle; they are available to their children to help out, explain something, or offer interesting suggestions, responding to their children's requests of their time and interest rather than being the ones to decide when to spend time and how to spend it; their teaching time with their children is generally "on the fly" rather than in concentrated doses, responding to and capitalizing on their children's spontaneous, self-chosen interests with an answer to a question or suggestion of a related idea or activity; they are generally indulgent of their children's behavior, letting them do most things they choose; but they also are not afraid to say no with strength and conviction when necessary. Their discipline is reasonable and consistent, not arbitrary. In sum, these mothers are supportive of and responsive to their children, following their lead and responding to their needs while providing an interesting, stimulating, and warm environment in which they can learn and grow.

Infants learn to feel toward themselves what they sense in response from others to their activities. If others are impatient with their attempts to do things for themselves, or if they are never allowed to explore toys or cupboards and closets, or if they always sense fear from others when they climb up on chairs, they will begin to feel unworthy, incompetent, afraid and useless. This stage of development is fairly fragile even in an approving world. Feelings of great power and success over their newly learned skills can suddenly switch to feelings of smallness and weakness when babies find they cannot do what they tried to do or cannot do what another person has done. They need to be encouraged in their independence and made to feel proud of their new skills in doing things for themselves by adults who allow them to use their new skills and praise them for doing so. How this stage in babies' development is handled will have a significant impact on their future relationships with other people as well as on their feelings about themselves.

Between eighteen and twenty-four months, children begin to call themselves by their name and to talk about things as "mine." They recognize that some things belong to them and they can distinguish between "mine" and "yours," a beginning step in defining themselves in relation to others. They are beginning to think of themselves as individuals, separate from the world around them.

Children from one to two years are becoming increasingly better at expressing their needs. They may begin, toward the end of this period, to play with other children (i.e., in the same room, not yet at the same activity), though they still like to play alone.

Some children by age two are sensitive to the feelings of others and form strong attachments to others of the same age or older or younger. Two-year-olds can tell a man from a woman by what they do, wear, and look like. You should provide good, flexible models for male and female roles so that children learn that although men and women may look different, they can do the same things and act in the same ways.

At two years, most children can play on their own, choosing for themselves what to do. When children play in the same area with other children, it is usually without much interaction. They may play side by side, doing the same thing, but they usually won't do it together. Two-year-olds should be treated as persons and allowed as much independence as they want and need *as long as it does not infringe on anyone else's rights or endanger them.*

The essence of independence is to be able to do something for one's self.

—MARIA MONTESSORI (1870–1952)

4

Two to Three Years: I Want It My Way

The child becomes largely what it is taught, hence we must watch what we teach it, and how we live before it.

—JANE ADDAMS (1860–1935)

Parents who wish to train up their children in the way they should go, must go in the way in which they would have their children go.

—FRANCIS BACON (1561–1626)

From two to three years, children begin to use the basic skills developed in the first two years as the basis for more skilled motor development and more learning about how the world around them is organized. In most of the first two years of their life children learn through direct contact with objects and people; that is, they must experience everything in order to learn about it. By age two, children begin to be able to represent their experience; they have pictures or other images in their head about the things in their world. Also, they are beginning to understand and use the names of the things around them, which is another kind of representation. As a rule, children's most striking growth between two and three is the development of their ability to understand and use language for communication. This is also a time that children begin engaging in role playing and make-believe, other ways for children to represent their experience.

Finally, this period in children's lives is infamously known as "the terrible twos." It is characterized by a stance on the child's part that might be summarized by the words of this chapter's title: "I want it my way." We urge you to try to keep your patience during this period, particularly when your children have temper tantrums. (These of course, are not new to this period; they usually begin around fourteen to fifteen months.) How you handle your child's temper will have a durable effect on his behavior in the future, including how he will treat your grandchildren.

Don't try to stop a tantrum by yelling or striking out physically; you'll only teach, through your model, that those are acceptable behaviors, and it won't help much to stop the tantrums. Usually the best way to handle a tantrum is to remain very calm yourself (if you possibly can), and, without getting in the way of kicking feet, reach out to the child with a gentle but strong hand on her arm and talk to her in very soothing tones; it doesn't matter what you say, since she probably won't hear you, but the tone of your voice will calm her down. After the temper is done, you can deal with what caused it. But don't try to stop a tantrum by yelling; you'll most likely prolong it, and your behavior will have long-term effects you might not want to live with.

In general, your model to your children is becoming increasingly important now. Children are in the process of defining themselves as persons, and they do this in large part through observing, and adapting to themselves, behaviors they see in those around them, particularly those they love. So watch your behavior with your children and make sure what you teach them through the way you treat them and others (*and* yourself) are behaviors you're going to be proud to see in them, now and in the future. The wonderful or terrible thing about having children, depending on how you raise them, is that you will get to see in them and in their children and perhaps in their children's children all of what you are and have been to them. Don't forget, therefore, that what you do now is an investment in your own as well as your children's future.

MOTOR DEVELOPMENT

From two to three years, most children make gains in gross motor control and coordination which enable them to march in time to music with a repetitive beat, walk on tiptoe, jump over a string or off a chair, stand momentarily on one foot, and run well. They can learn to balance on a wide board or walk a line on the floor, forwards and backwards. They can be trusted to carry breakable objects and can run carrying an object in their arms.

By three years, most children are really beginning to master the upright posture: They toddle less and can walk without needing to watch their feet as they move them. They walk with a rhythmic gait pattern, arms relaxed and moving in coordination with their feet. They are learning to speed up, slow down, dodge obstacles, turn corners, make sudden stops, and start up again. They can run holding hands with another child, and they can run with greater speed than before. Occasionally, however, children may still stumble or trip when running. Through movement, children are beginning to learn a sense of up and down, front and back (left and right awareness develops later, about six to seven years). Most children at age three can walk upstairs alternating feet, but they still bring both feet together at each step when walking downstairs. They can step over low obstacles, taking an exaggerated step, and they can imitate simple actions to familiar songs.

From two to three years, most children can learn to throw a large ball with some accuracy, kick a ball with ease, and catch a large ball thrown from about five feet away using their arms and body. Children of this age enjoy wagons, to fill with things and haul around or to get halfway into (one knee in the wagon, one foot on the floor) and steer around. By three years, children will climb on low inclined planks, packing boxes, jungle gyms, fences, ladders, and similar things if they have access to such equipment. By this time, also, most children can pedal and steer a tricycle, and some children may be able to ride a two-wheeled scooter. Games that require children to throw a ball or beanbag into a box or basket provide good practice in motor control. Such a game can be made more fun for two- to three-year-olds if the box is sometimes the mouth or stomach of an animal and the children are pretending they are feeding it. Children this age may enjoy a jumping platform such as a large box set above a mattress that they can practice jumping on in all the different ways they can think of without worrying about getting hurt.

Children from two to three love motor activities; they're still busy developing more skilled movement. They may enjoy "Monkey-See-Monkey-Do" and "Follow-the-Leader" games using the variety of movements they can now do. Also good at this age are activities in which children walk between two lines on the floor, and later, on one wide line. You can have them walk to the steady beat of a drum or clapping or music; they can practice changing speeds, slowing down and speeding up as you or a child leader calls it; you can put small blocks along the line for the children to step over, and so on. These types of activities are good for developing balance and coordination.

Children continue to need plenty of space for moving freely. They need grass to romp on, hills to hike up and down, and lots of open space to run in. If you live in the city, an occasional trip to the country or to a forest preserve would be a welcome break from concrete streets and sidewalks and small, crowded playgrounds.

Children are becoming increasingly more interested in finer manipulations of play materials, e.g., puzzles, toys with simple parts to assemble, crayons, pencils, and paint brushes. Their hand and finger coordination is fairly good now. They can make a fist and wiggle their thumb and move each finger separately. Finger-play games and songs such as "Eency-Weency Spider" are now appropriate and can be included as part of group activities. These are good for developing strength and flexibility in children's fingers as well as language and singing skills. Most children from two to three years can take things apart with moderate skill now, implying some sort of plan and not destructiveness. They will enjoy simple toys with big pieces to take apart and put together again. At first they'll be better at taking apart than putting back together and may need your help with the latter.

From two to three years, children learn to do other things with their hands such as string beads on a shoelace, copy lines and circles (though crudely), do simple puzzles, unscrew lids and close all sorts of jars, cut dough or clay with a cookie cutter, turn water fixtures on, build simple structures with blocks, fold a piece of paper lengthwise and crosswise (but not diagonally yet), turn crank handles (e.g., on an egg beater or a music box), use a pair of tongs to pick up small objects, and use scissors to cut a small piece of paper in half.

You can think up games and activities and make or buy toys for children to use in practicing the hand skills described above. In addition, they will enjoy developing fine coordination of their hands and fingers through practical activities which will give them real competence in self-help and adult-valued activities. They will enjoy doing such things as learning to set a low table (use unbreakable dishes), carrying dishes on a tray and serving food, wiping, washing, and drying dishes, helping to care for a pet, gardening, and so on. Children can accept a great deal of responsibility when you trust them to do so, and assumption of responsibility is its own reward; it gives children increased independence and freedom (over their own competencies and from need of help from others).

From two to three, children really enjoy art activities such as drawing, painting, molding with clay, snipping paper and pasting. They still enjoy the process of using their hands and a few simple tools more than they care about producing anything. They're not very interested in the things they make; they're more interested in the making.

Most children hold a crayon in their fingers now instead of in their fist. They can smear finger paints and roll, pound, and squeeze clay. Art expression is really important for children. It gives them a medium for expressing themselves and communicating with color, form, and texture. It also helps them develop hand and finger skills and gives them practice in the use of tools. Introduce children to different art materials, giving them the opportunity to experiment with them and see how they look and feel and what can be done with them. Process is still all-important, and messiness is part of the process. You can put protective materials around children, but you'll still need to learn to tolerate a certain level of mess.

Between two and three years, most children are becoming more competent at dressing themselves with help. They can put on their shirt, pants, and coat with help and can learn to button one large button. Many children at this time are becoming very interested in buttoning and unbuttoning, and by three years they can button front buttons, close front snaps, and put on their shoes, though not necessarily on the correct feet.* They still cannot manage any small or difficult fasteners or ones that they can't see to manipulate. Most children can hang their clothes on a hook situated at their level and can learn, by age three, to hang them up on hangers if their closet has a bar at their level.

By three years, most children can wash and dry their hands on their own, turning on the faucet, soaping their hands, using a wash cloth for their face, wringing it out and hanging it up when they're done. With your supervision, they can use a brushing motion on the surfaces of their teeth. And, if their clothes are easy to unfasten and the toilet is low or easy to reach, they can usually take care of themselves for urination.

Children are becoming increasingly better at feeding themselves, using a small fork or spoon. They may be beginning to use their fingers to hold them and give up their "fist grip." They can learn to pour from a small pitcher into a cup without pouring more than the cup will hold. All these self-help skills (feeding, dressing, and grooming oneself) are important for children to learn because it helps make them more competent and self-reliant, which is an important part of their developing a good self-concept. They should be learned at the children's own pace, not with your pushing, in order for them to be viewed as positive accomplishments rather than tasks.

LANGUAGE DEVELOPMENT

At two years, children still use words mostly to "point to" objects and actions in their world. They are just beginning to use language as a means of getting things they want from other people. Between two and three, most children increase the number of words they use from around 250 to about 900.

In addition, children begin to include language as a part of their experiences; while playing, they talk about what they're doing. They begin to be able to control their behavior through language. They learn to wait through understanding the concept of time words and phrases such as "in a while" and "pretty soon." By three years, many children begin to use past and future verbs and other time designa-

---

* You can help children get their feet in the correct shoes by laying out their shoes for them. You can help them learn how to do it themselves by activities such as the following. Make a print of both your child's feet by tracing around them and cutting out the prints. Make multiple copies and tape them to the floor like footprints. Have her walk on her "feet," being sure to match her feet to the ones on the floor. Point out to her the way each foot curves, and show her how her shoes do the same. Let her put her shoes on her hands and practice "walking" them on her footprints.

tions, such as "last week," "last night," "one day," and "tomorrow." They often use plurals for more than one thing and adjectives to describe quality. Most children's speech is becoming less telegraphic and is beginning to include a greater variety of words. The two-year-old's "more milk" becomes the three-year-old's "I want some more milk." By three years, most children can think in words. They begin to use language easily; they can invent their own sentences based on the rules they have learned from listening to adult models.

Usually between two and three years, children also learn to identify action in pictures and begin to use pronouns more often to refer to themselves and others. Most children learn to identify large and smaller body parts and to name at least one color. They can remember and repeat two or three things in the right order. Children learn these things through hearing a good adult model and by having opportunities to practice these different language skills.

Children from two to three typically cannot say many of the speech sounds correctly, esepecially in the middle and at the end of words. Sounds that they usually can say correctly are $p, b, m, k, g, w, h, n, t,$ and most of the vowels.

Some suggestions for stimulating children's use of language follow. These ideas are also appropriate after two years. The important thing to remember in teaching language skills to young children is to connect the words to the experiences they represent. Therefore, specific language "lessons," especially for the two- to three-year-old, should not be a major part of an educational program. Instead, every experience the child has should be accompanied by language learning. Talk with children about what they're doing. An awareness of what kinds of language skills children normally develop at each age level should enable you to direct your talking with children to build on the kinds of ideas about the world they are forming during that period.

You can teach children adjectives through experiences with different sounds, textures, colors, and objects of different sizes. For example, listen with the children to loud and soft sounds, high and low sounds, and talk about sounds, saying for example, "This is a soft sound. What kind of sound is this one? Who can make a high sound?" and so on. Have balls made of soft, hard, smooth, or rough materials, such as cotton, wood, or sandpaper. Give a child one of the balls and say, "Is it a soft ball or is it a hard ball?" Or, "Is it rough or smooth?"

Plan experiences with color and size words too. For example, have pictures and objects of big and little things, red and blue things, and ask a child, "Tell me about this picture (or object)." You may have to ask leading questions, keeping the choices down to two at first. For example, say, "Is this an apple or a banana? Is it red or yellow?" After a child has answered, ask him again: "Tell me about this. What color is it? What is it called? Is it big or little?" After a while, he'll learn to look for and talk about the qualities of things on his own. By doing this activity in small groups, children also learn from each other.

You can read books which have action pictures and ask children questions such as, "Show me the boy who's running" or "Show me the duck swimming." Then, instead of just "naming" pictures, the children can begin to answer questions like "What is the boy doing? Is he walking or running?" Picture cards made for the children from old magazines provide opportunities for naming: "What's this?" and telling use: "Show me the one you eat" or "Let's find all the ones you can wear."

Confusion often occurs for children two to three in using opposite-meaning words, such as hot/cold, up/down, give/take. Use the words together many times with actions. For example, give Michelle a toy and tell her, "Give the ball to Tommy." Then after she's done it, say, "Take the ball from Tommy." Emphasize the words you're trying to teach and provide examples where needed.

Poems such as Mother Goose rhymes with a lot of activities to go with the verses are good for language development. At first, children will only be able to join in on phrases or single words. Eventually, they will be able to say a whole poem they have heard often.

Storytelling time or book-reading time can be used also for role playing and learning about sequence of actions. As you turn the pages of the book, the children can act out what happens. They may wear masks or pictures of characters hung by string around their necks. Flannel board figures may be placed on the board by the children at appropriate times, or the children may arrange pictures from the story in the proper order to tell the tale. These activities also are appropriate any time after three years.

Activities may be planned for two-and-a-half-year-old children for "this morning" or "this afternoon" or "tomorrow." Use of these terms will help children learn about time and planning and waiting.

You can help children use the past tense by talking about what they did yesterday or by using pictures that show a sequence of actions, such as a baby dropping a bottle or a truck leaving the gas station and by then asking such questions as "What happened?" or "What did he do?"

Have a Show-and-Tell time, when children show and tell about a picture or something they bring to the group. (You can play "show and tell" with your child at home too.) Help children by asking, "Tell me something about this." "What do you use it for?" "Where did you find it?"

COGNITIVE DEVELOPMENT

Children from two to three years are learning new ways of organizing and representing their world. As discussed above, the major strides made in this direction during this period are those related to learning the principles of organization, classification, and representation of their world through language symbols. Although at this age children still understand more about the world than they can communicate in words, language may help them in their efforts to develop rules for grouping and ordering objects and events.

The learning of time words such as "in a minute" or "after a while," based on an increased understanding of time relationships, seem to help children in controlling their behavior. When told, "We'll go in a little while," children learn that they must wait a short time. Learning past and future words as well as words which divide the present into parts, such as "this morning" and "this afternoon," helps children understand order in terms of time.

Another example of the way in which language can help children in their rule-making about the world is in the developing of classes—things which can be grouped together because of likeness among themselves and differences from other things. Every object has many attributes or features which describe it, such as size, color, shape, material, and weight. Some of these are important to the definition of that object, and others may alter without changing what the object is. For example, a person may change his hair color and still be a person. Children get taller and heavier as they grow up. They are still persons when these changes occur, but they are no longer children. An apple may be green or red and still be an apple; but an apple is never orange and does not have the same kind of covering as an orange. An apple and an orange are both things to eat; children can learn this without knowing the names for these objects. Learning that they are both part of the category "fruit," as are bananas and grapes, is much easier for children once they have learned the word for that category.

Between two and three most children begin to learn about number and amount. They learn to tell the difference between "one" and "many" and to use plural nouns to mean more than one of a thing. You can use pictures or objects of just one of a thing and of more, and ask children to point to "just one duck," "more than one bird," "many dogs" or to "the cat" and then to "the cats." Most children at this age can give "just one" of something when asked to. Ask the child to take "just one cookie" or to bring "one toy." Puzzles can be made also which require that children match a picture of one of a kind with a picture of more than one of the same kind. Use the time when a child is working on such a puzzle to communicate these words. Also take advantage of any opportunities to use number words to describe things around your child, including body parts, clothes, and toys.

Though many children begin to use words like "another," "all gone," "big," "little," "no more," and "much," which help them learn about how much is meant by certain words and help them compare things by amount, they may not yet be able to tell which is "bigger." With pictures or toys, ask for the "big doll" or "another teddy." Have two sizes of things. Have children put the big ones in one pile, the the small ones in another. Then ask them, "Show me the big doll," then, "Show me the small doll," and conclude, "This doll is bigger than this one."

Children may learn to count to two when presented with more than one of something. You can count with children, using concrete objects and dropping each object into a container as you say its number. Use a container that makes a noise as the object is dropped.

Activities such as playing store with pictures can also be used to help exercise children's short-term memory. You can give children a pile of pictures of foods and say, for example, "Storekeeper, I'd like to buy some apples, oranges, and bananas." Ask the "storekeeper" to repeat the order after you, before giving you the pictures, or have the pictures spread out on another table for her to get for you.

Between two and three, children begin to learn about things by taking them apart (not to destroy them, but to explore what they are like). They will enjoy toys that come apart and go back together again, such as stacking toys, simple puzzle blocks, or cars which can be taken apart and put back together. Many toys of these types can be made from household and kitchen things. For example, you can make a stacking set by covering tin cans of successively smaller sizes with attractively colored paper.

Most children around this age will put things where they belong. Let them help in putting toys away after play. Have places for each of their toys and perhaps put a picture or drawing of the type of toy where it should go. Putting things that are alike together (e.g., all the art materials, all the puzzles, all the cylinder blocks) helps children learn classification skills. Putting things back when they're done with them can help children learn such principles as fairness to others (through taking care of and replacing shared materials), organizational skills, and understanding that if you want something again in the future, you will be sure to know where to find it if you put it back where it belongs.

Although this period of time in children's development is marked particularly by their growth in language development, and that occurrence in turn affects their thinking skills, it should be remembered that children still know most of what they know through means other than words. For example, children who learn to apply the words "rough" and "smooth" to objects possessing those characteristics do not learn about those qualities through learning the words. First they must perceive the qualities—they must understand how rough and smooth things *feel*. But the words can help them, in this example and others, to generalize what they know to other situations. The words help children abstract rules from concrete experiences and apply them in more generalizable ways.

SOCIOEMOTIONAL DEVELOPMENT

From two to three years children are beginning to organize and represent their world in ways other than language. They begin role playing, imitating actions and behaviors they have observed in others, such as "feeding" a doll or talking on the telephone. They will also transform a thing into something else as "make-believe." For example, a stick could be a wand, or a horse. Role playing is a very important avenue of learning for young children. It helps them learn to take the point of view of others, to observe people, and to generalize about the important aspects of their behavior. From two to two and a half, children may play together, but usually they are simply playing at the same thing and not interacting with each other. From two and a half to three and a half, most children become more involved in group activities such as playing house or in games such as hide and seek, or tag.

Between two and three, children are becoming more independent and are really beginning to think of themselves as having their own identity, separate from others in their world; this is a very important step for later development in all areas. Children should have certain things set apart as theirs, as, for example, a coat hook with their name and picture above it, or a place of their own to keep things. In art activities, you and the children can make materials so that each child can have some of her own things. Mark each child's things with a picture of her and her name on it.*

As described in relation to motor development, children are learning a large number of self-help skills including feeding themselves competently, taking care of their own toileting, washing their own hands, and beginning to dress themselves (leaving only the hard parts for you). These are important steps toward self-reliance and, consequently, toward feelings of competence and self-worth. Encourage and praise their successes, but be careful not to pressure them. Many children can play on their own, choosing what to do, or with only a simple suggestion of what they might do. Children at this age have some idea about danger. They come in out of the rain, are careful about falling, avoid matches, knives, and sharp things, and stay out of the street. Development of self-awareness depends on the development of children's memory, the experiences they encounter, and the development

---

* These and some other references in this chapter and the ones that follow are worded to refer to children in play groups, nursery schools, kindergartens, or day care and child development centers. Parents whose children are at home should translate these references into terms more specifically appropriate for them.

of language. If you encourage your child to use language to learn about herself and how she feels, and help her handle problem situations and learn from them, she will come to feel confident in her own abilities.

The time period between two and three years is known popularly as the "terrible twos." * Some people who study young children suggest that at about two and a half years, children's behavior is characterized by rigidity and inflexibility. They want things just so and no other way. They don't like change, can't wait, and won't give in; they often do just the opposite of what they're told.

A few words of warning are in order. If you expect "bad" behavior, you'll usually get it. The behavior of children this age is not bad. There's a very good reason for it. They've just begun to figure out things about the world they live in. They're beginning to have "ideas" about the way things are. But their ideas aren't yet secure. Therefore, they don't feel comfortable with a lot of change; that makes it harder to be sure about things. Also, children this age are beginning to gain command over many new skills, most notably understanding and using speech. Much of their behavior is the result of their checking out the power of their new skills. For example, if you say "Come here" and they walk in the other direction, they're showing that they understood you well enough to do just the opposite—quite an accomplishment. Finally, this is an age when children's "eyes are bigger than their stomach," in terms of trying to do things. They can't do everything they try to do and that's frustrating. You can help most by being patient and understanding and by not adding too much to what they can't do. Don't choose this time to pile on the "no's." It will only cause trouble for you and the children.

To feel that you have cheered the heart and brightened the life of a little child for even an hour, is sufficient reward for any effort.
—MARY C. MC CLEES (1887)

* Children who have passed successfully through the ten-to-eighteen-month period discussed in the last chapter—who, at that time, were able to establish themselves as independent and self-reliant persons who could positively affect their own lives and the world they live in—will probably have less difficulty with the "terrible twos," particularly because those caring for them are likely to cope effectively with this period also. Nevertheless, this is a time when children typically make up their own rules about the way things should be and are likely to become upset if things don't follow their plan. This is a period characterized by "Me do it."

5

Three to Four Years: The Age of Reason

The first duty to children is to make them happy.—
If you have not made them so, you have wronged them.—
No other good they may get can make up for that.

—SIR THOMAS FOWELL BUXTON (1786–1845)

The year from three to four is a time of great strides in children's cognitive development. By now, for example, they have good motor skills, so they can put puzzles together not just for the practice of fine motor, manipulative skills, but according to a simple plan (e.g., to make a body or tell a simple story). Most important at this age, children are beginning to realize that language can be used as a tool for finding out about things. This is the period of questions. It is an important stage in children's development because if their attempts to find out about the world meet with success, they will continue to be active learners. If their exploration or questioning is interfered with or not responded to, they will lose some of this natural curiosity which is so important to learning.

MOTOR DEVELOPMENT

Most children three to four years old have very good gross motor coordination and control.* They can jump high and far, and walk downstairs one foot per step, using right foot, then left foot, then right, and so on. Children's running is smooth and they can now run slowly or quickly, as they choose. They can walk a circular path without step-

---

* Some children, however, go through a period about this time when they are uncoordinated at things they could do before—they may stumble and fall or walk into things. This may be because they're no longer paying attention to their movements as they did when they were younger and less secure about them.

ping off, and can balance on a walking board, walking backwards, forwards, and sideways by the time they're four. They can hop on one foot and in place on both feet. By four years, some children may be beginning to try to skip, but they do it with just one foot. Some children also practice galloping at this time.

With these motor skills children can learn to play games such as "Simon Says," "Mother May I," and "Red Light-Green Light." They begin to be able to play catch-and-throw games and will enjoy playing on slides, jungle gyms, and other such play equipment. By age four, children can learn to use roller skates and a small bicycle with training wheels. Playground activities also can be used to teach language concepts and body awareness: "Trenton is going down the slide and through the tunnel, up the steps." You can set up an obstacle course for the children in which they have to go over, around, under, behind, and inside different obstacles. Talk about what the children are doing as they do it. You might direct them verbally, saying, for example, "Go around the chair. Now crawl under the table." The activities described in the last chapter for walking on a straight line can now be done on a circular line drawn on the floor.

Children who can ride wheeled toys should be able to do so without bumping into things. Set up an obstacle course for the children to ride through:

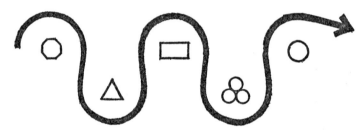

You could also set up play "streets" for them to ride through, with traffic signs to obey, bridges to ride under, and corners to turn.

From three to four years most children's motor coordination develops well enough for them to be able to copy with pencil or crayon not only a circle, but also a square and a cross. Their ability to copy these forms, of course, lags behind their ability to produce the same forms in their spontaneous drawing. You can play drawing games with the children using lines, circles, squares, and crosses. These forms can be combined to draw figures such as bunnies, kitties, houses, trains, ice cream cones, step by step, as shown below. More examples are found on pages 122–123.

The purpose of this type of activity is to help develop children's

NOTE: *Illustrations in chapters 5 and 6 designed by Skip Williamson.*

fine motor coordination, as well as to show them the separate parts of a whole. It should *not* be used as a substitute for a child's own free artistic expression.* The important thing here is the process, not the final product; therefore, although you may help children who are having trouble, you should never do the drawing for them. That would defeat its purpose.

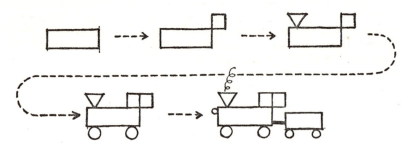

In addition to drawing with pencil or crayon, at this age children will enjoy learning to use many different art media, including water color, tempera, and finger paints, and will have fun exploring such activities as string painting, making collages from everything from buttons to macaroni, printmaking using potatoes and various fruits and vegetables to make the prints, sponge painting, and so on. Whatever medium they are using, children will work best on the floor, where

* Research done in recent years on the development of children's ability to draw (See R. Kellogg, "Understanding Children's Art," in P. Cramer (ed.), *Readings in Developmental Psychology Today*, Del Mar, Calif.: CRM Books, 1970, 31–9) has shown that, when given the opportunity to draw, all children go through the same developmental stages in learning to use crayon or pencil and paper and in learning to make basic forms and to combine them in various aesthetically pleasing ways. Conclusions drawn from this research are that we should not "teach" children to draw any more than we teach them to talk and that, in fact, concern on the part of adults in the past with children's ability to reproduce geometric forms and draw realistic pictures served to interfere with their natural ability to draw. We agree wholeheartedly that children should have unlimited opportunities (from the time they can first hold a crayon awkwardly in their fist) to draw on their own, at their own pace, following their own inner developmental guide. We do not feel, however, that it is harmful to the development of children's natural artistic ability to offer them the opportunity to combine forms they know how to make into fun, cartoonlike productions as we suggest in the above activity, any more than it interferes with children's "natural" language development to talk to them on an adult level. What *is* detrimental to children's natural development of anything is to teach them something through correcting their way of doing it. The important thing is the style with which something is introduced, and just as it's unwise to correct children's language, so it's not a good idea to present drawing games as superior alternatives to children's own spontaneous productions. It has been our experience that children this age enjoy such activities, and as long as it gives them pleasure, there's no reason not to do it.

they have lots of elbow room and can move their whole body as they work. Children can use large arm movements before they can be expected to accomplish restricted hand and finger movements. They might sometimes enjoy having music to draw or paint by. Put on a selection with different moods and tempos, and invite the children to paint the way the music makes them feel.

Between three and four years, many children begin to develop good enough pencil grasp and fine enough motor coordination to copy *capital letters.* (Small letters require much finer coordination and should not be attempted before school age. Even then, many children cannot manage the fine coordination which is necessary for forming small letters.) It can be a very gratifying experience for children to be able to print their own name if they're ready to learn it. Different devices and experiences should be made available for children who want to learn to write, *but a preschool child should never be forced to learn reading and writing.* Examples of devices which can be used to prepare children for writing are letters and numbers cut from different materials such as cardboard, burlap, or other heavy-textured cloth, and fine sandpaper for them to trace with their finger in the same way as if they were forming the letter; stencils (of capital letters—start with the child's name); and "follow-the-dot" outlines of letters. They should be given crayons or fat "primary" pencils, not skinny ones.

At this age children can string beads by colors and shapes. A variation which can be used in developing left to right skills for reading readiness is to have children copy one made by another child or adult, or match theirs to a model drawn on a card. They can also use a blunt needle and heavy thread to string macaroni and make jewelry. Give the children simple puzzles to put together. Sometimes you can work with a child in putting together a hard puzzle and use the opportunity to build some language at the same time. For example, say "What fits here? That looks too big. Try turning it. Put the head in now. Where's the tail?" and so on. Have blocks and other materials available so children can build things.

Between three and four years, children's improved fine motor ability enables them to learn to dress themselves completely including putting their shoes on the correct feet and lacing them. It will still be a couple of years before they can tie their own shoes, however. They can comb their hair, brush their teeth, and wash and dry their face and hands fairly well by four years, though they may need some adult checking to make sure they've done it right. Be a guide, though, not a watchdog. With adult supervision, many children can bathe themselves by age four. By this time, also, most children can feed themselves completely except for cutting. They are motorically competent enough at eating now that they don't have to put all their energy and attention into it; they can talk and eat at the same time.

LANGUAGE DEVELOPMENT

Between three and four years, language begins to be used as a tool to help children find out about things in their world. The two-year-old acquired words; the three-year-old uses them. You can help children use language to figure out things by using experiences and real objects to build their vocabulary. At three years children use, on the average, about 900 words; by four years, they use an average of about 1,550. More important than increase in number of words, however, is the expansion that occurs during this time period in the complexity of language children are able to use.

Between three and four most children begin to expand their language—to use different kinds of words, sentence forms, and rules for grammar. For example, most children begin to use auxiliary verbs now and forms of them such as "want" or "wanna," "would," "could," "got" or "gotta," "be," "have," "can." Using these forms, children begin to make longer sentences such as: "This is a car" and "I want to go." They will begin to use different sentence forms, including declarations, such as "Get the ball," and questions, such as "Do you want a cookie?"

Most children between three and three and a half begin to learn to use negatives to change sentence order for uses of "no" and "do," as in sentences such as "That's not a toy" and "I don't see you."

Between three and four most children begin to be able to understand and use at least three prepositions. A guessing game will help develop this skill. For example, hide a small toy. Say to the children, "Is it *under* the box?" "Is it *behind* the board?" Later, children can ask these questions of one another.

From three and a half to four and a half, most children begin to learn to use the following word-changing rules: (1) when using "she" or "he" there is an "s" added to verbs in the present tense: "she walks," "he runs"; (2) "ed" added to a verb means a past event: "Today I walk to school," "Yesterday I walk*ed* to school"; (3) "s" added to a noun indicates more than one: one dog, two dog*s*, many dog*s*; (4) when something belongs to someone you use words like: my/mine, your/yours, his/hers or her, their/theirs. Children learn to use words by hearing them used.

Children do not learn to speak by copying adults; they listen to adults, learn the rules, and then make up their own sentences based on the rules they have at the time. Children have a built-in language-learning device which lets them learn to use certain word and sentence forms when they're ready. They learn from listening to adults and other children talking and from extracting rules about their language from what they hear. They thus learn the rules for using different kinds of sentence structures, and in the process of learning they make many mistakes, often in a very systematic way. For example, when they begin learning the rules for making plurals, children who previously had used the correct plural form for mouse and foot will now say mouses and foots. This is called overgeneralization and is a sign of growth— that they are learning the rules. Later, they'll learn the exceptions to the rules (again through listening, not through lessons), and they'll again say mice and feet.

Therefore, try not to correct your child's language. Fear of failing or being corrected can make a child become silent, anxious, or even develop stuttering. Correcting doesn't work, anyway. Studies have shown that young children repeat sentences not as they hear them from the adult speaker, but using their own language level. When children make a mistake, answer them or repeat what they said, using the correct sentence form. For example, if a child says, "I no want no juice," don't correct her. Instead, try something like, "You don't want any juice? All right, don't have any juice," or "I don't want any juice either."

When children make mistakes in the way they use words, help them by showing them the object while saying the correct word or by explaining the correct meaning if the object is not there where they can see it.

Most children's sentences at this stage average three to four words per sentence. They now use language to get things they want. They should be encouraged to *ask* for things, rather than just pointing to them. Children are beginning to ask "why," "how," "what" and "where" questions. The period from three to four years is the peak of "why" questions. Try to be patient and answer them in the best way you can. Three-year-olds may ask questions to which they already know the answer; they do this to check out their knowledge. They will begin more and more to ask information-seeking questions and to view adults as resources if they get good reactions to their questioning.

Most children at this age begin to discover the meanings of general concepts of length, weight, number, size, and color by playing with real things. Children now practice words to suit their actions and actions to fit their words. When you're playing with children you can help them learn concepts and words by directing their play with appropriate words: "Let's put the big things here and the little things here. Which pile has more, this one or that one?" To begin learning these concepts, children should have two choices: big, little; long, short; red, blue, and so on. Not until three and a half to four and a half years do most children begin to use words such as "best," "most," "biggest," and "hardest" to compare things.

In the age period between three and four years, children begin to use most of the sounds of their language fairly well. Most English-speaking American children use about 90 percent of the American English vowels during this time and can use most of the consonants at the beginning, middle, and end of words by four (for example pig, apple, top). Most children can be understood fairly well now.

Many children during this period are ready to learn to listen for sounds. From three to four, children learn to listen, and then they listen to learn. For those who are ready, different activities can be used to work into this gradually. For example, start with a key picture of a "man." Have two other pictures, only one of which begins with "m" (e.g., mop/fan). Have the children identify which of the two pictures begins with the same sound as the word "man." Have them listen to the two words together to see if they sound the same at the beginning, saying "man . . . mop. Do these words sound the same at the beginning?" and so on.

As the children develop this skill, you might ask them to pick from a group of pictures all those which begin with a certain sound. Or you could go around the room and have the children identify all those whose names begin with a certain sound, or have them identify objects in the room which begin with certain sounds. You can make up special short stories (for example, a story about *B*ertha the *B*ear who didn't like *b*ees) which contain a lot of words which begin with a particular sound. Then read them and have the children clap every time they hear that sound. When teaching children to listen to sounds, begin with those that are easy to hear, such as *m*, *b*, *d*, and *z*. When talking about letter sounds, say the sound, rather than the letter name.

Children at this age enjoy playing with words, their sound and rhythm. They may enjoy rhyming games too. More than once, we've heard stories about children engaged in this fun activity who had the unlucky experience of rhyming words with "luck" in front of an adult. If it happens that your child does this, please remember that he doesn't know yet that certain words are taboo. You'll only frighten him if you get upset, and he probably won't even know which was the wrong one.

Many children now enjoy stories for as long as twenty minutes at a time. Stop often as you read stories to look at the pictures and sometimes to ask questions such as "Why did Peter hide from the farmer?" or "Where is Little Red Riding Hood going?" or "How would you feel if you saw a wolf in the woods?" Let the children take turns "reading" familiar stories to each other. Children may memorize the order of familiar stories, and they will object if that order is changed. Follow a familiar story with questions about what happened "when . . ." or "after . . ." and "What do you think will happen next?" Also, you might cut up the pictures from an extra book or draw pictures on cards for the children to put in the right order. Children really enjoy going through picture cards and books naming what they see. Naming can be varied by asking children to "Name all the red things" or "Name all the animals."

At age three most children can tell winter from the rest of the year in a climate where winter is different from other seasons. The only holiday known is Christmas or another major ethnic holiday. Present, future, and past time words are all used a great deal. Both past and future verbs are used, often correctly. By three and a half, most children can tell summer from the rest of the year as well, and they are likely to know both Christmas *and* Easter or other special holidays, depending on their cultural background. They use more time words at three and a half than they did at three, but they may be confused at this age and misuse some terms they had used correctly before, saying, for example, "I'm not going to take a nap yesterday."

Common time phrases used by children in this stage include "almost juice time," "lunch time," "time for music," "next time." Many children now pretend to tell time by watches or clocks, but they still cannot give the correct clock time.

By age four, most children can imitate a six-syllable sentence. You can play the circle whisper ("Telephone") game to practice this skill. Have three or four children sit in a circle. Whisper a very short sentence, such as "Apples are red" to the first child. Have each child whisper what he has heard to the child next to him, and let the last child say aloud the sentence he has heard.

Most children between the ages of three and four know the names of two colors. One example of an activity to teach color names as well as some connections between colors and objects is to give children a picture and ask them to color the pictures the same colors as the objects. For example, they would color a banana yellow and an apple red or yellow. Have the children choose the crayon which is the same color as the object she is coloring a picture of, and name the color. Ordinarily, except with a special activity like this, children should be encouraged to use any colors they want, not necessarily "realistic" ones. You might also go around the room finding all the red things or all the blue clothes, and so on.

Show-and-Tell or picture descriptions should be used to help children use more kinds of words. You can coach children who need it by asking questions like "Tell me about this" or "What is he doing?" or "Whose mittens are those?" It is important that Show-and-Tell or storytelling or talking about a past or future field trip be a time to listen to *what* children say, not to how they say it.

From three years on, you can teach children to play guessing games which help them use language skills. For example, clip different pictures to the backs of pieces of bright-colored felt. A child chooses a piece of felt by naming its color: "I want the red one." Then she describes what her picture is, giving one clue at a time, such as: "Mine has something that grows on trees." "It is round." "It is red." "It is good to eat." The child who guesses correctly chooses the next one. Younger children may need some assistance in learning how to describe. To help, you might ask questions such as, "Where do you see it?" "Is it big or little?" "What color is it?" or "What do you do with it?" You should be the first player, so that you can show how the game is played.

COGNITIVE DEVELOPMENT

Now that children are beginning to sort out some of the ways in which the world around them is ordered, they begin to be able to create an ordering of it for themselves. A child of three to four enjoys building things with blocks and tinker toys, modeling clay, and so on. He is learning how things are related to each other. For example, he learns how parts of a thing go together to make a whole, and how objects are arranged in space in relation to one another and to him.

The following are examples of activities to build on children's growing knowledge of the relationship between parts and wholes: Children can choose the correct bottom half to go with the top half of the picture of something. Pictures of objects from magazines may be cut in half. Ask the children to find the ones that belong together. Limit the number of choices that are given to the children to two at first, and then add more as the children show they can do them. Also, if there is a camera available, take pictures of the children. (Teach them how to use the camera, too.) Cut the pictures in half and see if the children can mix two or three sets up and put them back together. Do this with different kinds of shots: face, full body, profile. This is also a good activity for building children's self-concept.

Most children three to four years old will understand the concepts and use the words "back," "over," "over there," and "fits." When children are playing with puzzles, you can ask them questions such as, "Does this piece *fit?*" "What if you turn that piece *over?*" And at other times, "Put the truck *over there;* put the blocks *back.*" *Use* the words.

Children know the relation of rooms indoors to one another. In addition to beginning to understand spatial relationships, children from three to four are beginning to have a good understanding of temporal relationships. They are beginning to use and understand most of the common time words. They can often understand a length or duration of time, too, such as "all the time," or "for two weeks." Many children can answer some basic questions about time, can tell how old they are, and what they do on Christmas and during the winter. Children now are able to plan things better over a length of time either within the day or the week. Time games may be played with children that involve asking what time they go to bed, what they will do tomorrow, or similar questions about the events in time in a favorite story.

You can make puzzles that help children practice skills of time sequencing. For example, show photographs of the children in different regularly scheduled daily activities. Mix these up, and have the children put them in order, saying, "What picture shows what we do when we get here in the morning?" "What picture shows what we do next?" or "Do we have lunch before or after we go home?" You may also cut pictures from magazines of daily activities such as eating breakfast, playing, and going to bed, and have the children put these in order.

Calendar work, too, can be included in activities for children at this age. It is a good device to teach time words, sequencing (what things follow each other), use of past tense, and vocabulary and concepts about seasons, weather, temperature, clothing, and so on.

Have a big monthly calendar with spaces for days large enough that you can draw small pictures on them. Each morning after the children have settled down, have one child (give children turns) cross off yesterday. Let another child tear off yesterday's page from another daily calendar. Then talk about "What did we do yesterday? Mona painted a picture; Tash played with blocks; we had spaghetti for lunch," and so forth. Give each child a turn to tell what she did. Then talk about today. "What is the weather like? What kind of clothes did you wear to school?" Give the children choices if no one answers: "Is it sunny or cloudy? Is it raining or snowing?" Let one of the children draw a picture of the day's weather using simple symbols they can draw. Using real dolls, paper dolls, or a drawing, dress a doll with the proper clothes for the day's weather.

After discussing the kind of day it is, talk about the day's activities. Say, for example, "What are we going to do today?" and ask each child what he or she wants to do this morning, this afternoon, or after lunch. More time can be spent on this activity as the children get older and more concepts can be developed. With children as young as three, you may have to do some of the talking and directing at first, and the children may have trouble at first with the time word, "yesterday."

One of the reasons that temporal concepts are hard for children is that time is intangible and invisible—you can't touch it and you can't see it. Calendar work translates temporal order into a spatial context: children can "see" that yesterday came before (to the left of) today and that tomorrow will come after (to the right of) today. This is also good preparation for learning to read later on.

Children from three to four years also are beginning to understand relationships between things on the basis of certain attributes that they share, such as what they are used for, their color, size, and shape. They begin to recognize likenesses and differences in things and thus to group things together (classification). For example, children of this age can put a third picture of something with two of the same kind: they will choose a Teddy bear to put with two other Teddy bears instead of a different toy, or a hat to put with a coat and suit rather than with something to eat. Children should be able to understand "same" even when, for example, the three Teddy bear pictures are of three different Teddy bears. You can make sets of things for children to group by how they are used, or where they are found, or by color, shape, size, or texture. Classification skills are best learned through their application to real-life situations, e.g., sorting laundry, finding things in the grocery store, choosing clothes to wear that go together. Try to think of ways in which you use classification skills in your day-to-day life and make up games based on those situations.

Children at this age can tell how to get to another place, for example, "in a car" or "on the bus." Plan pretend trips, using pictures from magazines for how to travel and what to see. You can even set up chairs for a pretend bus or plane trip. Let the children lead the way, since they're better at pretending than most adults; but you should play too.

Children between three and four begin fantasizing, exaggerating and making up stories. This is not a sign that children are becoming liars but, rather, it shows that their thinking processes are growing. It is another way for them to apply their own processes of ordering to things in their world. There's nothing wrong with telling a good story. We all do it. Children shouldn't be forced to tell the truth all the time. A little fantasy is healthy as long as you know what's fantasy and what's not.

Between the ages of three and four, children begin to understand how things are related to one another in terms of number and amount. At about three years, most children count, saying, "one, two, a lot" for anything containing more than two, or by saying "one and one and one" as they point to each thing. Children understand how many things "two" means: they can give "just two" when asked.

To give children practice with number and amount, you can have flannel board cut-outs of turkeys with detachable tail feathers or Easter baskets with eggs, with instructions to "Put two big feathers on the turkey" or "Put just one blue egg in the basket." Ask children to put "just one" block in a box, then, "just two" blocks. When this becomes easy, ask them to put "just one red block," and so forth.

Count things with children, giving them one of a thing and yourself one, and say, "One for you, one for me; one more for you, one more for me. Now you have two and I have two. See, we both have the same." Even though they only understand the concept of two, many children can now count in correct order up to five.

Between three and four, children learn to tell which of two things is *bigger*. Use the word with objects. For example, tell the story of a man and a giant. Use pictures of food, clothes, furniture, and have children give the "bigger" one to the giant, and the "smaller" one to the man.

Children are also beginning to understand weight and can tell fairly often which one of two things is heavier. It is helpful to have a scale for children to play with and for them to have different experiences with weighing, comparing weight and amount—seeing, for example, how many feathers it takes to equal the weight of one jelly bean. They should have a collection of things to weigh including bottles of water, different size cups of sand, clay shapes, buttons, feathers, bottle caps, dried beans, shells, pine cones, blocks, and so on. Have children feel which is heaviest, and then check out their choice, using the scales.

You should understand that children discover how to group things together in a number of ways. Things can be grouped according to (1) how they look, feel, react to actions on them; (2) time and space relations, size, number, color relations; (3) concepts which are socially derived and named, such as what things are for and what people do. The first two involve children actively constructing the understanding from within their mind in reaction to their direct experience with objects. The third is imposed by the adult and serves to give the child a common means for organizing and communicating about them. For example, children learn what breaks, bends, stretches, floats, or melts through their own experiments. They learn about the bigness and smallness and amount and color of things, and what comes before and what after through their own observations. You can provide them with opportunities to experiment and observe, but you can't do it for them. But you need to teach them the social rules about who does what, and what's acceptable and expected, and what things are called. Experiences and materials should be provided for children that allow them to invent and learn ways to order the world through all these means.

SOCIOEMOTIONAL DEVELOPMENT

As a result of having so many skills at their command and because of their growing consciousness of their own identity in relation to others, children from three to four years are beginning to be conscious of and concerned about others also. They are beginning to understand that other people have feelings just as they do, and you can appeal to this in dealing with many problem situations—by helping children look at a specific occurrence from the other person's point of view (perhaps through talking about how they felt when something similar happened to them). Children this age are typically friendly and enjoy being together. Most are beginning to develop strong attachments to other children and are learning to sympathize with others. They are learning to share, take turns, and play cooperatively. It is very important that you capitalize on these growing social skills and help children become increasingly more concerned with others in this very human way (as opposed to the unhealthy way too many adults are concerned with others—in terms of what other people think of them or what someone can do for them).

Most children at this age enjoy participating with others in group activities and can now be expected to play group games. They will explore being a leader or a follower in these group activities. Give all the children chances to lead and follow, but don't embarrass a child by asking him to do something that he doesn't feel secure about doing, and be sensitive to the fact that some children aren't able to do some things well. Try to explain to all the children through play activities that everyone has things which she does and does not do well.

Children three to five should be allowed and encouraged to play together, not separated into age groupings. Children often can learn more, especially language, from a slightly older child than from an adult. And the older children will benefit from leading and sticking up for those younger than they are.

During this time period children are learning to handle their emotions in productive ways and find reasonable solutions to their negative feelings. By three, many children will have learned not to kick and fight. A child may, instead, scold another child, for example, who has taken her toy. This child is beginning to be able to express anger or discomfort by words or by finding a practical solution. Children should be helped to learn to use words to express emotions, and to seek specific solutions to specific problems, through patient suggestions and encouragement from adults. For example, when a child gets upset because he wants to play with a toy someone else has, he can be encouraged to ask for a turn.

Children can begin to tell whether a person is happy or sad, pleased or angry, by watching her face. You can make scrapbooks of faces and of events that might lead to happy faces, surprised faces, and so on. Play pretend games with the children, having them pantomime the expression that goes with a picture or a situation that you describe. Talk about the feelings that go with the facial expressions. Even more important, talk with children about *their* feelings in their own day-to-day lives—how it made Thom feel when James took his toy; why Mary is sad today; what Rachel is so excited about. Help your children become more sensitive to their own *and* others' feelings.

Children may try to "hide" from unhappy situations by withdrawing or pulling into themselves, or by insisting that a problem is not true and does not exist, or by blaming the whole matter on someone else. Children need patient guidance in learning to accept their mistakes without letting it change their feelings of worth as persons. For example, you might respond to wrongdoing by saying, "I care about you, but I don't like what you're doing" or "I'm mad at what you did, but not at you."

Children from three to four are becoming more independent as they learn to do more things for themselves and to control their own behavior. We already mentioned (in motor development) the competence children age three to four typically have in relation to self-help skills (assuming they've been allowed to do things for themselves). Encourage your child's new independence. Let him know you're proud of his ability to care for himself. Also be understanding when there are times that he'd rather have your help than do something himself.

Children at this age often enjoy helping to do little things like straightening up, running errands, setting the table, feeding pets, or dusting. Not only will allowing children to help do such things strengthen their feelings of confidence and self-worth, but they also can be made very valuable learning experiences in terms of cognitive and language development. For example, children can learn classification by putting away together things that are alike. They will learn about one-to-one correspondence, a necessary beginning math skill, by setting the table with one dish, one glass, and so forth, to each chair or placemat.

Children are learning to control the ways in which they explore things and play with them to meet adults' expectations about not tearing or breaking things. They can be reminded with a firm but gentle "careful," but the best control is what children use themselves.

Some time between three and six years, most children learn to give their name, tell what street they live on, and what city they live in. Children should be taught to give names and addresses and told how to call an operator for help. Most children between three and a half and four and a half can tell how old they are.

Between the ages of three and four, children culminate the development of the foundation of their self-concept and how they feel and think about themselves. By three years, children have a fairly steady self-concept in that they call themselves "I" and have a set of feelings about themselves. They already have their own personal world view that affects the way they will interpret and influence all their future human interactions to reinforce how they already feel about themselves.

Children's self-concept is at all times greatly affected by attitudes and behaviors of those around them. They still see themselves as they think others see them and, therefore, must feel that others think they are worthy persons and that they care about and accept them. This is especially important when disciplining children. They must be made to realize that, while some particular action or behavior was not acceptable, they are not bad persons.

In this period, children are beginning to become aware of cul-

tural attitudes. An important part of learning self-confidence is learning to be proud of who you are. Children must never be made to feel
that what they learn in their cultural setting is any less valuable (or
any more valuable) than what is learned in other cultural settings. If
their language or dialect is different from yours, do not correct their
language or in any way make them feel it is wrong.

Fear of being punished for something should be becoming less
important to children than their own set of standards by which they
judge themselves. Rules should be explained to children, so that they
can understand and then apply the appropriate rule to themselves.
They should be praised for trying to do what they feel is right. When
children misbehave, they should be given a chance to explain why.

From three years, most children begin to learn that some activities and things are more acceptable for boys (e.g., wrestling, playing
cops-and-robbers) and some more acceptable for girls (e.g., playing with
dolls), according to what society encourages or discourages. Identifying
with the model of an adult of the same sex is an important part of
building a self-concept. Boys should have a chance to have male models
in any school setting as well as at home. However, the models afforded
both little girls and little boys should present the children with *choices*
of behaviors, activities, and goals, *not* with stereotyped roles. It is important, for example, that children see men and women doing different
things, not always the man doing a job and the woman taking care of
the house and children. Children learn about their sexual identity—
what is expected of and appropriate for boys and for girls—from the
men and women they see, especially parents, but also teachers, people
on TV, in books, and so on. It's good for children to hear stories about
and see women doing things that men usually do and men doing things
women usually do. This allows children of both sexes to see that they
can do and be anything they want and do not have to be limited by
what sex they are.

Girls and boys should also be encouraged to play together in all
games, and not to separate into games for boys and games for girls. Not
all socially accepted role behavior is necessarily good for the growth
of a healthy child. For example, it is not good to allow or encourage
boys to fight simply because "that's what boys do"; they must be
helped to learn to harness their anger and to find other, more productive ways of expressing it. Nor is it good to discourage a girl from
playing with tools and trucks because "that's not what little girls do,"
or to discourage little boys from playing with dolls. Don't cut off children's options and force them to be only a part of what they can be if
they become full human beings and not simply males and females.
Children learn by exploring and experiencing. They should be encouraged to learn in many ways and not be restricted by their sex.

Between three and four, children begin to enjoy doing stunts, singing or dancing for the entertainment of others. This is not showing off, but, rather, it is an attempt to communicate and make others laugh. A simple "stage" may be set up by putting a large cloth, sheet, or blanket over a clothesline. Dress-up clothes can be used as costumes. Drawing on paper sacks is an easy way to make masks. This may be made into a group activity if a theme or plot is taken from folk stories, fairy tales, or current history. The more difficult parts can be filled by the older children because they have longer memories and more skills, but younger children should be allowed to take part in the "cast" too. This type of activity can provide good stimulation for language development and growth of self-concept.

Dramatic play at this age can involve such activities as playing house and simple dress-up play, playing mail persons, busdrivers, office workers, teachers, and so on, or having tea parties or coffee breaks. Through acting out the way things are in the world around them, children come to understand more about that world. This is one of the most important avenues children have for learning social skills and they should be encouraged to use it.

For children this age and older, socio-dramatic play also can begin to be used to act out and work out feelings, problem situations, attitudes, and values. For example, you might have one child play the role of a child who is rejected by the group—whom nobody wants to play with—perhaps because of the way she looks or acts. (It's best to use examples, at first, of situations that actually occur in your classroom.) Have two more children play the roles of children who are excluding the other child from their play. Use other children than those actually involved in a similar situation. Stop the action periodically for comments from the audience and for role switching. Encourage all the children to talk about how they would feel if they were really involved in such a situation. At first, especially with the younger children, you may have to guide their acting out and the later questioning. You could also take one of the roles to show the children how to do it. *Use this as a chance to listen to the children, not as an adult-directed moral lesson.*

> *. . . Of a good leader*
> *who talks little*
> *When his work is done,*
> *his aim fulfilled,*
> *They will say,*
> *"We did this ourselves."*
>
> —LAO-TZU

6

Four to Five Years:
The Calm
Before the Storm

*You cannot teach a child to take care of himself
unless you will let him try to take care of himself.
He will make mistakes; and out of these mistakes
will come his wisdom.*

—HENRY WARD BEECHER (1813–1887)

Four-year-olds already understand that the things in their world have an order, that they can put them back in that order once they have taken them apart, and that many things can be compared or related to each other in an orderly way. Between four and five years, children are free to explore more complicated ways of ordering more and more objects in their world.

The period from four to five is one in which children appear to be approaching a culmination of their development. During this year, they become increasingly more organized in their thinking and able to relate to the world in conventional and acceptable ways. They seem to be becoming delightful, mature beings who can care for themselves as well as show a concern for others. But, as our title suggests, this is the calm before the storm. Enjoy this period, because it is followed by what has been called by some "the first adolescence" and which can be compared in certain ways also to the terrible twos. What is common to all these periods is that they are stages of transition—from one period within which the child has reached a mature state, to another in which he must, in essence, start over. But if you prepare your children well in this "calm before the storm," helping them to develop feelings of competence and self-worth, they (and you) will be better able to handle the period that follows.

MOTOR DEVELOPMENT

Children from four to five years continue to make gains in control and coordination of their gross motor skills. They can now move in a variety of ways. Most children have a good sense of body awareness, including where their bodies are and how to move them in relation to other things in the world. They are developing greater balance and control, which enables them now to begin to use movement not just for getting around in the world, but also for learning to play games requiring complex motor skills, and for learning gymnastic or body-building skills and stunts. For most children this is a period of growth in cooperative play, and the gross motor skills they now have allow them to begin to participate in a number of group games involving good control of movement and balance.

During this period children learn to run well with a good reciprocal arm action. Most children have learned the basic movements of galloping, and they can do simple dances, rhythms, and jigs. By five years children walk and run with a flow and ease of movement which is really graceful. They can run with reasonable speed by this time, and many can skip smoothly. Because of their balance and coordination, children are now ready pupils for dance and physical exercise.

At five years, most children can play, without help, on roller skates, sleds, and junior bikes if they have had the opportunity to learn to use them. They can learn stunts such as whirling, swinging, and somersaulting. Gross motor exercise can now include gymnastic skills and games such as "Statues," "Mother May I," and so on. They can play "Follow the Leader," walking straight lines, hopping, jumping, running, skipping, galloping, walking on tiptoes, and balancing.

Children will enjoy free-form movement to music of different moods and tempos. Tell them to listen to the music and move the way it makes them feel. Use a variety of types of music from rock to gentle waltzes. Children this age may also like learning simple folk dances with easy-to-learn, repetitive steps. Marching, especially with rhythm band instruments (many of which can be made as arts and crafts activities), is also a favorite.

Other activities that children this age will enjoy are relay races and creeping (moving on hands and feet) races—fast and slow and through obstacle courses in which they will have to combine creeping and walking. An obstacle course might be set up to go under tables, around chairs, over boxes, along boards, between markers, up and down steps. Gymnastic stunts such as somersaults and leapfrog might be enjoyed on a mattress put on the floor. Children from four to five may also enjoy simple ball games; walking through a maze; playing on climbing equipment such as rings, parallel bars, jungle gyms, and ladders; skating; and riding a small bicycle with or without training wheels.

Gross motor activities for children this age might include a few body exercises such as toe or knee touching; making "angels in the snow," lying on the floor; and deep knee bends. This is a good time to begin children on a good program of physical exercise. Anything that includes a balance of flexing and extending all the muscles is fine. Hatha Yoga is particularly good because it is a very systematic approach to exercise and relaxation.

By four years, most children have developed fine motor skills which enable them to handle scissors, pencils, and crayons fairly well. At this age, most children use the same hand all the time for drawing, eating, cutting, and so on. (Research stresses that whether children use their left or right hand should not be made an issue or a problem.)

Children from four to five can begin to use their fine motor skills in a number of ways. At four, most children can cut on a line with scissors. By five years most children use scissors more skillfully, following the general outline of a form. Cut-and-paste activities in which the children cut out pictures and paste them in consecutive order can be built around field trips, seasons, or stories. At this age most children can draw out of simple mazes. You might make up some for children to use, built around stories—for example, a maze of the path Little Red Riding Hood follows to get to her grandmother's house. Other examples of mazes may be found in coloring books for young children.

When the children draw things, they are now able to fill in the outlines. Most children also now enjoy coloring books. These can be used for free play during a quiet time or to build language with color words, and so on. Filling in outlines should not be stressed as a goal in children's coloring. Further, although coloring books should be available to children if they enjoy them, they should never replace free artistic expression, nor should children, when coloring, be directed how to do it.*

* We have visited far too many preschool situations where we have observed all the children involved at the same time in coloring or cutting out or pasting exactly the same "art" project—20 orange pumpkins, green Christmas trees, etc. drawn from a pattern by the teacher. Please don't stifle children's real, spontaneous artistic expression by engaging in this kind of activity. If it's Christmas, then let each child do her own chosen representation of the season. You can show the children how you draw something if they ask, but don't have them all doing one just like yours. We have suggested a number of art activities throughout involving coloring books or putting geometric forms together to make a cartoon-like picture. These are acceptable to offer children occasionally *if* they are used flexibly and according to individual children's interests and developmental needs; but, as we've said repeatedly, the majority of children's art experiences should be open-ended and directed by them—just coloring or painting or scribbling what they want in the way they choose.

Between ages four and five, most children learn to draw circles and squares and copy a triangle, and their spontaneous drawings contain recognizable forms of people, animals, trees, houses. You can play drawing games with children by, for instance, talking about the shapes as they are drawn, then looking around the room for other shapes that are the same. Drawing should usually be open-ended to allow children freedom; it may also be used to teach specific skills or as a group experience, such as drawing a mural of what was seen on a field trip.

The following drawings can be made by most children from four to five. (Some of them could be done with three- to four-year-olds also.) They all use only straight lines, circles, squares, triangles, and rectangles. Draw with the children, one shape at a time, until the whole figure is drawn. It will give them great pleasure to be able to draw recognizable objects. After doing a few, the children may think of others on their own. Let different children lead the activity. Again, remember that these activities are suggested for fine motor training and for the fun of drawing recognizable things, and are not a substitute for children's free expression.* Let the children draw on their own; don't draw the figures for them. Children who have trouble drawing may find it easier if you provide dotted lines to guide them. Do not force or even coax children to participate in this or any other kind of activity. It's meant to be fun, not tedious, and should be undertaken only if the children express an interest in it.

Between four and five, most children develop enough fine motor coordination to be able to write the numbers 1, 2, 3, 4, and 5, but they may write ᄅ for 2 and ᕮ for 3. Give them models to trace and then copy, with arrows showing the direction to draw in. For example:

Some children this age learn to print simple words such as their first names in large, irregular letters, though they may make mistakes

---

* Most of children's drawing should be spontaneous and self-directed. When a child has done this kind of drawing, don't ask her what it is or tell her what you think it looks like. Rather, ask her to tell you about her creation, why she used the colors she did, what things she likes about it, how it makes her feel.

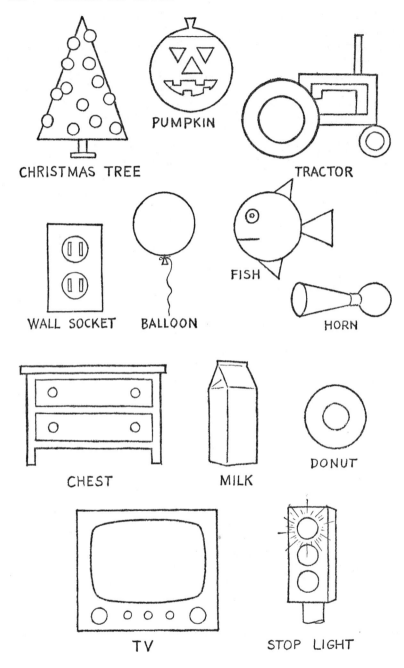

CHRISTMAS TREE   PUMPKIN   TRACTOR

WALL SOCKET   BALLOON   FISH   HORN

CHEST   MILK   DONUT

TV   STOP LIGHT

CLOWN

HOUSE

TRUCK

ICE CREAM

TEDDY BEAR

DOOR

OPEN WINDOW

CAT

BUTTON

KITE

BOAT

TRAIN

such as Я for K or ꟻ for B. If they have learned how, children can write their names on drawings, paintings, and cut-paste projects. Scrapbook projects might now include a couple of words written by you and copied underneath by the child.

Some children will want to learn to write; materials and activities for this purpose should be available. But no child should be forced to learn to write. If controlled drawing and writing is hard for a child, it is a sign that his fine motor skills are not yet well enough developed to do those things. Making him do them will only cause problems. When he's ready to learn them, he will do so easily and enthusiastically.

Between four and five most children will have learned to lace their shoes easily and dress themselves without help except for tying. By five most children are ready to learn to tie a bow knot. Some can do so after seeing it done. Most children can use a knife to butter bread and for cutting soft foods by five, but they still need you to cut their meat.

For children this age, formboards, puzzles, pegboards, parquetry blocks, counting blocks, and other manipulative materials may be used for developing cognitive abilities through copying patterns, learning about number and amount, sequencing, and so on. Most children already have developed the fine motor skills to use these materials. By five years, children can in fact build complex and intricate structures with blocks which they often use in their dramatic play over a period of days.

LANGUAGE DEVELOPMENT

From four to five, most children make great strides in language development. They increase their vocabulary, learn to say more of the speech sounds correctly, increase the length of their sentences, and learn to use new sentence forms, as well as use more correctly the ones they already know. They begin to use language to find out about things in their world; they're beginning to use words to learn, whereas before they were learning to use words. Finally, talking and listening, communicating with others, becomes an enjoyable activity for children four to five.

Between four and five, the number of words children can use increases rapidly from an average of about 1,550 at four years to an average of about 2,050 words by five. Sentences of children this age are usually on the average of four to five words long. Children learn new words by hearing them used with the things or events they refer to: each new field trip or game can bring new words. Talk to children about their experiences; ask them questions about what they did and what they saw. Draw pictures and write stories together about field trips. The best library is one with many books made by and with the children themselves.

Between four and five years most children learn to say some of the more difficult speech sounds such as *l, r, s, t, sh, ch,* and *j.* They can almost always be understood now—about 98 percent of the time. Children can be helped to hear the different sounds and then to say them through games or stories such as the story of a dragon who could not "grr" until he had eaten only food with "r's" like grapes and raspberries.

At four and a half children still sometimes alter the sequence of words in a sentence. When this happens, answer them with the words in the correct order, but don't correct them. By five years, word order will almost always be correct in most children's sentences. Most children begin to use the following language forms and rules correctly some time between four and a half and five years: *possessives* (Johnny is pulling *her* hair); *conjunctions* (The boy *and* girl climb. The boy jumps *but* the girl runs); *adjectives* (The *little* dog is running); *relative pronouns* (The girl *who* cries is very sick); *nominalizations* (Mother does some *cleaning* with a mop); *subordinations* (The boy will find out *what we're going to do*); *irregular verb forms* such as do (He *does* not wear a hat.); *indirect objects* (He throws the ball *to the girl*). Children also may begin to use clauses or phrases in the middle of sentences by five years ("I saw the boy *who lives next door* at the store."). Picture stories should provide chances to use these types of sentences; encourage children to use them in play too.

Not until between five and six years will most children complete their learning of the following sentence forms: *passives* (The boy *is pulled* by his sister); *inversions* (Joyfully he rang the bell); *reflexives* (*He pulled himself* up into the tree); and *questions*. During Show-and-Tell times or story times, help children learn to use language by discussing things with them. Encourage them to ask you and other children questions and to give answers with much meaning. For example, if a child said only "He rang the bell," encourage her to explain more by asking how he might have *felt* ringing the bell, what kind of a sound the bell made, and so on.

By four years most children will use most of the different kinds of words. Children are likely to know four prepositions, and be able to use them in phrases such as "*off* the table," "*in* the yard," "*next* door," "*on* the sidewalk." Children should be able to put into words what they do when they are hungry or cold or tired. When reading stories, you can now ask questions such as "What should Goldilocks do?" or "What would *you* do if you were hungry?"

The children should be able to define a few words by saying how they are used. For example, if you ask them what an orange is, they probably will answer "to eat." Ask the children questions such as "What are clothes?" "What do you do with a spoon?" Encourage them to act out or show the answer as well as say it.

Many children begin using slang and may swear around age four. If swearing bothers you, explain that to the child. Give the child a choice of either not using the word or playing by himself for a while. Children most often use these words not to be naughty, but because they enjoy playing with words and perhaps because of the emotional responses their use may cause. Children also may make up words or make word play with words they know (e.g., "trun" for throw away).

Many four-year-old children will tell long, detailed stories, carry on long conversations, and ask for detailed explanations from others. The questions of children this age are a form of practicing speaking. By five their questions will be fewer and more clearly for the purpose of gaining information. Answer children's questions briefly; then wait for them to ask more questions. Make sure, by asking them questions in return, that children understand your answers. Field trips provide a great chance to talk about what children did and saw; in the discussion, children will learn new words and find out how some things work, such as how boxes are made or that milk comes from cows.

Between four and six most children will be able to understand the prepositions "in," "out," "over," "under," "in front of," "behind," and "on top of," when used in relation to their own body, things around them, and in pictures. These concepts may be used in many different activities. For example, make a mural of a recent field trip with pictures from magazines or the children's drawings. When putting it together, talk about where the pictures should go. "Should the tiger go under this tree?" "Put the elephant behind that fence," and so on.

Motor activities such as the obstacle courses described earlier provide opportunities for children to gain understanding of the concepts in relation to their own body. Make a game out of having children say what they're doing as they go through the course, or direct their movements through language, saying, for example, "Walk around the chair, now crawl under the rope, and then climb up the ladder." Don't give children more than two or three commands at once. Their memory isn't good enough yet to remember more than that.

Most five-year-old children will be able to describe the things and actions in pictures. "Read" books by pictures; go through picture books, asking children to tell the story by describing what's happening in the pictures. They should be able to tell stories without making too many errors. Acting out favorite stories or parts of stories with masks or signs for costumes can provide great fun and good language practice too.

By five, most children understand the words "backwards" and "forwards." Games like "Simon Says" and "Mother May I" help to develop children's awareness of space and of their own bodies. They also help them put the correct words with these body feelings. In addition, these words and movements can be used to introduce the mathematical skills of addition and subtraction.

One game the children can play is to walk forward and backward on a large number line on the floor, the number that appears on a die or on a spinner. Using five pieces of construction paper taped together, make a "line" divided into five sections, marked 1, 2, 3, 4, and 5. Mark "Start" before the 1 and Finish after the 5, and mark on each space something like "Move forward one step," "Move backward two steps." Tape the line on the floor. Have the children throw a die or spin a spinner with six numbers. If they fall on six, they can't move. If they get any other number, they move that many spaces forward and then follow the instructions on the space they land on. The goal of the game is to reach the finish. You'll have to help a bit on reading at first and making sure they move the right number of spaces. Once they understand the game, you can explain addition and subtraction to them in terms of movement on the number line and use the line to "add 2" or "take away 1."

Five-year-old children often ask what words mean. Always give them an answer, making it as simple as possible, and check to make sure that they understood it (not by asking if they understand; they may not understand *that* word). Also, whenever possible show them the object they're asking about or draw them a picture of it, and relate the answer to something they know already.

Children of this age enjoy using language. They like to talk to people and have them listen and talk to them. They very much enjoy listening to stories, poetry, and rhyming in songs. And they like to tell stories, recite poems, and sing songs themselves.

COGNITIVE DEVELOPMENT

Children from four to five are learning more complex ways of ordering things in their world. This is a time for them to "try out" the rules they have been developing and to change them and make up new ones to adjust for the new information they have. This is a very active period of learning for children; it is a time for them to begin to build on the foundations of all the areas in which they have developed in their first years, including perceptual, motor, language, socioemotional, and cognitive, in order to learn new information and skills through the integration of the skills they already have learned.

One of the ways in which children are able to integrate their previously learned skills to develop new ones is through increased ability to remember things, both over a long period of time and immediately. Many people, when they hear the word *remember,* think only of information that is a part of one's memory storehouse. They think of "calling up" to consciousness something they already know or of retaining some bit of information over a long period of time. But there's more to the process of remembering than that. Do you recall at the beginning of the book that we said that newborns had no memory and that they gradually learned to *recognize* familiar things? This is the first stage of remembering—recognizing something you've experienced before. Next, there is *short-term memory.* This involves two processes: (1) remembering something for a short time and (2) recalling it—repeating and/or using the information right away. This is the kind of memory you use when you remember a phone number just long enough to make a call. If you want to remember that same number over a long period of time, you'll have to put it into storage —transfer it to *long-term memory.* In order to do this, you'll have to *rehearse* it enough times that you can *retrieve* it from your memory store whenever you need it. When you *forget* something it may be for one of two reasons—(1) You may not ever have put the information into storage. Perhaps you didn't really pay enough attention for it to register in the first place or perhaps you did not rehearse it sufficiently, or (2) You may have trouble retrieving the information even though it is in your memory store. Perhaps you haven't used it recently, or perhaps you don't have any easy cueing devices or associations that can help you bring the information you want to consciousness.

All these principles apply to understanding memory processes in young children. Children's long-term memory at any age is reflected by what they know, both in information and skills. Their short-term memory—what they can remember over a short period of time—increases as they get older; they can remember a greater number of items of information over a greater length of time within the limits of short-term memory (usually considered a matter of seconds). It is important to keep in mind that young children's memories are limited. Don't expect them to remember everything you tell them. If it's important for them to remember something, make sure they're paying attention, and have them repeat after you what they're supposed to remember. Then tell them again later and ask them to repeat it again. Do this at different times until you can ask the child and get the necessary answer.

As children grow older, their attention span increases so that their learning becomes more efficient and takes less time and practice. Most children of four to five can remember and repeat four numbers or a sentence with eleven syllables. They can also remember to do three things told them in one sentence. For example: "Pick up the book, close the door, and then come over by the window." They can remember more if the material is meaningful to them and presented in a meaningful sequence. This is important in terms of teaching young children; they should be given experiences which are meaningful to them and which are organized in a meaningful way in order for them to learn.

Children (and all of us, for that matter) can remember a limited number of bits of information. In order to increase the amount of information that a person can remember, you can "chunk" it—organize separate but related bits of information into a limited number of units. An example will illustrate the principle: Look at these two series of numbers: 5937426; 198419741964. If you were asked to remember and repeat both, the second would be far easier, even though it contains almost twice as many numbers, because you can chunk it into three units: 1984, 1974, and 1964. What is more, there is a system to those units, making it even easier to remember them. This same principle applies in teaching children both to remember information and to use these techniques themselves.

The following activities suggest just a few ways to give children this age practice in remembering things over a short period of time. Such activities teach children to *attend* to what they are doing, and they also teach them ways to "chunk" the information they receive, by organizing it into small meaningful pieces.

Tell a short story and have children retell it. For example, "Joyce went to the store. She bought some milk. She went to grandma's." Play "Follow My Directions." Say to the child, for example, "Walk to the door and hop to the record player." Then have him do what's been said. Extend the number of directions as the child is able to follow more correctly. This can be played as a paper-and-pencil game also; e.g., "Draw a circle around the apple and make an X on the pear." Play store with the children. Give a child your "order," ask her to repeat it and then find what you ordered from a group of pictures. Say the names of three or four children, and have a child point to them and say their names. Say the names of three or four animals and have the child find them in a group of animal pictures and name them. If the children know the alphabet, play the game "I packed my bag with apples, (berries, cherries, and so on)." After about four, it will probably end with peals of laughter, but they'll remember more as they practice.

By four to five, most children have learned certain information about the relationship of time to events in their lives which help them learn to order experiences and events in time for themselves, according to when they can expect them to happen. This learning serves also as the basis on which children can begin to understand the relationship between the amount of time which an activity can be expected to take and the amount of work that activity will involve.

This is very important for children to learn. (Many of us would have a much easier time as adults if we'd developed this skill in childhood.) You can help by having children estimate how long an activity will take (a few minutes, a whole day) and then, when they're done, comparing their estimate with the actual time. Do this regularly until children become very precise in their estimates.

By four years, many children pretend to tell time, but their attempts are incorrect. They can tell, in terms of the things done, when different times of the day and year occur. For example, they know that "afternoon is after lunch," that they get up "in the morning," and when they eat breakfast, dinner, and so on. They know when winter, summer, Christmas and Easter (or other important holidays) are, and can tell what happens on special days like Sunday (for example, that there is no school or work that day). Present, past, and future verb tenses are all used correctly, most of the time, reflecting an awareness of these time divisions.

You can play guessing games that will develop time skills. For example, say, "There are sleds. There is snow. What time of the year is it?" Have pictures of children doing activities based on the fact that they are taking place in different seasons. Have the children group together those pictures which are taking place in the same seasons. You may have the children find pictures to make a mural of seasonal activities. This will work for times of the day too, and will give many chances for language development.

By age five, most children can tell what hour they go to bed. Most children by now can tell what day it is, but usually they cannot tell correctly what hour it is until age six or seven or even later. Children now know winter, spring, and summer as different times of the year. Holidays they know include Thanksgiving and Halloween now. They use words such as "yesterday" and "tomorrow" correctly. Activities may now be planned using a calendar. A record of the children's main activities could be kept using a calendar too. This would provide good chances for developing a sense of time, as well as developing good language skills, using the past tense. Special days like holidays provide good opportunities for many activities, including practice with time words.

Children from four to five years usually will take pleasure in helping to follow routine activities. They will enjoy having a general schedule for such things as eating, playing outside, and so on, and should be given a chance to help plan the schedule. However, activities should not be forced into a rigid schedule. Children should not, for example, be made to paint at ten o'clock because that's the scheduled time for painting. Activities should be flexible so that children do things when they will enjoy them and when they're involved, not when it's "time to do them."

Most children this age have learned enough about the consistencies of certain things in their world to recognize the relationship of parts to wholes. For example, they can tell when something is missing from ordinary things they have seen before, such as the teeth of a comb. You can make puzzles by drawing pictures or cutting them from a magazine, cutting out a part of each picture, and then giving the children a choice of parts from which to fill in each missing part. Also you might make one large picture puzzle containing many objects with missing parts. Give the children the missing parts to fill in the spaces. The children should be able to help make the puzzles now.

Most children are able to cut a picture or paper shape into parts and then put it back together again. Help the children to make simple puzzles out of pictures of themselves or out of large magazine pictures.

At four years, most children begin to be able to copy designs both by drawing and by putting together pattern pieces to copy patterns already made as examples. You might make felt shapes to match sets of paper shapes for each child. Make designs on the feltboard for children to copy. Some designs can be put together to make pictures of houses, trains, and so on, and some can be used to make colorful designs. (See pictures of objects made from ○, □, △, and □ on pp. 122–23 for ideas.) Activities of this type are good for seeing geometric and part-whole relationships, but should never take the place of free artistic expression.

Most children at about four begin to be able to copy the order of a group of things in the same order or in opposite order. These activities are helpful in developing prereading skills. Activities might include copying the order from left to right of blocks, beads, letters, objects, or pictures. At first you should do the activity with the children, for example, by stringing beads in front of them, saying, "First a round one, next a square, now another round one, next another square one." As the children are able to do it, you can make the patterns more difficult. Finally, once the children have the idea, you can make up cards with patterns on them for them to copy on their own. Have the children put in order real objects and pictures of real events which have a real order also, such as a toy train with engine, cars, and caboose, or seasons with different foliage on trees, or the development of an animal from birth to adulthood.

Most children from four to five years are able to recognize likenesses and differences among objects and can group them together on that basis. For example, children will be developing skills which enable them to pick out the important characteristics of an object which make it the same as another, in order to match similar objects. Games can be made up with objects or pictures which are the same and ones which are a little bit different:

Have the children find the ones that are the same. Then have them describe why the ones that are different are not the same. Also, most four-year-old children can find one shape out of a group of different shapes that matches a model. Worksheets and games may be created that require the child to find the same object, picture, shape, or design out of a group.

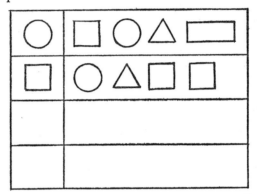

This can be done with sounds and smells and feelings as well as with things you can see. For example, you might put an object inside a bag for children to feel and try to match with one of a group of objects that they can see on a table, or make a sound and see if the children can find what made it.

By four years, children should be able to match all shapes such as squares, circles, stars, and so on in a ten-hole formboard.

Watching the method by which children do this should give you a good indication of the level of their rule-making and problem-solving abilities. Do they pick up each shape, look for its match, then put it in? Do they pick up a shape and try it out in several places before finding one that fits? Do they have difficulty putting the pieces in because they don't have them turned right? Do they look at all the holes in the formboard and then try to find shapes to match each one? The way a child goes about this and other tasks can tell you a great deal about how she thinks. If you know how children think and go about solving problems, you can help them better in their learning by choosing materials and teaching strategies which strengthen their present skills and help them develop new ones from skills they already have. For example, if their procedure is trial and error, you can help them take more time and think about what they're going to do before they do it.

Most four-year-olds who have been taught these things know what ordinary things are made out of—for example, that chairs are made of wood. Go around the room having the children find all the things made of wood, glass, and so on. Children usually find out about the properties of things around them by noticing the way those things look and feel. It helps children understand the physical properties of materials if they have an opportunity also to try things out on them: Can they float, or do they sink? Are they hard or soft, rough or smooth? Do they break, bend, stretch, fold? Collect a box of different kinds of materials: paper, soft and hard plastics, wood, rubber, acrylic, cloth, sandpaper, metal. Encourage children to try out different actions on the materials, including touching them, putting them in water, trying to cut or break them. Do not include anything that could hurt children, such as sharp metal or glass that they could break. They'll probably learn that glass breaks by dropping a glass or jar on the floor sometime, or you can explain it to them; but don't put it in the box with the other materials.

Between four and six years, most children can learn to follow one type of classification, rule, or plan throughout one set of things without forgetting. For example, given a set of shapes with many colors to group, children learn to put all the red shapes together in one group and all the blue in another without forgetting in the middle of the task, and, for example, putting a blue circle with a red circle because they're both circles. Four-year-olds change their idea of what they're doing as they go along; they find it hard to keep in mind one specific way of classifying things. Their thoughts seem more strung together than grouped together. Even in art and dramatic play, four-year-olds may start with one idea and go from one to another, changing as they go along. By five to six years, children will begin to have a plan first and to be able to follow it.

By the time they're six, most children have the practice and knowledge first to go all the way through objects and group them by color; then to mix them up and regroup them all by shapes; and then to mix them up again and arrange them all by size. Before that time they may need to be asked, "Can you think of another way to group them?" after they've already done it one way. Children should be given many chances to group things in different ways. For example, a set of colored flowers and fruits could be divided into those we do and do not eat, or by colors.

You can make some materials which are useful for developing classification skills; use your imagination. Some kitchen units which can be fitted together will make a sorting tray; egg cartons can be used for sorting small objects. For very little money you can buy different sets of objects for the child to sort, such as different colored chips, small animals, marbles, and so on.

"Grouping" circles also can be drawn on paper or made from large hoops, and used for sorting: If there are two groups—big, little; square, triangle; red, blue; and so on—then each object in one group would be put with ones like it into the same circle. You can also have more than two circles or overlap the two, for example, for red squares and triangles vs. blue squares and blue triangles. The latter is a much harder task.

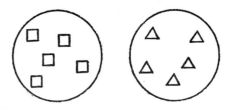

You develop your child's classification skills at home by letting him do such things as help sort the laundry, and put away groceries (soups together, vegetables together, fruits with fruits).

Most four-year-old children can tell the front from the back of their clothes. Have mirrors set up so that children can see the back of themselves also. When they draw a person, you might suggest that they draw the back of the person too, on the *back* of their paper.

Children from four to five years should be increasing their understanding of number and amount. They usually are able to say and even write numbers before they have a consistent concept of amount, just as they are able to say and write letters before they can read words for meaning.

At four years, children usually can say numbers in order from one to ten. They should be able to count correctly (by pointing to each thing as they count) at least three things. Count toys, blocks, beads, and so on, one by one together with children—one set for them, one for you. Have a box for yourself and a box for the child; then put each object in a box as you say the number. Also count objects with children, guiding their finger at first, if necessary, to make sure that they touch each thing as they say the number.

Four-year-olds should be able to tell the biggest and the longest of three things. Have them put in order three different lengths of candy, straws, sticks, or dolls. Draw pictures of things of different length and ask them which is the longest or tallest. Explain the meanings of long or tall, if necessary.

At four years most children will be able to tell the biggest of three circles. Play games with pretend pies, cookies, pillows, or plates to be grouped by children for each of the three bears. Use words like "biggest" and "smallest."

By using trial and error, most four-year-old children will be able to order five blocks from heaviest to lightest with only two mistakes. Have children arrange blocks, balls of clay, boxes, or marbles from lightest to heaviest. Help them check their choices with scales, if available.

At four most children will be able to tell which bunch of things has the "most," and which bunches have the "same" number of things. Put marbles, blocks, and so on into boxes or pails of the same size and shape. Ask the children which has the most. Have them put "more" in one and then ask which has the most and which has the same. Do this also with sand, water, or whatever else you can think of in clear containers of the same size and shape so the children can see the amount. Pile objects on a table or within grouping circles to compare amounts.

Between four and five, most children should know the names of coins and that they have certain sizes and colors. You may make or buy a play cash register and use play money which looks as much like real money as possible. Also give the children at least one real coin of each type to put in the cash register. Playing store or restaurant with real prices on items will help the children learn about money. When it fits into planned activities, take the children to the store to buy needed things and let them pay and get change.

From four to six years most children learn the beginning of mathematical thinking by arranging one of one thing for every one of another (one-to-one correspondence). For example, children will put enough place settings at the table for all the chairs at the table, but not too many. You can use many different sets of materials to help children learn this concept: forks and knives, ice cream and cake, socks and shoes, cups and saucers, dolls and hats. This skill can be practiced through role playing, having tea parties and setting places for the children or dolls, and having children help set the table for snacks and meals.

At four to five years, children's ideas about things are based on how they look to them. If, for example, you line up forks and napkins so that they're next to each other, children this age agree that there are the same number of each. But if you then spread the napkins out so they take up more space than the forks, they'll say there are more napkins—because it *looks* like more.

Children four to five years old have the same problem with amount if you take two groups of things (each with the same number) and bunch one in a pile while leaving the other in a line. If the two groups of things are lined up together, children think they have the same number, but not when one group is put in a pile. You can make up games based on these observations, but although they may be enjoyed, the games won't make children change their way of thinking. It will change in time through many kinds of experiences and doesn't really need to be trained.

Children from four to five should be getting practice in telling whether there is a lot or a little of something; most children will be able to say so correctly by six. When children are playing with clay or water or painting, or whatever, there are many chances to talk with them about "which has a lot," "there's too little," and so on.

By four and a half, most children are able to give "just three" and no more. Most are able to count correctly up to nine things. By now children should be able to count by themselves, putting blocks or marbles in a container, or using an abacus. Check to see that they count each thing once and don't skip any.

Cut out pictures or have children draw pictures of different objects, ten of each kind. Then play games asking a child to give you just three apples, carrots, dolls. Do this with real objects too. When this gets boring, play grocery store and order two chickens, three onions, and so forth.

At five years, many children can say the numbers at least up to thirteen but they know most of the numbers only because they've memorized them; they don't understand number concepts beyond about the number five.

Most children at this age can tell you how many fingers are on one hand but they may not know how many are on both. Play number games with fingers; ask the child to hold up two, to hold up all except one, and so on. In number activities, you may sometimes write numbers on children's fingers with magic marker that washes off.

Children should learn that something cut in half has two pieces. Cut pictures and real things such as apples, balls of clay, and shapes once and ask children how many pieces there are; then cut them twice. Ask children to put the pieces back together again too.

By five years, most children have begun to know how to write the numbers up to five but will often put them in the wrong order and just not write the ones they do not know. Practice putting numbers with groups of things up to five. First have the children say how many; then have one child write the correct number on a blackboard. Other good materials for this skill are puzzles which fit together only in the order of 1 to 5, with the correct number of dots or pictures on each piece or holes for pegs corresponding to the number on the piece.

Even by the age of six most children will not be able to arrange things in order of smallest to biggest without a lot of trial and error to check them out first. There are many things to be learned by children before they can put things in order correctly; for instance, children should be able to pick one thing from a group of objects that is bigger than all the others or bigger than one other. They also should be able to choose one that's smaller than one or all the others. Children should be able to make four balls of clay or draw four lines on a piece of paper, each one a little bigger than the last. Arranging things from smallest to biggest can be taught by using stories like "The Three Bears" or ones you make up. Have the children put things for the bears in order—big, middle-sized, and small. Make or draw different-sized bowls, beds, chairs, and so on for the bears.

Children under seven usually are *not* able to do the following:

(1) arrange objects from smallest to largest, shortest to longest or lightest to heaviest without any trial and error or without making mistakes due to using incorrect cues;

(2) see that one group of objects which have been lined up and another group of the same number of objects which have been put into a pile still are equivalent in number, or that one group of objects lined up with another group of the same number spread further apart also contain the same number;

(3) know that when liquid is poured from one container into another that is longer and thinner it still is the same amount as before;

(4) know that two sticks of the same length are still the same when the end of one is moved up from the other (the child only looks at one end);

(5) know that a ball of clay still has the same amount of clay when it's flattened out or rolled into a snake or that it can be rolled back into the same size ball once it has been flattened.

Young children under about seven years still base their rules on the way things look to them. They don't understand that the quantity of a thing remains the same even when it is arranged differently (principle of conservation.) They need more experience in many arenas —seeing the relationship between how something looks and what it is, and observing that things can change in some ways and yet still remain essentially the same—before they can understand this particular aspect of that general principle. They *should not* be asked to do academic tasks which assume understanding of the above principles.

SOCIOEMOTIONAL DEVELOPMENT

From four to five years, children continue to develop as individuals. Most children are able to adjust to changes and deal with situations more easily, without getting upset. Children are better able to adjust because they are better able to understand things and have had more practice in dealing with situations. Encourage them to use language to seek solutions to problems rather than just crying and getting upset.

Children are becoming better able to handle their own emotions in productive ways, to help them settle problems rather than to get in their way. Discomfort is talked about and children are more willing to accept situations as they are. Help children talk about difficulties, seek solutions if there are any, and to accept situations realistically if there is no way to change them.

Fears decrease as children learn more skillful responses through practice, greater understanding of the world, and greater confidence in their own abilities to act appropriately. Encourage children to tell you if they are frightened of something. Help them understand what is new to them and help them feel comfortable with their own ability to handle new, unknown situations.

Children are beginning to learn to avoid aggression when angry and to look for a compromise. Praise children for talking out anger and seeking agreement to arguments. When they act out their aggression, help them to calm down and talk about the situation. Direct them toward finding a solution on their own.

Most children this age should be continuing to develop a stable self-concept (based, we hope, on their own inner definition of who they are; a self-concept that is based on others' opinions of you cannot be stable). Children are beginning to internalize social rules and to rely on their own judgment of their behavior. They begin to understand the words "good" and "bad" in terms of what happens as a consequence doing those things called good or bad by parents and other adults and older children. Children still may not be able to understand all the reasons for sharing with others and for being "good." They will learn best if things are explained in terms of themselves *as well as in terms of others:* "If you share your toy with Milly, then she will share hers with you too." Although children may not be able totally to "put themselves in another's shoes," they can understand if it's explained in terms of themselves.

Most children from four to five tend to seek approval less from adults and more now from other children. They are becoming more aware of and concerned about others, particularly other children. Most children play both competitive and cooperative active games in small groups of three or four such as tag, marbles, hide-and-seek, and jump rope.

Children's drawings now contain recognizable forms of people, houses, and so on. Help children learn to use drawing to tell how they feel, about themselves and others, and to describe things that are happening to them. Drawing is for some children a much easier way of communicating feelings than is talking.

Most children at this age seldom play alone, but they can work by themselves when directed to by you, without bothering others. Children can now be given a project to work on by themselves at a desk or table and will stay with it until they are finished, without wandering off to find others to play with instead. Persistence, continuing to work at something until it is completed to the child's own satisfaction, should be encouraged. It is a critical part of problem-solving behavior, and is necessary for self-directed learning.

Between four and five, children should begin to learn on the basis of intrinsic motivation. That is, children should be beginning now to do things less to seek the approval of others and more to increase their own feelings of competence and self-worth. Their learning of skills, and their actions, are influenced by their own efforts to become more like a model whom they respect or admire and whom they see as being like themselves in some ways. This means that they must see the person they want to be like doing those things. A good model is accepting and competent and has things or is able to do things the child wants to have or to be able to do.

Children should be beginning to form a "conscience" to help them judge their own actions. At this stage it is very fragile, and children need to be encouraged for good behavior. Praise children for trying to behave in ways that seem right to them and that show concern for others. Don't ever hit a child. Disapproval shown through eye contact with the child is one of many means which are far more effective in dealing with misbehavior than any kind of physical punishment or restriction. There is no excuse for striking a child. It has been found that children learn violent behavior toward others through violence shown them by adults. Encourage and help children learn to judge their own actions rather than relying on others to reward and punish them.

From four to five years, children are becoming more capable of doing things for themselves. They can dress themselves without help, eat with a fork and use a knife to spread and to cut soft things. Most children recognize their own neighborhood and can go around the block and to school without getting lost. They can go out in the neighborhood and play, for example, if traffic is not a problem. When possible, children should be given chances to do things on their own. This helps build their self-confidence and independence.

Children are now becoming increasingly aware of the different roles played by people, such as grocers, bakers, police people, nurses, social workers, and pilots. They should be given the chance to meet different kinds of people by having them invited to come to the school, if they are in a school setting, and also by taking field trips when possible. Dramatic play now includes playing doctor, delivery person, and so on. As children learn more about their world, they try it out and practice it through dramatic play. Children will enjoy having hats and costumes to wear when playing these roles, as well as some examples of different kinds of equipment used by people with different jobs. Some of these things could be made as an art activity.

Most children are beginning to become aware of others and will defend their rights, especially the rights of younger children. Encourage and praise this sensitivity to and responsibility for others. Children begin now to have feelings of really belonging to a group. The group is important to the child. Be aware of and concerned about how each child is accepted by the group. Don't put a child in an uncomfortable position with the group, and try to help him work out problems he might have with it.

It takes an exceptional person to see the common humanity in all human beings, and recognizing it, to devote one's life to the work of lifting the whole human race to a higher level.

—SUSETTE TIBBLES (1887)

7

What about School?

*If we were willing to lose a bit more time and let the
children be active, let them use trial and error on
different things, then the time we seem to have lost
we may have actually gained. Children may develop
a general method that they can use on other subjects.*

—JEAN PIAGET (1896–   )

*The true order of learning should be: first, what is
necessary; second, what is useful; and third, what is
ornamental. To reverse this arrangement is like
beginning to build at the top of the edifice.*

—LYDIA H. SIGOURNEY (1791–1865)

It is more fatal to neglect the heart than the head.

—THEODORE PARKER (1810–1860)

*If the emotions are free, the intellect will look
after itself. . . . The cure for the sickness of man does
not lie in politics or religion or humanism; nay,
the cure is freedom for children to be themselves.*

—A. S. NEILL (1883–1973)

Just for a moment, think back on your years in school. Think about
the amount of time and energy you put in (and that some of you may
still be putting in). Now think of all the things you learned that are
of use to you, directly or indirectly, in your day-to-day life. Unless you
had a very unusual educational experience, chances are that you'll find
the scales tipped almost embarrassingly toward your output of time
and energy in contrast to what was provided you by your school. The
point is that our schools do very little to prepare us for life, and they
don't even teach us to learn how to learn so that we can take over our
own educations when we finish our enforced time there. What they do
teach us of value could be accomplished in a very small fraction of the
time we put in, much more efficiently and certainly more enjoyably.
The real crime is that school teaches too many children to hate learning, since they come to associate learning with schooling. Human be-

ings who are not learning are not growing; and since development is basic to the nature of human beings, human beings who are not developing are not in tune with their nature and are thus seriously handicapped in their ability to find peace and happiness.

Our point is not to indict the schools or the individuals who make up the system. As with so many problems that exist in our society today, on group and individual levels, the issue is not that the institution or the people in it mean deliberate harm. Rather, our schools have developed some nonproductive, nonadaptive habits, and habits are hard to break, especially when they're so widespread. The schools are not going to change unless individuals with conviction begin to insist that they become more responsive and accountable *to the people they are supposed to serve,* and that means children. And since children have no voice in our society, we who care for them must speak for them. *

The world is not getting any easier to cope with, and we can hardly imagine what kind of a world our children are going to have to face. They deserve the best possible preparation we can give them in order to have a chance in coping with the unknown challenges ahead of them. We've tried, in this book, to offer you a few tools so that you can do that for your children in their preschool years. But what *about* school? If you've done your job well, the schools, no matter how bad they are, cannot undo the foundation you've given your children. But they *can* waste their time. And time is too precious a resource in our finite human existence to throw away so easily.

Further, there is a trend in some states, now, toward attaching early childhood education programs to the elementary schools—simply extending downward to age three or four the age range that the schools will encompass. The question of those of us who are concerned with early childhood education as a vehicle for child development is whether this linking of the schools and early childhood education will result in the early years following the pattern of the other parts of the system—to prepare children for the next grade in school—or whether the early childhood education programs will have the beneficial effect of helping the schools to refocus their own priorities and methods. It's your choice.

In order for the schools to become more responsive to their consumers, parents are going to have to become more active in their concern for their children's educational future. What we are suggesting is not that you go in and scream and yell and insist that the schools do a better job educating your children. It is never productive to put people on the defensive, especially when you have no workable alternatives to offer. Rather, we recommend two lines of action.

* "What the best and wisest parent wants for his own child, that must the community want for all of its children."—John Dewey (1859–1952)

First, give your active support to school programs which *are* daring to try something new and different. There are some schools operating today that are providing children with just the kind of education they need. If you're fortunate enough to live near one, get involved—find out what the staff is doing and how you can help. You should also lend your support to schools that are trying new programs, even if they're not totally successful; the fact that they're willing to question their old habits means that they'll be more likely to be open to ideas that will enable them to become increasingly more successful. We've seen too many really promising programs discontinued because of lack of support from parents.

Second, do some reading and especially some serious thinking about the ways you think the schools need to refocus to become more consistent with the developmental needs of growing human beings. Think, for example, of some of the things you wish you'd learned in school, of skills that would be useful to you now. Get together with other parents and teachers who share your concerns and try to come up with some positive proposals that you could offer.

And, finally, when you do eventually get the ear of someone who could make a difference, speak with strength of conviction. If you really believe in what you're saying and you communicate your belief with strength and conviction, you *can* make a difference. The problem with the schools and many other arenas that are not serving the people they're supposed to serve is that there are never enough people who are willing to put in the time and energy to make a difference. It's too easy for individuals to take the easy out: "What can one person do, anyway?" You can do that too, and that's your choice. But it just isn't so. We leave you with two statements as food for thought on the issue:

"Behold the turtle who makes progress only when he sticks his neck out"

and

"Almost always, the creative, dedicated minority has made the world better."
—Dr. Martin Luther King, Jr. (1929–1968)

WHAT SHOULD THE SCHOOLS TEACH?

We've asked you to give some thought to what the job of the schools should be. It's only fair that we share some of our thoughts on the issue. Our answer to the question is that schools should teach children, not subjects. They should help children gain the tools through which they can then learn to use their mind as a tool. What the world needs more of is human beings who, when faced with an important decision, problem, or question, whether personal or social, can bring to bear on it their resources to search for and find a solution and then take positive action based on their decision. At this time, too many people feel helpless when confronted with a problem; they do not feel in command of the skills necessary to solve many of the problems they face, and they tend to look to someone else to solve their problems for them. It is not their fault that they feel this way; no one ever taught them how to approach and solve their own problems.

How do we translate this into specifics of how children's time in school should be spent? First, we would suggest that the importance of children's self-concept as a determinant of what, how much, and how well they are able to learn does not end with the preschool years. If a child doesn't feel very good about herself, she is less likely to feel capable of success in learning than if she believes in her ability to learn. So a primary focus in educating children should be to help them achieve successes which will increase their feelings of competence and self-worth. This is more possible in a learning environment that does not stress competitiveness but rather concentrates on finding ways of reaching each child where he is and helping him grow from there at his own pace and in his own way.

In addition, teachers need to relate to their children as human beings and let them know they care about them. Children who do not believe enough in themselves to want to learn in order to achieve feelings of competence and self-worth *will* work in order to receive praise and nurturance from someone they care about. And children, like all of us, tend to care about those who care about them. So a prerequisite to being able to teach children skills that will be personally meaningful to them is that the classroom atmosphere be one of mutual caring and respect in which the children can feel safe enough to play around with ideas, take risks, and pursue their own interests.

Next, the teacher must provide a model to her students. In order to get them excited about learning, she must be excited about learning too. That means that she must participate in the learning experience with the children, not simply pass information on to them. She should constantly be learning new information and skills with which she can help guide her children in their self-chosen interests, and she should continuously be learning from her children as she sees how they look at things and what interests them. The role of the teacher* should be the same at all levels of school as it is in the preschool—she should be a guide and resource to children, a catalyst and facilitator for their

---

* Remember, parents are teachers too; they are, in fact, children's primary teachers.

learning. She should help them, through providing stimulating materials and through asking them questions that enable them to focus their thinking, to find and pursue areas of learning that interest them. The principle of assimilation and accommodation that we discussed in relation to preschool children applies to learning at all levels. Children will learn what is close to what they already know but is also slightly different, a bit more difficult, puzzling, and thought-provoking. In order to find things that will provoke learning in his children, then, the teacher will need to get to know them and find out what they already know and what interests them. Then he can search for ways to capitalize on what each child already knows and can do. The *ultimate* goal of this kind of education is to get children involved enough in their own learning that they don't need a teacher, that they can use their own resources to follow through for themselves on ideas that interest them.

What we're really talking about is motivation—what moves people to act as they do. The goal of the kind of education we've been discussing is to get children to operate primarily on the basis of intrinsic motivation—motivation from within themselves. The kind of schooling that most of us received taught us to operate primarily on the basis of extrinsic motivation—motivation from outside. A person who is intrinsically motivated does what she does because it feels right to her; she relies on her own judgment as the final determinant for what she does. Although she is open to others' ideas, feelings, and opinions, she weighs them against her own in making her judgments of what is right, rather than making her judgments about things primarily on the basis of other people's input. In contrast, a person who is extrinsically motivated acts as he does primarily because of how it will affect how others respond to him. Although he may have opinions of his own, they are easily swayed by others' contrary opinions. He is primarily concerned with how others feel about him rather than how he feels about himself, and he *bases* his feelings about himself on how others feel about him.

Most people in the world today operate in their day-to-day lives primarily on the basis of extrinsic rather than intrinsic motivation. This is not their fault. First, when they were small children, of necessity they had to choose the wishes of those caring for them over their own when the two were in conflict. Then, when they got to school, the whole system rewarded them for meeting others' expectations: grades, approval from teachers, competition with other students—all are extrinsic reinforcers. And studies have shown that even when children are naturally motivated from within, the strength of the extrinsic rewards to act in a way consistent with other people's standards and punishments for acting on the basis of their own standards is sufficient to make them become extrinsically motivated.

Then, television, movies and other media tell people, through the models they show them, what they should be like—what is "normal," acceptable behavior. (Unfortunately, these "roles" we're shown have little resemblance either to what people are really like or to what they can be; they present people with unattainable models, adding to their insecurity.) And of course advertising plays on people's insecurities, selling them things they don't need by promising their product will make them more attractive and acceptable to others. The pictures people get from advertising of what they should be like are even more unrealistic than the role models they get from TV, movies, magazines, and books. All this adds up to giving people a very distorted view of what human beings really are, making it very difficult for them to rely on their own judgment for the answer. There are very few who have the strength of belief in themselves to do so. They are the ones who were fortunate enough to have a loving, supportive childhood such as we have described.

This world is in desperate need of people who have the strength of their own convictions, who don't blow with the wind on important issues because of their fear of what others will think of them. We *must* help our children learn to follow their own inner conscience, to accept responsibility for their own behavior. We can do this only through an educational system that encourages the growth of intrinsic motivation from preschool education all the way through.

WHAT ABOUT THE 3 R's?

We are not suggesting that children no longer be taught to read, write, do math, and learn other useful skills included in traditional school programs. An education based on concern for children's total development will not neglect these skills; it will simply approach them in a different way. For example, a teacher might put up labels around her classroom giving each visible object a "name tag." In this way her children could see the connection between a thing, its name, and the written symbol used to represent it. Then she could make a game out of taking the name tags down and having the children see if they can match them up again with their referents. Math skills, instead of being taught through drill and rote memorization, would be taught through understanding of the relationship of number and amount to real-life situations within the kind of educational context we describe.

And, most important, all skills taught would be related to an understanding, in depth, of how children develop. Just as you should have a knowledge of child development in the years before school in order to be an effective guide in your children's learning and growing, so teachers in the schools should have a knowledge of how children develop in the school years that they can use as a guide to their teaching. For example, in Chapter 6 we included a list of basic understandings related to math concepts that most children under age seven haven't yet developed. Teachers of children below this age should certainly be aware of such information. Many of the learning problems children experience in schools today could be avoided if they were not forced to learn skills before the time that they were developmentally ready to learn them. That is why teachers must teach children, not subjects. Not all children are ready to learn to read at age six. An understanding of child development, including knowledge of prerequisite skills necessary before children are ready to learn many school subjects, would do a great deal to change educational practice in the schools.

> *Education is not something which the teacher does, it is a natural process which develops spontaneously.*
>
> —MARIA MONTESSORI (1870–1952)

8

Materials
and Resources

*What we do today is important, for we are
exchanging a day of our life for it. When tomorrow
comes, today will be gone, leaving in its place
whatever we have exchanged it for.*

ANONYMOUS

*If we save the children today,
we have saved the nation tomorrow.*

—MARY H. HUNT (1878)

In this chapter, we offer some guidelines for choosing materials to use
in your work with young children. In addition, we include lists of
resources which will give you more information about (1) materials
and equipment for use with young children, (2) child development,
(3) early childhood education, (4) day care, (5) learning problems, and
(6) testing and evaluation.

MATERIALS

It is important that as you work with children and develop appropriate
activities, you remember that the most important single thing for
children's development is not toys and materials but rather their relationship with the people around them. The people in a child's life provide the basis for the development of all of his skills; they help him
learn how to respond to others, and affect how he comes to feel about
himself, as well as influencing his development of language, cognitive,
and other skills. It is not so terribly important that children have any
one toy or kind of equipment at any age; it *is* essential that they have
people who care about them, support them, provide for and help them

148

learn to provide for their own needs. Becoming tuned in to your children and understanding how children develop will help you identify and meet their needs.

Your awareness of children's levels of development and your ability to take advantage of the situation around you is more important than the particular materials you use. For example, if a child at one or two years seems interested in throwing objects into a container, provide her with a large can and some objects (such as a sock rolled into a ball, crumpled up pieces of paper or aluminum foil, or a beanbag) to throw into it. You need not always arrange counting activities for children three to four years old; just count things you're working with, like barrettes for a little girl's hair or shirts that you're ironing. Talk to your child regularly about what both of you are doing or seeing. For example, she'll learn colors better if you talk about the red apple when you're handing her one or red shirts when she's wearing one, than if she practices recognizing colors only during special activities.

Nevertheless, there are materials that can be useful to you in your work with children or that children will enjoy and learn from. Since there are so many "educational toys" on the market today and other materials advertised as useful for teaching young children, we felt it might be helpful to provide some general guidelines for selection of toys and materials.

Materials and equipment should be chosen with the following in mind:

(1) They should provide enjoyment for children. A good toy is, first of all, one that your child likes, that's interesting and fun to him. An empty box may therefore be a better toy for your child than the toy that it contained if the former is more interesting to him.

(2) They should be flexible in their usefulness for children of different ages and abilities. For example, infants use small wooden blocks to practice picking up and grasping. Later they'll use them for dropping and letting go. Still later they'll use them to put in and take out of containers and to begin building simple structures. By preschool age, they'll use them for building more complex structures and for counting, sorting by color, and as props in sociodramatic play and other "pretend" activities.

(3) They should be in some ways suggestive to children of what to do with them, but at the same time they should be flexible—able to be used in a large variety of ways. For example, clay can be pounded, rolled, flattened, cut into pieces, used to make things, and so on.

(4) They should require some action on the part of the child. Many commercially advertised toys for children are not involving; the child looks at them or does one thing which makes the toy work, and

they work the same for each child. A good toy should be different for each child who plays with it because of how she, as an individual, acts on it.

(5) They should be stimulating to a child in learning skills or concepts appropriate to his developmental level. You should check the text for ideas of toys and materials that are developmentally appropriate at different times and will thus help children exercise their developing skills.

Different materials are used to develop different kinds of learning skills. For example, stringing beads is a motor skill for the very young child; stringing them according to a pattern once he's developed the motor skill develops his cognitive skills. As children get older they apply skills from more areas of learning to any one kind of activity.

(6) They should not require much adult direction although they may be conducive to adult involvement—your role should be to observe the children in play and to suggest new materials or new ways of using the old materials in relation to what you know about the child's skills and level of development.

But a toy should be usable by the child without the necessity of your help. For example, a complicated erector set that a child couldn't put together without you would be a poor toy. A set of oversized tinker toys that she could enjoy on her own would be a good toy.

(7) They should be well made and sturdy enough to hold up under steady use with no sharp, jagged edges or parts which could break easily.

(8) Finally, materials should be chosen with reference to the children's cultural background and interests. This is particularly important in terms of choice of materials and equipment for role playing. (Dress-up clothes and hats, and types of equipment in the housekeeping area, for example, should relate to adult models the child has in his home and community.) Some play equipment also can be adapted to reflect the children's cultural heritage.

The type of materials and equipment chosen, of course, should relate not only to the children's cultural heritage but to their present environment as well. So, for example, children living in a large urban area would need different kinds of materials than children living in a rural area. Books should be chosen also that relate to the children's cultural background and are written in their native language if it is other than English.

As sources for materials, we recommend, first, that you look around you at the common household things you might ordinarily throw away. A cardboard or styrofoam egg carton is a good container for an infant to put in and take out small objects such as balls made from crumpled paper; for an older child, it's a sorting tray. A toilet paper roll is a trumpet or a spy glass for the dramatic play of your child of two or three. And a shoe box is a good home for your preschooler's collection of rocks or bottle tops (or whatever her particular "specialty" is). Old socks make good puppets, and worn-out shoes can be mounted on a board and used for practicing lacing and tying.

Second, we suggest you look through magazines for teachers of preschool and elementary school children for advertisements of toy and equipment manufacturers. Send for their free catalogs and use them to get ideas for materials you could make. For example, one company makes a very expensive set of touching materials—a number of plastic pieces with tops made of different-feeling materials such as sandpaper, cotton, foam. You can make such a toy for very little money, and the activity of putting it together can be a fun-shared experience with your child.

Finally, use your common, daily experiences as the basis for many of the materials and activities you make available to your children. We mentioned in the text using times like grocery shopping, putting away groceries, cleaning the house, and doing laundry for giving children practice at classification, beginning math skills, and motor skills. Children should be expected to keep their own spaces and possessions in some order, to help you out, to develop responsible habits, and to learn the skills of putting things where they go, putting like things together, and so on. Baths can be a time for learning about wet and dry, hot and cold, warm and cool, floating and sinking, and so on. Mealtimes can be a good source of learning experiences—comparing different tastes, smells, and textures; classifying different kinds of foods; trying new and interesting things; practicing motor skills and math skills by pouring and serving portions.

CHOOSING CHILDREN'S BOOKS

When choosing books for children, it is important to think of the child's stage of development. Children like books for somewhat different reasons at different ages. Thus, you should think about what a child likes, what she does, and how she thinks when you are choosing a book for her. You should take children from three to five to the library and let them choose their own books. Infants first like books for their colors. They are not particularly interested in specific pictures, but they like pictures with bright colors, especially red and yellow.

As children are developing language skills in their second year, they will enjoy books which have simple pictures of things with which they are familiar. Pictures should still be colorful, and they should be realistic and simple. Gradually children begin to be interested not only in pictures of things but also in pictures of activities familiar to them. Their interest then develops from pictures of simple activities to interest in picture sequences which show the progression of a simple activity. For example, the first picture in a sequence might show a girl getting out of bed in nightclothes; a second picture might show the girl brushing her teeth, and on through a whole series of activities.

As children develop language skills, they enjoy the words in books more. Children from one to two may enjoy naming, and having others name, simple pictures in books. Children from two to three enjoy being read to from books with word play, such as rhymes.

By three to four children are developing more advanced language skills and the ability to think in terms of whole situations. Children at this age usually like stories with a simple plot. This includes traditional simple children's stories such as "The Three Bears." The pictures in the book should be clear and identifiable. Children should be able to see easily what's happening in the picture, and the picture should help to explain the story or relate directly to what the text is saying. At age three to four children generally still prefers bright, primary colors in pictures and pictures that have good, sharp contrast. Children at this age may also enjoy acting out short stories.

From four to five most children will enjoy stories with slightly more complicated plots than before. Children at this age also begin to like stories that give information, such as stories about what a post-person does or how bread is made. At this age, in addition to bright colors some children may begin to like softer colors, such as pastels, in pictures. Pictures should still be clear, and they should either directly support and illustrate the story or they should supplement it, giving extra details not contained just in the verbal material.

In addition to borrowing books from the library and buying ones that they really like, children should be helped to make their own. For very young children, homemade books can be illustrated by you or by pictures they choose from magazines. Each page can contain one picture and perhaps the name or a caption written underneath. Pictures of things and people should come first, then, later, pictures of activities. Older preschool children will enjoy making their own books. Some of their books might be on themes—e.g., color books, containing pictures of red things only or yellow things only; a family book; an animal book, and so on. Some of their books might describe a field trip or excursion they took. Some books might be made as a group project and others by individual children.

The words to stories can be dictated to you; they should be written exactly as the child says it. This will help children learn to read. In some experimental preschool education programs children as young as three have been taught to type by color coding their fingers and the typing keys. They have then produced their own newspapers, magazines, and books. Even if you don't have the equipment to do this with children, you can act as a recorder for them so that they can engage in similar projects.

Reading and writing are best taught together if you can find ways of getting past children's problems with the fine motor coordination needed to produce words themselves. You can write for them; they can use a typewriter; you can make up letter sets like scrabble pieces made from pieces of cardboard covered with clear contact paper. But, whatever methods you use, if children can see their own spoken words written down, they'll learn to read better than if they're just reading someone else's words.

PLAY AREAS

There is a new movement in designing playgrounds for children to get away from expensive, conventional, and fairly static, inflexible kinds of equipment and move back to providing children with interesting spaces and flexible, unstructured kinds of materials that children can work with and combine in various ways. Nancy Rudolph describes such a movement:

> Once upon a time, childhood meant a spontaneous adventurous quality of life. There was no such thing as a designated place for playing —as distinct from other places. The first "playgrounds" in this country were basically vacant lots. . . . Since then, play spaces have increased in quantity and changed in quality. While most recent designs are sophisticatedly landscaped and architected and are aesthetically pleasing to the adults who conceive and build them, the playgrounds themselves are often a source of frustration and potential danger for the children who use them. At the same time, the traditional play areas—open fields, empty lots, dense woods, uncluttered seashore, and moderately trafficked streets—are becoming increasingly scarce.
>
> "Workyards" are an alternative to this trend; they can begin to provide some of the freedom to explore and experiment that has been lost in the rush to make playgrounds as demonstrably modern and advanced as the rest of the culture. Workyards are quite simply places to play in—in any way a child elects. The only limitations are set by available space and materials. Here children are the architects, designers, inventors, builders. Quiet spaces for just thinking, dreaming, reading, and writing co-exist with noisy spaces for ball playing, building huts and bridges, and singing and dancing. The children do the planning and the changing. Adult supervisors suggest how things *can* be done, not how they *should* be done.

These play leaders guide children to explore their own possibilities. The leader is there to be a friend, lend a hand, mediate disputes, and fill in where needed." *

The kind of playground described above is being tried out in Europe and the United States.† What is included in a particular "workyard" depends upon available resources, but some of the things that have been found to work are big tires for sandboxes and other uses the children think of; rope ladders for climbing or swinging, and long pieces of rope for other uses; old furniture for storing things and playing; wood and other building materials for children to use in creating structures (some of which they might keep for playing on; many are built, torn down, and rebuilt another way); large telephone wire spools for tables and climbing up and jumping off; the body of an old car as a prop for dramatic play; engines and other mechanical objects to take apart and rebuild; strainers, funnels, pots, pans, and other kitchen utensils for playing in sand and dirt. The play area might also include a garden for the children to plant and harvest and pets for them to care for and feed with the plants they grow. The whole idea behind this kind of playground is a growing recognition that children need to be busy, productive, and constructive in their play. As we said at the beginning of the book, *learning is child's play, and playing is child's work.*

* Nancy Rudolph, "What are playgrounds made of?" *Ms.* magazine, June, 1974, p. 103.
† *Some European Nursery Schools and Playgrounds,* a resource listed in the following section, contains descriptions and pictures of such playgrounds.

RESOURCES

In spite of the length of the resource lists that follow, you should be aware that they are by no means inclusive. The amount of material available in the area of child development and its companion fields is immense, and much of it is very good. It is always difficult to filter and to choose from all that exists; in trying not to omit valuable references we hope that we do not overwhelm you with material, and we hope, equally, that we did not leave out anything that you might have found of use.

We thought it might be helpful to point out to you which of all the books and other materials cited in each section were particularly readable, informative, or good places to begin your investigation of an area. Therefore, we have placed asterisks by those resources we consider outstanding in these characteristics.

SOME SOURCES OF FREE AND INEXPENSIVE LEARNING MATERIALS

A Useful List of Classroom Items That Can Be Scrounged or Purchased. Available for 50 cents from Early Childhood Education Study, Educational Development Center, 55 Chapel Street, Newton, Mass. 02160.

*Beautiful Junk. Office of Child Development, Head Start, Washington, D.C. 20201.

Big Rocky Candy Mountain. Catalog listing of educational resources. Available for $4.00 from: Portola Institute, Inc., 1115 Merrill Street, Menlo Park, Calif. 94025.

Elementary Teachers' Guide to Free Curriculum Materials. Available for $9.75 from Educator's Progress Service, Randolph, Wisc. 53956.

Free and Inexpensive Learning Materials. Available for $1.50 from George Peabody College, Division of Surveys and Field Services, Nashville, Tenn.

*Group for Environmental Education, *The Yellow Pages of Learning Resources.* Available for $1.95 from M.I.T. Press, Cambridge, Mass. 02142.

MONAHAN, R. *Free and Inexpensive Materials for Preschool and Early Childhood.* Available for $2.25 from Lear Sieger, Inc./Fearon Publishers, Belmont, Calif., 1973.

O'HARA, F. *Over 2,000 Free Publications.* 1968. Available for $.95 from New American Library, 1301 Avenue of the Americas, New York, N.Y. 10019.

SALISBURY, G., *Catalog of Free Teaching Materials.* 1970. Available for $2.50 from G. Salisbury, P.O. Box 1075, Ventura, Calif. 93001.

SCHAIN, R. and POLNER, M. *Where to Get and Use Free and Inexpensive*

Teaching Aids. Available for $1.95 from Atherton Press, 70 Fifth Avenue, New York, N.Y. 10011.

Teacher Shop. Catalog available on request from The Teacher Shop, The Children's Museum, The Jamaicaway, Boston, Mass. 02130.

The Scrap Book. A pamphlet describing ways to use household scraps to provide activities for 3–5-year-olds. Available for $2.00 from the Friends of Perry Nursery School, c/o Perry Nursery School, 1541 Washtenaw Avenue, Ann Arbor, Mich. 48104.

THOMAS, J. *Free and Inexpensive Educational Aids.* 1962. Available for $1.75 from Dover Publications, Inc., 80 Varick Street, New York, N.Y. 10014.

WEISINGER, M. *1001 Valuable Things You Can Get Free.* 1968. Available for $.75 from Bantam Books, New York, N.Y.

RESOURCES ON MATERIALS AND EQUIPMENT

*ASCHEIM, C. *Materials for the Open Classroom.* New York: Dell, 1973.

CAMPBELL, E. (ed.) *Small World of Play and Learning.* 1970. Available from the LINC Children's Center, 800 Silver Avenue, Greensboro, N.Y. 27403. Also request a listing of other available publications.

Early Childhood Education: How to Select and Evaluate Materials. Report No. 42. 1972. Available for $4.25 from Educational Products Information Exchange Institute, 386 Park Avenue South, New York, N.Y. 10016.

Equipment and Facilities. 1970. Available from Appalachian Regional Commission, 1666 Connecticut Avenue N.W., Washington, D.C. 20235.

Found Spaces and Equipment for Children's Centers. 1972. Available for $2.00 from Educational Facilities Laboratories, 477 Madison Avenue, New York, N.Y. 10022.

HAASE, R. *Designing the Child Development Center.* 1969. Available for $.40 from Project Head Start, U.S. Government Superintendent of Documents, Washington, D.C.

Patterns for Designing Children's Centers. Available for $2.00 from Educational Facilities Labs, 477 Madison Avenue, New York, N.Y. 10022.

Planning Playgrounds for Day Care. Available for $2.00 from Day Care and Child Development Council of America, Inc., 1012 14th St. N.W., Washington, D.C. 20005

Preschool Equipment for a Multi-Use Center and Children's Things. Booklets giving instructions for making inexpensive indoor and outdoor equipment. Available for $2.00 each, from Stone Mountain, 60 Broad Street, Westfield, Mass. 01085.

Safe Toys for Your Children. Available on request from Children's Bureau, U.S. Department of Health, Education and Welfare, Washington, D.C., 20201. Also request a listing of other publications.

Some European Nursery Schools and Playgrounds. ECF/2, 1970. Available for $3.50 from University of Michigan, Publications Distribution Service, Ann Arbor, Mich.

The Further Adventures of Cardboard Carpentry. Available for $2.50 from the Workshop for Learning Things, Inc., 5 Bridge Street, Watertown, Mass. 02172.

RESOURCES FOR SELECTION OF BOOKS FOR CHILDREN

Bibliography of Books for Children. Available for $1.50 from Association For Childhood Educational International, 3615 Wisconsin Avenue N.W., Washington, D.C. 20016.

*GRIFFIN, L. *Books in Preschool: A Guide to Selecting, Purchasing and Using Children's Books.* 1970. Available for $2.00 from NAEYC, 1629 Twenty-first Street N.W., Washington, D.C. 20009.

*GRIFFIN, L. *Multi-Ethnic Books for Young Children.* 1970. Available for $2.00 from NAEYC, 1629 Twenty-first Street N.W., Washington, D.C. 20009.

HAVILAND, V. (Ed.) *Children's Literature: A Guide to Reference Sources,* 1966. Available for $2.00 from U.S. Government Printing Office, Washington, D.C. 20402.

*LARRICK, N. *A Parent's Guide to Children's Reading.* 1969. New York: Pocket Books.

RIF (Reading Is Fundamental) Guide to Book Selection. Available on request from Reading Is Fundamental, Smithsonian Institution, Arts and Industries Building, Washington, D.C. 20560.

RESOURCES FOR THE SELECTION OF MEDIA MATERIALS

Catalog of Films and Services. Available on request from National Audio-Visual Center, Washington, D.C. 20409.

COOKE, G. *Films in Early Childhood Education,* ED075069. Available for $3.29 from ERIC Document Reproduction Service, LEASCO, Box O, Bethesda, Md. 20014.

Educator's Guide to Free Films. 1972. Available for $10.75 from Educator's Progress Service, Randolph, Wisc. 53956.

Exposure: Media Evaluations. 1972. Available free from Pennsylvania Bureau of Academic and General Education, Department of Education, Box 911, Harrisburg, Pa. 17126.

Films on Early Childhood, 1972. Available on Request from Project Quest, P.O. Box 426, Pitman, N.J. 08071.

Films Suitable for Head Start Child Development Programs. Available from Project Head Start, Office of Child Development, Washington, D.C. 20201.

JOHNSON, H. *Multimedia Materials for Teaching Young Children: A Bibliography of Multi-Cultural Resources.* 1972. Available on request from National Leadership Institute, U-173, University of Connecticut, Storrs, Conn. 06268.

Learning Directory: A Comprehensive Listing of All Instructional Materials.

1972. Available for $99.50 from Westinghouse Learning Corporation, 100 Park Avenue, New York, N.Y. 10017.

CHILD DEVELOPMENT

*AUSUBEL, D. and E. SULLIVAN. *Theory and Problems of Child Development*, 2nd ed., New York: Grune & Stratton, 1970.

BAR-ADON, A. and W. LEOPOLD (eds.) *Child Language*, Englewood Cliffs, N.J.: Prentice-Hall, Inc., 1971.

*BEADLE, M. *A Child's Mind*. New York: Doubleday/Anchor Books, 1971.

*BEARD, R. *An Outline of Piaget's Developmental Psychology for Students and Teachers*. New York: Mentor/New American Library, Inc., 1969.

BERNARD, H. *Child Development and Learning*. Boston: Allyn & Bacon, Inc., 1973.

BIJOU, S. and BAER, D. *Child Development, Vol. I: a Systematic and Empirical Theory*. New York: Appleton-Century-Crofts, 1961.

———— *Child Development, Vol. II: Universal Stages of Infancy*. New York: Appleton-Century-Crofts, 1965.

BLOOM, B. *Stability and Change in Human Characteristics*. New York: John Wiley & Sons, 1964.

*BRACKBILL, Y. (ed.) *Infancy and Early Childhood*. New York: Free Press, The Macmillan Co., 1967.

*BRACKBILL, Y. and G. THOMPSON (eds.) *Behavior in Infancy and Early Childhood*. New York: Free Press, The Macmillan Co., 1967.

*BRAGA, J. and L. BRAGA. *Child Development and Early Childhood Education: A Guide for Parents and Teachers*. Chicago: Office of the Mayor and Model Cities-C.C.U.O., 1973. Available for $5.00 from Model Cities, Public Information Service, 640 N. LaSalle, Chicago 60610.

*———— *Growing With Children*. Englewood Cliffs, N.J.: Prentice-Hall, Inc., 1974.

*BRAZELTON, T. B. *Infants and Mothers*. New York: Dell Publishing Co., Inc., 1969.

BREARLEY, M. and E. HITCHFIELD. *A Teacher's Guide to Reading Piaget*. London: Routledge & Kegan Paul, 1966.

*BRECKENRIDGE, M. and M. MURPHY. *Growth and Development of the Young Child, 8th ed.* Philadelphia: W. B. Saunders Co., 1969.

BRODY, S. *Patterns of Mothering*. New York: International Universities Press, 1956.

BRUNER, J., R. OLIVER, and P. GREENFIELD. *Studies In Cognitive Growth*. New York: John Wiley & Sons, 1966.

CAPLAN, F. (ed). *The First Twelve Months of Life*. New York: Grosset & Dunlap, 1973.

CARMICHAEL, L. *Manual of Child Psychology*, 2nd ed. New York: John Wiley & Sons, 1954.

CAZDEN, C. *Child Language and Education*. New York: Holt, Rinehart & Winston, Inc., 1972.

Child Development. Society for Research in Child Development, 5801 Ellis Ave., Chicago, Ill.

Child Development Abstracts and Bibliography. Society for Research in Child Development, 5801 Ellis Ave., Chicago, Ill.

Children Today. U.S. Government Printing Office, Washington, D.C., 20402.

*CHUKOVSKY, K. *From Two To Five*. Berkeley, Calif.: University of California Press, 1966.

COFFIN, P. *1,2,3,4,5,6. How to Understand and Enjoy the Years That Count*. New York: Collier Books, 1972.

Cognitive Development in Children: Five Monographs of the Society for Research in Child Development. Chicago: University of Chicago Press, 1970.

*COLE, M. and S. SCRIBNER. *Culture and Thought: a Psychological Introduction*. New York: John Wiley & Sons, 1974.

*CRAMER, P. (ed.) *Readings in Developmental Psychology Today*. Del Mar, Calif.: C.R.M. Books, 1970.

ERIKSON, E. *Childhood and Society*, 2nd ed. New York: W. W. Norton Co., 1963.

FERGUSON, C. and D. SLOBIN (eds.) *Studies in Child Language Development*. New York: Holt, Rinehart, & Winston, 1973.

*FRAIBERG, S. *The Magic Years*. New York: Scribner's, 1959.

FRANK, L. *On the Importance of Infancy*. New York: Random House, 1966.

*GERHARDT, L. *Moving and Knowing*. Englewood Cliffs. N.J.: Prentice-Hall, Inc., 1973.

GESELL, A. *The First Five Years of Life*. New York: Harper & Row, 1940.

*——— and F. ILG. *Infant and Child in the Culture of Today*. New York: Harper & Row, 1943.

——— and F. ILG. *The Child From Five to Ten*, New York: Harper & Bros., 1946.

*GINSBURG, H. and S. OPPER. *Piaget's Theory of Intellectual Development: An Introduction*. Englewood Cliffs, N.J.: Prentice-Hall, 1969.

GORDON, I. (ed.) *Readings in Research in Developmental Psychology*. Glenview, Ill.: Scott, Foresman & Co., 1971.

GORDON, I. *Human Development: From Birth Thru Adolescence*, 2nd ed. New York: Harper and Row, 1969.

GOULD, R. *Child Studies Through Fantasy: Cognitive-Affective Patterns in Development*. New York: Quadrangle Books, 1972.

HELLMUTH, J. (ed.) *Cognitive Studies*, Vols. I, II. New York: Brunner/Mazel, Inc., 1970, 1971.

———— (ed.). *Exceptional Infant: the Normal Infant.* New York: Brunner/ Mazel, Inc., 1967.

HOFFMAN, M. and L. HOFFMAN (eds.) *Review of Child Development Research, Vols. 1 & 2.* New York: Russell Sage Foundation, 1964, 1966.

How Children Grow. U.S. Dept. of Health, Education, and Welfare, 1972. U.S. Government Printing Office, Washington, D.C. 20402.

HOWARD, N. *Education for Parents of Preschoolers: An Abstract Bibliography.* Publications Office, ERIC, University of Illinois, 805 W. Pennsylvania Ave., Urbana, Ill. 61801.

HURLOCK, E. *Child Development, 4th ed.* New York: McGraw-Hill, Inc., 1964.

———— *Child Growth and Development.* New York: McGraw-Hill, Inc., 1970.

HYMES, J. *The Child Under Six.* Englewood Cliffs, N.J.: Prentice-Hall, Inc., 1963.

ILG, F. and L. AMES. *Child Behavior.* New York: Harper & Row, Publishers, 1955.

*JERSILD, A. *Child Psychology, 6th ed.* Englewood Cliffs, N.J.: Prentice-Hall, Inc., 1968.

KELLOGG, R. *Analysing Children's Art.* (Palo Alto, California: National Press Book, 1969.)

*LANDAU, E., S. EPSTEIN, and A. STONE (eds.) *Child Development Through Literature.* Englewood Cliffs, N.J.: Prentice-Hall, Inc., 1972.

LANDRETH, C. *Early Childhood, 3rd ed.* New York: Alfred A. Knopf, 1973.

LAVATELLI, C. and STENDLER, F. (eds.) *Readings in Child Behavior and Development, 3rd ed.* New York: Harcourt Brace Jovanovich, 1972.

McCANDLESS, B. and E. EVANS. *Children and Youth: Psychosocial Development.* Hinsdale, Ill.: Dryden Press, 1973.

McGRAW, M. *Growth: A Study of Johnny and Jimmy,* New York: Appleton-Century-Crofts, 1935.

*MONTESSORI, M. *The Absorbent Mind, 2nd ed.,* New York: Holt, Rinehart, & Winston (Dell Paperback), 1967.

MURPHY, L. *Personality in Young Children, Vols. 1 & 2.* New York: Basic Books, 1956.

*———— *The Widening World of Childhood.* New York: Basic Books, 1962.

*———— and E. LEEPER. *Caring for Children, Vols. 1–5.* Washington, D.C.: U.S. Department of Health, Education, and Welfare, 1970. Available for $.40 each from the Superintendent of Documents, U.S. Government Printing Office, Washington, D.C. 20402.

MUSSEN, P. (ed.) *Carmichael's Manual of Child Psychology, Vols. I and II, 3rd ed.* New York: John Wiley & Sons, 1970.

*———— *The Psychological Development of the Child, 2nd ed.* Englewood Cliffs, N.J.: Prentice-Hall, Inc., 1973.

————, J. CONGER, and J. KAGAN. *Child Development and Personality, 2nd ed.* New York: Harper & Row, 1963.

PHILLIPS, J. *The Origins of Intellect: Piaget's Theory*. San Francisco: W. H. Freeman and Co., 1969.

PIAGET, J. *The Child's Conception of the World*. London: Routledge & Kegan Paul, 1951.

*———— and B. INHELDER. *The Psychology of the Child*. New York: Basic Books, Inc., 1969.

PIAGET, J., and B. INHELDER. *Memory and Intelligence*. New York: Basic Books, 1973.

Report of the Interagency Panel on Early Childhood Research and Development. Available on request. Washington, D.C.: Social Research Group, George Washington University, 2401 Virginia Ave., N.W., 1972.

*ROE, R. (ed.) *Developmental Psychology Today*. Del Mar, Calif.: C.R.M. Books, 1971.

ROSENBLITH, J., W. ALLINSMITH, and J. WILLIAMS (eds.) *The Causes of Behavior, 3rd ed.* Boston: Allyn & Bacon, Inc., 1972.

SHEA, M. *Social Development and Behavior: An Abstract Bibliography*. Publications Office, ERIC, University of Illinois, 805 W. Pennsylvania Ave., Urbana, Ill. 61801.

SHUEY, R., E. WOODS, and E. YOUNG. *Learning about Children*, Rev. ed. Philadelphia: J. B. Lippincott Company, 1964.

SIGEL, I. and F. HOOPER. *Logical Thinking in Children: Research Based on Piaget's Theory*. New York: Holt, Rinehart, & Winston, 1968.

*SMART, M. and R. SMART. *Children, 2nd ed.* New York: The Macmillan Co., 1972.

*SMITH, L. *Encyclopedia of Baby and Child Care*. Englewood Cliffs, N.J.: Prentice-Hall, Inc., 1972.

*SPOCK, B. *Baby and Child Care*. New York: Pocket Books, 1968.

*STONE, L. and J. CHURCH. *Childhood and Adolescence*, 3rd ed. New York: Random House, 1974.

TALBOT, T. (ed.) *The World of the Child*. New York: Anchor/Doubleday, 1968.

Today's Health. American Medical Association, 535 N. Dearborn St., Chicago, Ill. 60610.

VYGOTSKY, L. *Thought and Language*. Cambridge, Mass.: M.I.T. Press, 1962.

Young Children. National Association for the Education of Young Children (NAEYC), 1629 21st St., N.W., Washington, D.C. 20009.

**Your Baby's First Year*. Washington, D.C.: U.S. Government Printing Office, 1970.

**Your Child From 1 to 3*. Washington, D.C.: U.S. Government Printing Office, 1971.

**Your Child From 1 to 6*. Washington, D.C.: U.S. Government Printing Office, 1970.

Your Child From 3 to 4. Washington, D.C.: U.S. Government Printing Office, 1970.

*WEINER, I. and ELKIND, D. *Child Development: A Core Approach*. New York: John Wiley & Sons, 1971.

EARLY CHILDHOOD EDUCATION

This section contains books that (1) describe and compare early childhood education programs, (2) explain the kinds of materials and activities that are useful for young children, or (3) discuss parent and teacher roles in early childhood education.

Administrator's Handbook for Kindergarten. Available on request from Pennsylvania Dept. of Education, Box 911, Harrisburg, Pa. 17126. Also available without fee: *Kindergarten Guide*.

An Annotated Bibliography on Early Childhood. New York: Educational Facilities Laboratories, Inc., 477 Madison Avenue, New York, N.Y. 10022.

*ANDERSON, R., and SHANE, H. *As the Twig Is Bent: Readings in Early Childhood Education*. Boston: Houghton Mifflin Co., 1971.

*Appalachian Regional Commission, *Programs for Young Children: Part I—Education and Day Care, Part II—Nutrition, Part III—Health, Part IV—Equipment and Facilities, Part V—Funding for Young Children*. Washington, D.C.: Appalachian Regional Commission, 1666 Connecticut Avenue N.W., Washington, D.C. 20235, 1970.

ASHTON-WARNER, S. *Teacher*. New York: Simon & Schuster, 1963.

Association for Childhood Education International. *A Lap to Sit On . . . And Much More*. ACIE, 3615 Wisconsin Avenue N.W., Washington, D.C. 20016 ($2.00), 1972.

AUERBACH, A. *Parents Learn Through Discussion: Principles and Practices of Parent Group Education*. New York: John Wiley & Sons, 1968.

BAILARD, V. and STRANG, R. *Parent-Teacher Conferences*. New York: McGraw-Hill, 1964.

BALLESTEROS, D. *Understanding the Bi-Cultural Child*. Available on request from Leadership Institute, Box U-173, University of Connecticut, Storrs, Connecticut 06268, 1972.

BATEMAN, B. *Temporal Learning*. San Rafael, Calif.: Dimensions Publishing Co., 1969.

BEREITER, C. *Arithmetic*. San Rafael, Calif.: Dimensions Publishing Co., 1969.

BERNBAUM, M. (ed.) *Curriculum Guides at the Kindergarten and Preschool Levels: An Abstract Bibliography*. 1971 Available from Publications Office, ERIC, University of Illinois, 805 W. Pennsylvania Ave., Urbana, Ill. 61801.

———— *Early Language Development: An Annotated Bibliography*. 1971. Available from Publications Office, ERIC, University of Illinois, 805 W. Pennsylvania Ave., Urbana, Ill. 61801.

—— *Number and Concept Development: An Annotated Bibliography.* 1971. Available from Publications Office, ERIC, University of Illinois, 805 W. Pennsylvania Ave., Urbana, Ill. 61801.

BIBER, B., E. SHAPIRO, and B. WICKENS. *Promoting Cognitive Growth: A Developmental-Interaction Point of View.* 1971. Available for $2.50 from National Assn. for the Education of Young Children, 1834 Connecticut Avenue N.W., Washington, D.C.

BRAUN, S. and E. EDWARDS (eds.) *History and Theory of Early Childhood Education.* Belmont, Calif.: Wadsworth Publishing Co., 1972.

BRUNER, J. *Toward a Theory of Instruction.* Cambridge, Mass.: Harvard University Press, 1966.

*—— (ed.). *Learning About Learning.* Washington, D.C.: U.S. Government Printing Office, 1966.

—— *The Process of Education.* New York: Vintage Books/Random House, Inc., 1960.

BUKTENICA, N. *Visual Learning.* San Rafael: Dimensions Publishing Co., 1968.

*BUTLER, A. (ed.) Current Research in Early Childhood Education. 1970. Available for $5.00 from EKNE/National Education Assn., 1201 Sixteenth Street N.W., Washington, D.C. 20036.

*CANEY, S. *Toy Book.* New York: Workman Publishing Company, 1972.

CASS, J. *Helping Children Grow through Play.* New York: Schocken, 1973.

CHALL, J. *Learning to Read: The Great Debate.* New York: McGraw-Hill, 1967.

CHESS, S. A. THOMAS, and H. BIRCH. *Your Child Is a Person.* New York: Parallax Publishing Company, Inc., 1965.

Childhood Education. Association for Childhood Education International, 3615 Wisconsin Ave., N.W., Washington, D.C. 20016.

COLE, M. and J. BRUNER. "Cultural Differences and Inferences About Psychological Processes," *American Psychologist* 26, No. 10, October, 1971.

COLES, R. and M. PIERS. *Wages of Neglect.* Chicago: Quadrangle Books, 1969.

Continuing Education Publications. *Improving Motor-Perceptual Skills.* Available for $3.00 from DCE Books, Waldo 100, Oregon State University, Corvallis, Oregon, 1971.

*CROFT, D. and R. HESS. *An Activities Handbook for Teachers of Young Children.* New York: Houghton Mifflin, 1972.

Day Care and Early Education. Behavioral Publications, 2852 Broadway, New York, N.Y. 10025.

DELLA-PIANA, G. *How to Talk to Children.* Available for $2.00 from Bureau of Educational Research, University of Utah, Salt Lake City.

DENZIN, N. (ed.) *Children and Their Caretakers.* New Brunswick, N.J.: Transaction Books, 1973.

DINKMEYER, D. and R. DREIKURS. *Encouraging Children to Learn.* Englewood Cliffs, N.J.: Prentice-Hall, Inc., 1963.

Directory of Resources on Early Childhood Education. 1971. Available for $.75 from DCCDA, 1012 14th St. N.W., Washington, D.C. 20005.

DODSON, F. *How to Parent.* New York: New American Library, 1970.

DURKIN, D. *Teaching Young Children to Read.* Boston: Allyn & Bacon, 1972.

Early Childhood: A Publications Packet. Available for $3.00 from ACEI/NAESP Publications, 1201 Sixteenth Street N.W., Washington, D.C. 1972.

ERIC/ECE Newsletter. Publications Office, College of Education/IREC, University of Illinois, 805 W. Pennsylvania Ave., Urbana, Ill. 61801.

*EVANS, E. *Current Influences in Early Childhood Education.* New York: Holt, Rinehart & Winston, 1971.

*FARNHAM-DIGGORY, S. *Cognitive Processes in Education: A Psychological Preparation for Teaching and Curriculum Development.* New York: Harper & Row, 1972.

*FROST, J. *Early Childhood Education Rediscovered.* New York: Holt, Rinehart & Winston, 1968.

FURTH, H. *Piaget for Teachers.* Englewood Cliffs, N.J.: Prentice-Hall, Inc., 1970.

*GORDON, I. *Baby Learning Through Baby Play.* New York: St. Martin's Press, 1970.

———— *Children's Views of Themselves.* Available for $2.00 from Association for Childhood Education International, 3615 Wisconsin Avenue N.W., Washington, D.C. 20016.

———— (ed.) *Early Childhood Education: Part II, 71st Yearbook of The National Society for the Study of Education.* Chicago: University of Chicago Press, 1972.

*————, B. GUINAGH, and R. JESTER. *Child Learning through Child Play.* New York: St. Martin's Press, 1972.

GREER, M. and B. RUBINSTEIN. *Will the Real Teacher Please Stand Up?* Pacific Palisades, Calif.: Goodyear Publishing Company, Inc., 1972.

HARING, N. *Attending and Responding.* San Rafael, Calif.: Dimensions Publishing Co., 1968.

*HARTLEY, R. and GOLDENSON, R. *The Complete Book of Children's Play.* New York: Thomas Crowell Co. (Doubleday/Apollo Books) 1963.

HARTUP, W. (ed.). *The Young Child: Reviews of Research, Vol. II.* 1972. Available for $5.75 from NAEYC, 1629 Twenty-first Street N.W., Washington, D.C. 20009.

HASKELL, L. (ed.) *British Primary Education: An Annotated Bibliography.* 1971. Available from Publications Office, ERIC, University of Illinois, 805 W. Pennsylvania Ave., Urbana, Ill. 61801.

HERRON, R. and B. SUTTON-SMITH. *Child's Play.* New York: John Wiley & Sons, Inc., 1971.

HESS, R. and R. BEAR (eds.) *Early Education: Current Theory, Research and Practice*. Chicago: Aldine Publishing Co., 1968.

*HESS, R. and D. CROFT. *Teachers of Young Children*, Boston: Houghton Mifflin, 1972.

HOPKINS, T. and M. JESSEN. A Kindergarten Curriculum Guide for Indian Children: A Bilingual—Bicultural Approach. (Dallas, Texas: Jarvis Press, 1970.)

HOWARD, N. *Discipline and Behavior: An Abstract Bibliography*. Publications Office, ERIC, University of Illinois, 805 W. Pennsylvania Ave., Urbana, Ill. 61801.

HOWARD, N. (ed.) Self-Concept: An Abstract Bibliography. Publications Office, ERIC, University of Illinois, 805 Pennsylvania Ave., Urbana, Ill. 61801.

HUGHES, M. *Community Components in Teacher Education*. 1972. Available on request from National Leadership Institute, Box U-173, University of Connecticut, Storrs, Conn. 06268.

HYMES, J. *Teaching The Child Under Six*. Columbus, Ohio: Charles Merrill Publishing Co., 1968.

INGLIS, R. *A Time To Learn: A Guide for Parents to the New Theories in Early Childhood Education*. New York: Dial Press, 1973.

JOHNSON, A. *Preschool Programs: An Annotated Bibliography*. 1971. Available from Publications Office, ERIC, University of Illinois, 805 W. Pennsylvania Ave., Urbana, Ill. 61801.

JONES, D. *Teaching Children to Read*. New York: Harper & Row, 1971.

KAPLAN, F. and T. KAPLAN. *The Power of Play*. New York: Anchor/Doubleday Books, 1973.

KAPLAN, S., J. KAPLAN, S. MADSEN, and B. TAYLOR. *Change for Children*. Pacific Palisades, Calif.: Goodyear Publishing Company, Inc., 1973.

KARNES, M. *Structured Cognitive Approach for Educating Young Children*. 1972. Available on request from National Leadership Institute, Box U-173, University of Connecticut, Storrs, Conn. 06268.

KEISTER, M. *"The Good Life" For Infants and Toddlers*. 1970. Available for $1.50 from DCCDCA, 1012 14th St. N.W., Washington, D.C. 20005.

Kindergarten Bilingual Resources Handbook. 1971. Available for $1.50 from DCCDCA, 1012 14th St. N.W., Washington, D.C. 20005.

*KING, E. *Educating Young Children . . . Sociological Interpretations*. Dubuque, Iowa: Wm. C. Brown Co., 1973.

LAVATELLI, C. *Piaget's Theory Applied to an Early Childhood Curriculum*. A Center for Media Development Inc. Book. Boston: American Science and Engineering, Inc., 1970.

Learning. 1255 Portland Place, Boulder, Colorado 80302.

LEEPER, S. R., DALES, D. SHIPPER, and R. WITHERSPOON. *Good Schools for Young Children: A Guide for Working With 3, 4 and 5 Year Old Children*. New York: The Macmillan Co., 1968.

LEIPMANN, L. *Your Child's Sensory World*. New York: Dial Press, 1973.

*LEITMAN, A. and E. CHURCHILL, "A Classroom for Young Children: Approximation No. 1," mimeographed paper. Newton, Mass.: Educational Services Incorporated, Elementary Science Study, 1966.

LESHAN, E. On "How Do Your Children Grow?" New York: Warner Paperback Library Edition, 1972.

LEWIS, A. *Preschool Breakthrough: What Works In Early Childhood Education.* 1970. Available for $4.00 from DCCDCA, 1012 14th St. N.W., Washington, D.C. 20005.

LIEBERT, R., J. NEALE, and E. DAVIDSON. *The Early Window: Effects of Television on Children and Youth.* New York: Pergamon Press, 1973.

LIGHT, N. (ed.) *Early Childhood Education: Part II, 46th Yearbook of the National Society for the Study of Education,* Chicago: University of Chicago Press, 1947.

*LORTON, M. *Workjobs: Activity-Centered Learning for Early Childhood Education.* Menlo Park, Calif.: Addison-Wesley Publishing Company, 1972.

Manual for Communities: Student Volunteers. Washington, D.C.: National Student Volunteer Program, ACTION, 806 Connecticut Avenue N.W. 20525.

Manual for Students: Volunteering. Washington, D.C.: National Student Volunteer Program, ACTION, 806 Connecticut Avenue N.W. 20525.

MAYNARD, F., *Guiding Your Child to a More Creative Life.* New York: Doubleday & Co., 1973.

MONTESSORI, M. *Dr. Montessori's Own Method.* Cambridge, Mass.: Robert Bentley Co., 1965.

NEILL, A. S. *"Neill! Neill! Orange Peel!"* New York: Hart Publishing Company, Inc., 1972.

NEWMAN, S. *Guidelines to Parent-Teacher Cooperation in Early Childhood Education.* New York: Book-Lab, Inc., 1971.

*NIMNICHT, G., McAFEE, O. and MEIER, JR. *The New Nursery School,* New York: General Learning Corp., 1969.

O'DONNELL, P. *Motor and Haptic Learning.* San Rafael, Calif.: Dimensions Publishing Co., 1969.

**Open Home.* Media Projects, Inc. 201 E. 16th St. New York, N.Y. 10003.

Parents: Active Partners in Education. 1971. Available for $1.00 from EKNE/ National Education Assn., 1201 Sixteenth Street N.W., Washington, D.C., 20036.

Parents and Teachers Together: A Training Manual for Parent Involvement in Head Start Centers. 1970. Available for $2.50 from DCCDCA, 1012 14th St. N.S., Washington, D.C. 20005.

PARKER, R. (ed.) *The Preschool In Action: Exploring Early Childhood Programs.* Boston: Allyn & Bacon, 1972.

PAUL, A. and P. HAWKINS. *Kids Cooking.* New York: Doubleday & Co., 1971.

PERRYMAN, L. (ed.) *Montessori in Perspective.* 1968. Available for $2.00 from NAEYC, 1629 Twenty-first Street N.W., Washington, D.C. 20009.

PETERSON, M. *An Alternative Approach to Special Education Classes.* 1971. Available on request from National Leadership Institute, Box U-173, University of Connecticut, Storrs, Conn. 06268.

PINES, M. *Revolution in Learning: The Years From Birth to Six.* New York: Harper & Row, 1968.

Portable Workshop for Preschool Teachers, Nos. 1–10. New York: Doubleday & Co., 1966.

*Project Head Start. Booklets and Pamphlet Series: Available from Project Head Start, Office of Child Development, U.S. Department of Health, Education, and Welfare. Washington, D.C. 20201.

    1a. *Recruitment and Selection for a Child Development Center,* 1969.
    1b. *Evaluating Performance and Progress,* 1969.
    1c. *Career Planning and Progression,* 1969.
    1d. *Training Courses and Methods,* 1969.
    2. *Health Services,* 1967.
    3. *Nutrition,* 1971.
    3a. *Food Buying Guide and Recipes,* 1971.
    3b. *Nutrition Instructors Guide,* 1969.
    3c. *Leader's Handbook* (Nutrition), 1969.
    3d. *Nutrition—Staff Training Problems,* 1971.
    3e. *Nutrition Film "Jenny Is a Good Thing.",* 1969.
    4. *Daily Program I,* 1969.
    5. *Daily Program II,* 1969.
    6. *Parents Are Needed,* 1967.
    9. *Equipment and Supplies,* 1969.
    10. *Parent Involvement,* 1969.
    11. *Daily Program, III,* 1967.
    12. *Psychologist for a Child Development Center,* 1971.
    13. *Speech, Language, and Hearing Program,* 1973.

Parent Handbook Pamphlet Series

    1. *Your Part as a Parent*
    2. *Your Family*
    3. *Americans All*
    4. *Making It Easier to Keep Healthy at Home*
    5. *Your Growing Child*
    6. *Dealing With Family Upsets*
    7. *Your Child's Health*
    All About Me (Child's book)

PULASKI, M. *Understanding Piaget.* New York: Harper & Row, 1971.

*RASMUSSEN, M. (ed.) *Creating with Materials for Work and Play,* ACEI Bulletin No. 5, Washington, D.C.: ACEI, 1957. Available for 75¢ from ACEI, 3615 Wisconsin Avenue N.W., Washington, 20016.

*RATHS, L., M. HARMIN, and S. SIMON, *Values and Teaching.* Columbus, Ohio: Charles Merrill Books, 1966.

*READ, K. *The Nursery School: A Human Relations Laboratory* (5th ed.). Philadelphia: W. B. Saunders Co., 1971.

Resources for Creative Preschool Teaching. Available for $12.50 from KAEYC Book Acct., c/o Mrs. H. E. Hamilton, 6041 Sunrise Road, Lincoln, Neb. 68510.

ROBISON, H. and B. SPODEK. *New Directions in The Kindergarten.* New York: Teachers College Press, Columbia University, 1965.

ROHNER, W. *Cognitive and Perceptual Development in Children.* 1971. Available on request from National Leadership Institute, Box U-173, University of Connecticut, Storrs, Conn. 06268.

*SALK, L. *What Every Child Would Like His Parents to Know.* New York: Warner Paperback Library Edition, 1972.

SALK, L. and R. KRAMER. *How to Raise a Human Being.* New York: Warner Paperback Library Edition, 1969.

SCHWEBEL, M. and J. RATH (eds.) *Piaget in the Classroom.* New York: Basic Books, 1973.

SHAFTEL, F. and SHAFTEL, G. *Role Playing for Social Value.* Englewood Cliffs, N.J.: Prentice-Hall, 1967.

SMILANSKY, S. *The Effects of Socio-Dramatic Play on Disadvantaged Pre-School Children.* New York: John Wiley & Sons, 1968.

SPODEK, B. *Teaching in the Early Years.* Englewood Cliffs, N.J.: Prentice-Hall, 1972.

*STAKELON, A. *Early Childhood Newsletters: A Selected Guide.* Publications Office, ERIC, University of Illinois, 805 W. Pennsylvania Ave., Urbana, Ill. 61801.

STALLINGS, C. *Gifted Disadvantaged Children.* 1972. Available on request from National Leadership Institute, U-173, University of Connecticut, Storrs, Conn. 06268.

*STANT, M. *The Young Child: His Activities and Materials.* Englewood Cliffs, N.J.: Prentice-Hall, Inc., 1972.

STRANG, R. *Reading.* San Rafael, Calif.: Dimensions Publishing Co., 1969.

TORRENCE, E. *Creativity.* San Rafael, Calif.: Dimensions Publishing Co., 1969.

VANCE, B. *Teaching the Prekindergarten Child: Instructional Design and Curriculum.* Monterey, Calif.: Brooks/Cole Publishing Company, 1973.

*WEBER, L. *English Infant Schools and Informal Education.* Englewood Cliffs, N.J.: Prentice-Hall, Inc., 1971.

WOOD, N. *Verbal Learning.* San Rafael, Calif.: Dimensions Publishing Co., 1969.

YAMAMOTO, K. (ed.) *The Child and His Image: Self-Concept in the Early Years.* Boston: Houghton Mifflin, 1972.

ZIGMOND, N. and R. CICCI. *Auditory Learning.* San Rafael, Calif.: Dimensions Publishing Co., 1968.

DAY CARE

There are many publications about Day Care. This list includes references which should be primary resources to persons working in the field. They cover a range of concerns, including the impact of different administrative structures and educational programs, the purposes of day care and different ways to accomplish those purposes, and facilities for day care centers.

A Handbook for Family Day Care Workers. 1972. Available for $2.50 from Information Office DARCEE, George Peabody College, Nashville, Tenn. 37203.

BEKER, J. (ed.) *Critical Incidents in Child Care: A Case Book.* New York: Behavioral Publications, Inc., 1972.

*BLAKE, M. (ed.) National Federation of Settlements and Neighborhood Centers, *Day Care Aides: A Guide for In-Service Training,* 2nd ed. Washington, D.C.: Day Care and Child Development Council of America, 1972.

BREITBART, V. *The Day Care Book: the Why, What, and How of Community Day Care.* New York: Alfred A. Knopf, 1974.

Child Care Quarterly. Behavioral Publications. 2852 Broadway. New York, N.Y. 10025.

Child Care Reprints—II. 1972. Available for $1.50 from DCCDCA, 1012 14th St. N.W., Washington, D.C. 20005.

Child Development/Day Care Resources Project. 1971. Available for $3.29 from LEASCO Information Products, Inc., ERIC Document Reproduction Service, P.O. Box Draware O, Bethesda, Md. 20014.

"Day Care" Children Today. Available for $.35 from U.S. Government Printing Office, Washington, D.C. Ask for Vol. I. No. 1, 1972.

Day Care: Proceedings from the Governor's Working Conference on Day Care. Available free from Office of Community Relations, Department of Children and Family Services, 524 South 2nd Street, Springfield, Ill. 62706.

Day Care: Serving School Age Children. 1972. Available for $.70 from U.S. Government Printing Office, Washington, D.C.

EVANS, B. and G. SAIA. *Day Care for Infants.* Boston: Beacon Press, 1972.

EVANS, B., B. SHUB, and M. WEINSTEIN. *Day Care: How to Plan, Develop, and Operate a Day Care Center.* Boston: Beacon Press, 1971.

Federal Panel on Early Childhood, Good References on Day Care. 1969. Available on request from U.S. Department of Health, Education and Welfare, SRS/Children's Bureau, Washington, D.C.

*GROTBERG, E. (ed.) *Day Care: Resources for Decisions.* 1971. Available for $4.50 from DCCDCA, 1012 14th St. N.W., Washington, D.C. 20005.

Guide for Establishing and Operating Day Care Centers for Young Children. 1966. Available for $3.00 from DCCDCA, 1012 14th St. N.W., Washington, D.C. 20005.

HAITH, M. *Day Care and Intervention Programs for Infants Under Two Years of Age.* Cambridge: Harvard University Press, 1972.

HOWARD, N. (ed.) *Day Care: An Abstract Bibliography* (Supplement #2). Available for $1.50 from Publications Office, ERIC, University of Illinois, 805 W. Pennsylvania Ave., Urbana, Ill. 61801.

I'm Not Just a Babysitter. 1971. Available for $4.00 from Community Family Day Care Project, Pacific Oaks College, 714 West California Boulevard, Pasadena, Calif.

*Office of Child Development, *Day Care Handbooks 1–8.* 1971. Available from Office of Child Development, U.S. Department of Health, Education and Welfare, Washington, D.C. 20201.

PARKER, R. and J. KNITZER. *Day Care and Preschool Services: Trends and Issues.* Atlanta, Ga.: Avatar Press, 1972.

PRESCOTT, E. and JONES, E. *Day Care As a Child-Rearing Environment.* 1972. Available for $1.75 from NAEYC, 1629 Twenty-first Street N.W., Washington, D.C.

Report on the Joint Commission on Mental Health of Children. *The Mental Health of Children: Services, Research, and Manpower.* New York: Harper & Row, 1973.

Resources for Day Care. Available from Day Care and Child Development Council of America, 1012 14th St. N.W., Washington, D.C. 20005.

ROBY, P. (ed.). *Child Care—Who Cares?* New York: Basic Books, Inc., 1973.

RUOPP, et. al. *A Day Care Guide for Administrators, Teachers, and Others.* Cambridge: The MIT Press, 1973.

Some Sensible and Outrageous Ideas for the Future. ECF/3, Early Childhood Facilities, Architectural Research Laboratories. Ann Arbor: The University of Michigan, 1972.

*SWENSON, J. *Alternatives in Quality Child Care: A Guide for Thinking and Planning.* 1972. Washington, D.C.: Day Care and Child Development Council of America, 1012 14th St. N.W., Washington, D.C., 20005.

Voice for Children. Monthly newsletter of the Day Care and Child Development Council of America, 1012 14th St. N.W., Washington, D.C. 20005.

LEARNING PROBLEMS

The following are a few good references which will give you some solid information on the kinds of learning problems that children may have, the reasons for them, and techniques for dealing with them. Whenever there is suspicion of a learning problem, it should be evaluated at an appropriate agency. But there often are fewer places for dealing with the problems identified than are needed. With guidance from someone in special education and understanding of the nature of different kinds of learning problems, parents and teachers of young children can be helpful in dealing effectively with many of the problems.

Note: Information regarding assistance on questions and location of regional resources for all exceptional children or children suspected of learning problems is available from:

Closer Look
Box 1492
Washington, D.C.

* *A Selected Guide to Public Agencies Concerned with Exceptional Children, A Selected Guide to Government Agencies Concerned with Exceptional Children,* and *A Very Special Child.* All free from the CEC Information Center on Exceptional Children, 1920 Association Drive, Reston, Va. 22091.

ALLEN, R., A. CORTAZZO, R. TOISTER. *Theories of Cognitive Development: Implications for the Mentally Retarded.* Miami, Fla.: University of Miami Press, 1973.

BANGS, T. *Language and Learning Disorders of the Pre-Academic Child.* New York: Appleton-Century-Crofts, 1968.

BATEMAN, B. *Learning Disorders: Reading.* Seattle, Wash.: Special Child Publications, 1971.

BERRY, M. *Language Disorders of Children: Bases and Diagnosis.* New York: Appleton-Century-Crofts, 1969.

BUIST, C. and J. SCHULMAN. *Toys and Games for Educationally Handicapped Children.* Springfield, Ill.: C. C. Thomas, 1969.

DE HIRSCH, K., J. JANSKY, and W. LANGFORD. *Predicting Reading Failure.* New York: Harper & Row, 1966.

Exceptional Children. The Council for Exceptional Children. (CEC), 1920 Association Drive, Reston, Virginia 22091.

Exceptional Parent. P.O. Box 101, Back Bay Station, Boston, Mass. 02117.

GESELL, A. and C. AMATRUDA. *Developmental Diagnosis* (2nd ed.) New York: Paul B. Hoeber Publishing, 1954.

*HAUSSERMAN, E. *Developmental Potential of Preschool Children.* New York: Grune & Stratton, 1958.

HODGDEN, L. et al. *School Before Six: A Diagnostic Approach.* 1970. Available from New York State College of Human Ecology, Department of Human Development and Family Studies. MVR-Cornell Univ., Ithaca, N.Y. 14850.

*JOHNSON, D. and MYKLEBUST, H. *Learning Disabilities: Educational Principles and Practices.* New York: Grune & Stratton, 1967.

JOHNSON, W., DARLEY, F. and SPRIETERSBACH, D. *Diagnostic Methods In Speech Pathology.* New York: Harper & Row, 1963.

*KIRK, S. *Educating Exceptional Children* (2nd ed.) Boston: Houghton Mifflin Co., 1972.

Learning Disabilities Due to Minimal Brain Dysfunction. 1971. Available on request from National Institute of Neurological Diseases, National Institute of Health, Bethesda, Md.

*LERNER, J. *Children With Learning Disabilities.* New York: The Macmillan Co., 1971.

McLEAN, J., D. YODER, and R. SCHIEFELBUSCH (eds.) *Language Intervention with the Retarded: Developing Strategies.* Baltimore, Md.: University Park Press, 1974.

MYKLEBUST, H. *Auditory Disorders in Children.* New York: Grune & Stratton, 1954.

SATZ, P. and J. Ross (eds.) *The Disabled Learner: Early Detection and Intervention.* New York: International Scholarly Book Services, 1973.

SCHAIN, R. *Neurology of Childhood Learning Disorders.* Baltimore, Md.: Williams & Wilkins, 1972.

Serving Children with Special Needs. Available for $.75 (stack #1791-0176) from the Superintendent of Documents, U.S. Government Printing Office, Washington, D.C. 20402.

Teaching Exceptional Children, CEC, 1920 Association Drive, Reston, Va. 22091.

*TILTON, J., D. LISKA, and J. BOURLAND (eds.) *Guide to Developmental Training.* Lafayette, Indiana: Wabash Center for the Mentally Retarded, Inc., 1972.

TESTING AND EVALUATION

This section may not be useful to everyone who has read this book. But those working in educational and child-care situations in which they must demonstrate learning gains made as a result of the educational program may find the books listed here helpful in selecting tests and test procedures which really measure what they have been trying to do and which also help to make the program better suited to the children's needs by showing what their strong and weak areas are.

Note: Information, pamphlets, and publications regarding the *Head Start Test Collection* and other related information is available on request from Educational Testing Service, Princeton, N.J. 08540.

ALMY, M. and R. CUNNINGHAM. *Ways of Studying Children.* New York: Teachers College Press, Columbia University, 1959.

ANASTASI, A. *Psychological Testing* (3rd ed.) New York: The Macmillan Co., 1968.

*BLOOM, B., HASTINGS, J., and MADEUS, D. *Handbook of Formative and Summative Evaluation of Student Learning.* New York: McGraw-Hill, 1971.

BRAGA, L. *Development and Evaluation of a Test Analysis System for Describing Intra-Child Variables in Learning Disabled Preschool Children.* Ann Arbor, Mich.: University Microfilms, 1972.

BRAZZIEL, W. *School Testing and Minority Children.* 1971. Available on request from National Leadership Institute, U-173, University of Connecticut, Storrs, Conn. 06268.

* BRUNER, J. *Guidelines for Testing Minority Group Children.* 1972. Available from National Leadership Institute, Box U-173, University of Connecticut, Storrs, Conn. 06268.

COHEN, D. and V. STERN. *Observing and Recording the Behavior of Young Children.* New York: Teachers College Press, Columbia University, 1958.

CRONBACH, L. *Essentials of Psychological Testing* (3rd ed.) New York: Harper & Row, 1970.

DYER, H. *Testing Little Children: Some Old Problems in New Settings.* 1971. Available on request from National Leadership Institute, U-173, University of Connecticut, Storrs, Conn. 06268.

*HOEPFNER, R., NUMNEDAL, C., and STERN, C. *Preschool Kindergarten Test Evaluations.* 1971. Available for $5.00 from Center for the Study of Education/Early Childhood Research Center, University of California, Los Angeles, Calif.

JOHNSON, O. and BOMMARITO, J. (eds.) *Tests and Measurements in Child Development.* San Francisco: Jossey-Bass, Inc., 1971.

KERLINGER, F. *Foundations of Behavioral Research.* New York: Holt, Rinehart & Winston, 1964.

MEEKER, M. *The Structure of Intellect: Its Interpretation and Uses.* Columbus, Ohio: Charles Merrill Books, 1969.

MERCER, J. *Sociocultural Factors in the Educational Evaluation of Black and Chicano Children.* 1971. Available on request from National Leadership Institute, U-173, University of Connecticut, Storrs, Conn. 06268.

SATTLER, J. *Assessment of Children's Intelligence.* Philadelphia: W. B. Saunders Company, 1974.

Tests and Measurement Kit. Available on request from Educational Testing Service, Princeton, N.J. 08540.

A final statement and wish for the children of the world:

Some people see things as they are and ask "Why?" But we dream things that never were and ask "Why not?"

after
—Robert F. Kennedy (1925–1968)
and
George Bernard Shaw (1856–1950)

REFERENCES

The following list of references consists of those books and articles consulted in developing *Learning and Growing*, especially those parts referring to developmental norms, which have not already been included in the resource lists in Chapter 8.

Having already devoted so much space to the listing of resources, we decided not to burden you by repeating here those references used in composing the hard data of the book; but we did feel it important to add this list so that those of you who are interested in looking even further into a particular aspect of developmental information would have at your disposal such specific references.

ADAMS, D. "The Development of Social Behavior," in Y. Brackbill, *Infancy and Early Childhood*. New York: Free Press, 1967, pp. 397–429.

Advances in Child Development and Behavior, Vols. 1–7. New York: Academic Press, 1963–73.

AMES, L. "The Development of the Sense of Time in the Young Child." *J. Genet. Psychology*, 68: 97–125, 1946.

———— "Postural and placement orientations in writing and block behavior: developmental trends from infancy to age ten," *J. Genet. Psychology.*, 73: 45–52, 1948.

———— "Bilaterality," *J. Genet. Psychology*, 75: 45–50, 1949.

———— "Sense of self in nursery school children as manifested by their verbal behavior." *J. Genet. Psychology*, 81: 193–232, 1952.

AMES, L. and F. ILG. "Development trends in writing behavior," *J. Genet. Psychology*, 79: 28–46, 1951.

ANTHONY, E. and T. BENEDEK. *Parenthood: Its Psychology and Psychopathology*. Boston: Little, Brown & Co., 1970.

ASIMOV, I. *The Human Brain*. New York: The New American Library, Inc., 1963.

ATKINSON, R. *Readings From Scientific American: Contemporary Psychology*. San Francisco: W. H. Freeman and Co., 1971.

BAKER, H. and B. LELAND. *Detroit Tests of Learning Aptitude*. Indianapolis: Bobbs-Merrill Co., 1959.

BALDWIN, A. "Socialization and the parent-child relationship." *Child Development*, 19: 127–136, 1948.

———— *Behavior and Development in Childhood*. New York: Dreyden Press, 1955.

BALDWIN, J. *Mental Development in the Child and the Race*. New York: The Macmillan Co., 1906.

BAYLEY, N. "The development of motor abilities during the first 3 years." *Monogr. Soc. Res. Ch. Devel.*, No. 1 (1) 1–25, 1935.

───── and H. JONES. "Environmental Correlates of Mental and Motor Development": A Cumulative Study from Infancy to Six Years." *Child Development*, 8: 329–341, 1937.

───── *Bayley's Scales of Infant Development.* New York: The Psychological Corporation, 1969.

───── "Development of mental abilities," in *Carmichael's Manual of Child Psychology* (3rd ed.) by P. Mussen. New York: John Wiley & Sons, Inc., 1970, 1163–1209.

BEERY, K. and N. BUKTENICA. *Developmental Test of Visual Motor Integration.* Chicago: Follet Publishing Co., 1967.

BELLUGI, U. and R. BROWN (eds.). *The Acquisition of Language.* Chicago: University of Chicago Press, 1970.

BELMONT, L. and H. BIRCH, "Lateral dominance and right-left awareness in normal children," *Child Development*, 34: 257–270, 1963.

BERKO, J. "The Child's Learning of English Morphology," *Word*, 14: 150–77, 1958.

BORGATTA, E. and W. LAMBERT (eds.). *Handbook of Personality Theory and Research.* Chicago: Rand McNally and Company, 1968.

BOWERS, P. and P. LONDON "Developmental Correlates of Role-Playing Ability." *Child Development,* 30: 499–508, 1965.

BOWLBY, J. *Maternal Care and Mental Health.* New York: Schocken Books, 1966.

BRIDGES, K. *The Social and Emotional Development of the Pre-School Child.* London: Kegan Paul, Trench, Trubner & Co., Ltd., 1931.

BROWN, R. *Words and Things.* New York: Free Press, 1958.

───── *Social Psychology.* New York: Free Press, 1965.

───── *A First Language: The Early Stages.* Cambridge: Harvard University Press, 1973.

BUHLER, C. *The First Year of Life.* New York: John Day Co., 1930.

BUTLER, A. and E. GOTTS, N. QUISENBERRY, R. THOMPSON (eds.). *Literature Search and Development of an Evaluation System in Early Childhood Education. Vols. I–V.* Report to the Office of Education, U.S. Department of Health, Education and Welfare, Washington, D.C., April, 1971.

BZOCH, K. and R. LEAGUE. *Receptive-Expressive Emergent Language Scale.* Florida: Computer Management Corp., 1970.

CARROLL, J. "Language Development in Children," in S. Saporta (ed.) *Psycholinguistics: A Book of Readings.* New York: Holt, Rinehart & Winston, 1961.

CASTNER, B. "The Development of fine prehension in infancy." *Genet. Psychol. Monogr.,* 12: 105–93, 1932.

CATTELL, P. *The Measurement of Intelligence of Infants and Young Chilren.* New York: The Psychological Corporation, 1940.

CHURCH, J. *Language and the Discovery of Reality.* New York: Vintage Books, 1966.

────── *Understanding Your Child from Birth to Three: A Guide to Your Child's Psychological Development.* New York: Random House, 1973.

COLE, M. and I. MALTZMAN (eds.). *Handbook of Contemporary Soviet Psychology,* New York: Basic Books, 1968.

CONEL, J. *The Postnatal Development of the Human Cerebral Cortex, Vols. L–VII.* Cambridge: Harvard University Press, 1939–1963.

CRANDALL, V., A. PRESTON and A. RABSON. "Maternal Reactions and the Development of Independence and Achievement Behavior in Young Children." *Child Development,* 31: 243–251, 1960.

CRATTY, B. *Active Learning.* Englewood Cliffs, N.J.: Prentice-Hall, Inc., 1971.

────── *Perceptual and Motor Development of Infants and Children.* New York: The Macmillan Co., 1970.

CROWELL, D. "Infant Motor Development," in *Infancy and Early Childhood,* ed. Y. Brackbill. New York: The Free Press, 1967, 125–207.

DEWEY, E. *Behavior Development in Infants.* New York: Columbia University Press, 1935.

DODWELL, P. "Children's Understanding of Number and Related Concepts." *Canadian Journal of Psychology,* 14: 191–205, 1960.

DOLL, E. *The Oseretsky Tests of Motor Proficiency.* Minneapolis: Educational Test Bureau, 1946.

────── *Vineland Social Maturity Scale.* Circle Pines, Minn.: American Guidance Service, Inc. 1965.

────── *Preschool Attainment Record* (PAR). Circle Pines, Minn.: American Guidance Service, Inc., 1966.

DOUGLAS, V. "Children's Responses to Frustration: A Developmental Study." *Canadian Journal of Psychology,* 19: 161–171, 1965.

DUNN, L. *Expanded Manual for the Peabody Picture Vocabulary Test.* Circle Pines, Minn.: American Guidance Service Inc., 1965.

ELKIND, D. "Discrimination, Seriation, and Numeration of Size and Dimensional Differences in Young Children: Piaget Replication Study VI." *J. Genet. Psychology,* 104: 275–296, 1964.

────── *Children and Adolescents: Interpretive Essays on Jean Piaget,* 2nd ed. New York: Oxford University Press, 1974.

ENGEL, R., W. REID, and D. RUCKER. *Language Development Experiences for Young Children.* Los Angeles, Calif.: School of Educ., University of Southern Calif., 1966.

ENGSTROM, G. *The Significance of the Young Child's Motor Development.* Washington, D.C.: National Association for the Education of Young Children, 1971.

ERVIN-TRIPP, S. *Language Acquisition and Communicative Choice.* Palo Alto, Calif.: Stanford University Press, 1973.

———— "Language Development," in M. Hoffman and L. Hoffman (eds.) *Advances in Child Development Research.* New York: Russell Sage Foundation, 1966, II, 55–105.

ESPENSCHADE, A. and H. ECKERT. *Motor Development.* Columbus, Ohio: Charles E. Merrill Books, 1967.

FLAVELL, J. *The Development of Role-Taking and Communication Skills in Children.* New York: John Wiley & Sons, 1968.

FRANKENBERG, W. and J. DODDS. *Denver Development Screening Test.* Denver, Colo.: 1967.

FREEDMAN, D., *et al.* "Emotional Behavior and Personality Development," in Y Brackbill (ed.), *Infancy and Early Childhood.* New York: Free Press, 1967.

FROSTIG, M. and P. HORNE. *The Frostig Program for the Development of Visual Perception.* Chicago: Follet Publishing Co., 1964.

GARDNER, E. *Fundamentals of Neurology.* Philadelphia: W. B. Saunders Publishing Co., 1968.

GEBER, M. "The Psycho-Motor Development of African Children in the First Year and the Influence of Maternal Behavior." *J. Social Psychology, 47:* 185–195, 1958.

GESELL, A. *The Mental Growth of the Pre-School Child.* New York: The Macmillan Co., 1925.

———— and H. HALVERSON. "The development of thumb opposition in the human infant," *J. Genet. Psychol.,* 48: (1936), 339–61.

———— and H. THOMPSON. *The Psychology of Early Growth.* New York: The Macmillan Co., 1938.

———— and B. SPOCK, *et al. The Complete Book of Mothercraft.* For the Parents Institute. New York: The Greystone Press, 1952.

———— "The ontogenesis of infant behavior," in L. Carmichael (ed.) *Manual of Child Psychology,* 2nd ed. New York: John Wiley & Sons, Inc., 1954.

———— and L. AMES. "The Development of Handedness," in *Behavior in Infancy and Early Childhood,* eds. Y. Brackbill and G. Thompson. New York: Free Press, 1967, 152–63.

GEWIRTZ, J. *Attachment and Dependency.* Washington, D.C.: W. H. Hinston & Sons, 1972.

GILMORE, J. "Play: A Special Behavior," in R. Haber (ed.) *Current Research in Motivation.* New York: Holt, Rinehart & Winston, 1967.

GOODENOUGH, F. *Anger in Young Children.* Minn.: U. of Minnesota Press, 1931.

GOSLIN, D. (ed.) *Handbook of Socialization Theory and Research.* Chicago: Rand McNally & Company, 1969.

GOUREVITCH, V. and M. FEFFER. "A Study of Motivational Development." *J. Genet. Psychology,* 100: 361–375, 1967.

GRAHAM, F. *et al.* "Development in preschool children of the ability to copy forms," *Child Develop.*, 31: 339–59, 1960.

GRIFFITHS, R. *The Abilities of Babies: A Study in Mental Measurement.* London, Eng.: University of London Press, 1954.

GUILFORD, J. P. *On the Nature of Human Intelligence.* New York: McGraw-Hill Book Co., 1967.

—— *Intelligence, Creativity, and Their Educational Implications.* San Diego, Calif.: Robert R. Knapp, 1968.

—— and R. HOEPFNER *The Analysis of Intelligence.* New York: McGraw-Hill Book Co., 1971.

GUTTERIDGE, M. "Study of motor achievements of young children," *Arch. Psychol.*, No. 244, 1939.

HALVERSON, H. "An experimental study of prehension in infants by means of systematic cinema records," *Genet. Psychol. Monogr.*, 10: 107–286, 1931.

—— "A further study of grasping," *J. Genet. Psychol.*, 7: 34–64, 1932.

—— "Studies of the grasping responses of early infancy: III," *J. Genet. Psychol.* 425: 449, 1937.

HARRIS, D. *Goodenough-Harris Drawing Test Manual.* New York: Harcourt, Brace & World, 1963.

HEATHERS, J. "Emotional Dependence and Independence in Nursery School Play." *J. Genet. Psychology, 87:* 37–57, 1955.

HEBB, D. *The Organization of Behavior.* New York: John Wiley & Sons, 1949.

HILDRETH, G. "The development and training of hand dominance: II. Developmental tendencies in handedness and III. Origins of handedness and lateral dominance." *Journal of Genetic Psychology,* 75: 221–75, 1949.

HISKEY, M. *Hiskey-Nebraska Test of Learning Aptitude.* Lincoln, Nebraska: University of Nebraska, 1966.

HOROWITZ, F. "Incentive Value of Social Stimuli for Preschool Children." *Child Development, 35:* 111–116, 1962.

ILG, F. and L. AMES. *School Readiness.* New York: Harper & Row, 1965.

INHELDER, B. and J. PIAGET. *The Growth of Logical Thinking from Childhood to Adolescence.* New York: Basic Books, 1958.

IRWIN, O. and H. CHEN. "Infant Speech. Vowel and Consonant Frequency." *Journal of Speech and Hearing Disorders, 13:* 31–4, 1948.

ISCOE, I. and H. STEVENSON (eds.). *Personality Development in Children.* Austin, Texas: University of Texas Press, 1960.

JERSILD, A. and F. HOLMES. *Children's Fears.* New York: Teachers College, Columbia University, 1935.

KAGAN, J. Interview in *Development.* Del Mar, Calif.: CRM Educational Films, 1972.

—— "The Many Faces of Response," in *Readings in Psychology Today,* 2nd ed. Del Mar, Calif.: CRM Books, 1972.

KELLOGG, R. "Understanding Children's Art," in *Readings in Developmental Psychology Today*, P. Cramer (ed.) Del Mar, Calif.: CRM Books, 1970, 31–9.

KIDD, A. and J. REVOIRE. *Perceptual Development in Children*. New York: International Universities Press, 1966.

KIMPLE, T. *Roadmap to Effective Teaching*. Monterey County, Calif.: Monterey County Office of Education, Special Education Department, 1970.

KIRK, S., J. McCARTHY, and W. KIRK. *Illinois Test of Psycholinguistic Abilities*, rev. ed. Urbana, Ill.: U. of Illinois Press, 1968.

KLATSTEIN, E., E. JACKSON and L. WILKIN. "The Influence of Degree of Flexibility in Maternal Child Care Practices on Early Child Behavior." *American Journal of Orthopsychiatry*, 26: 79–92, 1956.

KUHLMANN, F. *Tests of Mental Development*. Minn.: Ed. Testing Bureau, 1939.

LAVATELLI, C. (ed.). *Language Training in Early Childhood Education*. Urbana, Ill.: Univ. of Ill. Press (ERIC Clearing House on Early Childhood Ed.), 1971.

LAZERSON, A. and M. McKEAN (eds.). *Anthropology Today*. Del Mar, Calif.: CRM Books, 1971.

LEE, L. *"Developmental Sentence Types." JSHD, 31,* 311–30, 1966.

LEITER, R. *Leiter International Performance Scale*. Washington, D.C.: Psychological Service Center Press, 1952.

LENNEBERG, E. (ed.). *New Directions in the Study of Language*. Cambridge: MIT Press, 1964.

———— *The Biological Foundations of Language*. New York: John Wiley & Sons, 1967.

LEWIS, M. *Language, Thought, and Personality in Infancy and Childhood*. New York: Basic Books, 1963.

LICHTENBERG, P. and D. NORTON. *Cognitive and Mental Development in the First Five Years of Life*. Washington, D.C.: U.S. Superintendent of Documents, Government Printing Office, 1970.

LIPSITT, L. "Learning Capacities of the Human Infant," in Rosenblith et al (eds.) *The Causes of Behavior*, 3rd ed. Boston: Allyn & Bacon, 1972.

LISINA, M. and Y. VEROVICH. "Development of movements and formation of motor habits," in Zaporozhets, A. and D. Elkonin, (eds.) *The Psychology of Pre-school Children*, Cambridge: MIT Press, 1971.

LOWENFELD, V. *Your Child and His Art*. New York: The Macmillan Co., 1955.

LURIA, A. *Human Brain and Psychological Processes*. New York: Harper & Row, 1966.

———— *The Role of Speech in the Regulation of Normal and Abnormal Behavior*. New York: Liveright, 1961.

———— and F. YUDOVICH. *Speech and the Development of Mental Processes in the Child*. London, Eng.: Staples Press, 1959.

McCarthy, D. *The Language Development of the Preschool Child.* Minneapolis, Minn.: The Univ. of Minnesota Press, 1930.

Maccoby, E. (ed.) *The Development of Sex Differences.* Palo Alto, Calif.: Stanford University Press, 1966.

McGraw, M. *The Neuromuscular Maturation of the Human Infant.* New York: Hafner Publishing Co., 1969. (Reprint of 1945 Columbia University edition with new introduction and updated bibliography.)

Markey, F. *Imaginative Behavior of Preschool Children.* New York: Teachers College, Columbia University, 1935.

Maslow, A. *Toward a Psychology of Being.* 2nd ed. New York: Van Nostrand Reinhold Company, 1968.

——— *Motivation and Personality.* 2nd ed. New York: Harper & Row, 1970.

——— *The Farther Reaches of Human Nature.* New York: The Viking Press, 1971.

Mead, M. and F. MacGregor. *Growth and Culture.* New York: G. P. Putnam's Sons, 1951.

Mecham, M. *Verbal Language Development Scale.* Circle Pines, Minn.: American Guidance Service, Inc., 1959.

Menyuk, P. *The Acquisition and Development of Language.* Englewood Cliffs, N.J.: Prentice-Hall, Inc., 1971.

Merry, F. and R. Merry. *The First Two Decades of Life.* New York: Harper & Brothers, 1958.

Metropolitan Readiness Tests. New York: Harcourt, Brace & World, 1965.

Miller, G. *Language and Communication.* New York: McGraw-Hill Book Co., 1963.

——— "The Magical Number Seven Plus Or Minus Two: Some Limits On Our Capacity For Processing Information," in R. Anderson and D. Ausubel, *Readings In the Psychology of Cognition,* New York: Holt, Rinehart & Winston, 1965.

Milner, E. *Human Neural and Behavioral Development.* Springfield, Ill.: Charles C. Thomas Publishers, 1967.

Montagu, A. *Touching.* New York: Columbia University Press, 1972.

——— *The Direction of Human Development.* New York: Hawthorn Books, 1970.

Montessori, M. *The Discovery of the Child.* New York: Ballantine Books, 1967.

——— *The Secret of Childhood.* New York: Frederic A. Stokes Co., Inc., 1939.

Moore, T. (ed.). *Cognitive Development and the Acquisition of Language.* New York: Academic Press, 1973.

Oakes, M. *Children's Explanations of Natural Phenomena.* New York: Bureau of Publications, Teachers College, Columbia University, 1947.

O'DONNELL, P. *Motor and Haptic Learning.* San Rafael, Calif.: Dimensions Publishing Co., 1969.

OLDFIELD, R. and J. MARSHALL (eds.). *Language.* Baltimore, Md.: Penguin Books, 1968.

OREM, R. *Montessori and the Special Child.* New York: G. P. Putnam's Sons, 1969.

PEIPER, A. *Cerebral Function in Infancy and Childhood.* New York: Consultants Bureau, 1963.

PIAGET, J. *The Moral Judgment of the Child.* Glencoe, Ill.: The Free Press, 1948.

——— *The Psychology of Intelligence.* New York: Harcourt, Brace, 1950.

——— *Play, Dreams and Imitation in Childhood.* New York: W. W. Norton, 1951.

——— and A. Szeminska. *The Child's Conception of Number.* New York: Humanities Press, 1952.

——— *The Language and Thought of the Child.* London: Routledge & Kegan Paul, 1952.

——— *The Construction of Reality in the Child.* New York: Basic Books, 1954.

——— and B. INHELDER. *The Child's Conception of Space.* London: Routledge & Kegan Paul, 1956.

PIERS, M. (ed.) *Play and Development.* New York: W. W. Norton & Co., 1972.

PRATT, K. "The Neonate," in L. Carmichael (ed.) *Manual of Child Psychology.* 2nd ed. New York: John Wiley & Sons, Inc., 1954, pp. 251–91.

REBELSKY, F. and L. DORMAN. *Child Development and Behavior Readings,* 2nd ed. New York: Alfred A. Knopf, 1974.

ROTHENBERG, B. *Children's Social Sensitivity and the Relationship to Interpersonal Competence, Intra-personal Comfort and Intellectual Level.* Princeton, N.J.: Educational Testing Service, 1968.

SALZINGER, K. and S. SALZINGER. *Research in Verbal Behavior and Some Neurological Implications.* New York: Academic Press, 1967.

SEARS, P. and E. DOWLEY. "Research on teaching in the nursery school," in N. Gage (ed.) *Handbook of Research on Teaching.* Chicago: Rand McNally & Co., 1963, pp. 814–64.

SEARS, R., E. MACCOBY, and H. LEVIN. *Patterns of Child Rearing.* New York: Harper & Row, 1957.

SEARS, R., L. RAU, and R. ALPERT. *Identification and Child Rearing.* Palo Alto, Calif.: Stanford University Press, 1963.

SHIRLEY, M. *The First Two Years: Postural and Locomotor Development, Vol. I,* Minneapolis, Minn.: U. of Minn. Press, 1931.

——— *The First Two Years: Intellectual Development, Vol. II,* Minneapolis, Minn.: U. of Minn. Press, 1933.

—— *The First Two Years: Personality Manifestations, Vol. III,* Minneapolis, Minn.: U. of Minn. Press, 1933.

SIDEL, R. *Women and Child Care in China.* New York: Hill & Wang, 1972.

SINGER, J. *The Child's World of Make-Believe.* New York: Academic Press, 1973.

SLOAN, W. "The Lincoln-Oseretsky motor development scale." *Genet. Psychol. Monogr.,* 51: 183–252, 1955.

SLOSSON, R. *Slosson Intelligence Test for Children and Adults (SIT).* East Aurora, New York: Slosson Education Publications, 1963.

SMITH, F. and G. MILLER (eds.). *The Genesis of Language.* Cambridge: MIT Press, 1966.

STAUB, E. "The Use of Role Playing and Induction in Children's Learning of Helping and Sharing Behavior." *Child Development, 42:* 805–16, 1971.

STONE, L. J., L. B. MURPHY, and H. SMITH. *The Competent Infant: Research and Commentary.* New York: Basic Books, 1974.

STRANGE, R. *An Introduction to Child Study.* 4th ed. New York: The Macmillan Co., 1959.

STUTSMAN, R. *Scale of Mental Tests for Preschool Children.* New York: World Book Co., 1930.

SUTTON-SMITH, B. *Child Psychology.* New York: Appleton-Century-Crofts, 1973.

TEMPLIN, M. *Certain Language Skills in Children: Child Welfare Monograph,* No. 26. Minneapolis, Minn.: U. of Minn. Press, 1957.

TERMAN, L. and M. MERRILL. *Stanford-Binet Intelligence Scale: Manual for the Third Revision Form L-M.* Boston: Houghton Mifflin Co., 1960.

THOMAS, A. and S. AUTGAERDEN. *Locomotive from Pre- to Post-natal Life.* Lavenham, Suffolk, England: The Lavenham Press Ltd., 1963.

UZGIRIS, J. "Ordinality in the development of schemas for relating to objects," in B. Staub and J. Hellmuth (eds.) *Exceptional Infant. Vol. I: The Normal Infant.* Seattle: Special Child Publications, 1967, 315–48.

VINCENT, E. and P. MARTIN. *Human Psychological Development.* New York: The Ronald Press Company, 1961.

WALCHER, D. and D. PETERS (eds.). *The Development of Self-Regulatory Mechanisms.* New York: Academic Press, Inc., 1971.

WATSON, R. *Psychology of the Child.* 3rd ed. New York: John Wiley & Sons, 1973.

WECHSLER, D. *Wechsler Preschool and Primary Scale of Intelligence.* New York: The Psychological Corporation, 1967.

WEIR, R. *Language in the Crib.* The Hague: Mouton, 1962.

WELLMAN, B. "Motor achievements of pre-school children." *Childhood Education,* 13: 311–16, 1937.

—— "The development of motor coordination in young children." *Iowa Studies in Child Welfare,* 3: 1926.

WERNER, H. and B. KAPLAN. *Symbol Formation*. New York: John Wiley & Sons, 1963.

WHITE, B. *Human Infants: Experience and Psychological Development*. Englewood Cliffs, N.J.: Prentice-Hall, Inc., 1971.

WICKSTROM, RALPH. *Fundamental Motor Patterns*. Philadelphia: Lea Febiger, 1970.

WITMER, H. and R. KOTINSKY (eds.). *Personality in the Making: Fact Finding Report of Midcentury White House Conference on Children and Youth*. New York: Harper & Brothers, 1953.

WOLMAN, B. (ed.). *Handbook of General Psychology*, Englewood Cliffs, N.J.: Prentice-Hall, Inc., 1973.

Yale Clinic of Child Development, *The First Five Years of Life*. New York: Harper & Brothers, 1940.

ZAPOROZHETS, A. and D. ELKONIN (eds.). *The Psychology of Preschool Children*. Cambridge: MIT Press, 1971.

ZIMMERMAN, I., V. STEINER and R. EVATT. *Preschool Language Manual*. Columbus, Ohio: Charles E. Merrill Co., 1969.

Index